AIR
WAR
OVER
Russia ★

AIR
WAR
OVER
Russia

ANDREW BROOKES

Ian Allan
PUBLISHING

For Ollie and Leon

Page 1:
Oblt Klaus Quaet-Faslem, Kapitän 2./JG53, being strapped into his Bf109G during Operation 'Blue'. 'Quat' shot down some 24 VVS aircraft over southern Russia between 1 June and 30 September 1942. *Goss/Rauchbach Archive*

Previous page:
Soviet Major-General A. A. Kuznetsov insists on being the first Russian to fly a Hurricane brought by the RAF to Vaenga in late 1941. *Via Air Historical Branch (RAF). Crown Copyright 1941-2/MOD. Reproduced with permission of the Controller of Her Majesty's Stationery Office*

Left:
In their life-and-death struggle against the Luftwaffe, VVS pilots often resorted to the *taran*, or ramming technique, pioneered by the Tsarist Air Force in World War 1. This World War 2 propaganda poster proclaims, 'Taran Weapon of our Heroes. Glory to the Stalin Falcons'. *Author's Collection*

First published 2003

ISBN 0 7110 2890 7

© Andrew Brookes 2003

Published by Ian Allan Publishing

an imprint of Ian Allan Publishing Ltd, Hersham, Surrey KT12 4RG. Printed by Ian Allan Printing Ltd, Hersham, Surrey KT12 4RG.

Code: 0309/B

CONTENTS

LUFTWAFFE RANKS AND THEIR RAF AND USAAF EQUIVALENTS

Luftwaffe Rank	Abbreviation	RAF Rank	USAAF Rank
Flieger	Fl/Flg	Aircraftsman 2nd Class	Airman (Amn)
Gefreiter	Gefr	Aircraftsman 1st Class	Airman 1st Class (A1C)
Obergefreiter	Ogfr	Leading Aircraftsman	
Hauptgefreiter	Hptgefr		
Unteroffizier	Uffz	Corporal	Sergeant
Unterfeldwebel	Ufw		Sergeant
Feldwebel	Fw	Sergeant	Technical Sergeant
Fähnrich (Fahnenjunker)	Fhr		Flight Officer
Oberfeldwebel	Ofw	Flight Sergeant	Master Sergeant
Oberfähnrich	Obfhr	Warrant Officer	Flight Officer (senior)
Stabsfeldwebel	Stabsfw		Master Sergeant
Leutnant	Lt	Pilot Officer	2nd Lieutenant
Oberleutnant	Oblt	Flying Officer	Lieutenant
Hauptmann	Hptm	Flight Lieutenant	Captain
Major	Maj	Squadron Leader	Major
Oberstleutnant	Obstlt	Wing Commander	Lieutenant Colonel
Oberst	Oberst	Group Captain	Colonel
General Major	GenMaj	Air Commodore	Brigadier General
General Leutnant	GenLt	Air Vice-Marshal	Major General
General der Flieger/Flak	Gen dFl/Flak	Air Marshal	Lieutenant General
General Oberst	GenOb	Air Chief Marshal	4-star General
Generalfeldmarschall	GFM	Marshal of the Royal Air Force	5-star General
Reichsmarschall			

SOVIET AIR FORCE RANKS (1941-5)

Krasnoarmeyets	Private
Yefreytor	Corporal
Mladshiy serzhant	Lance-sergeant
Serzhant	Sergeant
Starshiy serzhant	Senior Sergeant
Starshina	Sergeant-Major
Mladshiy leytenant	2nd Lieutenant
Leytenant	—
Starshiy leytenant	Lieutenant
Kapitan	Captain
Major	Major
Podpolkovnik	Lieutenant-Colonel
Polkovnik	Colonel
General major	Major-General
General leytenant	Lieutenant-General
General polkovnik	—
General armiyi	General
Marshal	Field Marshal
Glavnyy marshal	Senior Marshal
Marshal Sovetskogo Soyuza	1st Marshal

To prevent confusion, this book uses the English equivalents of VVS ranks throughout. There were three Lt grades in the VVS but, for the sake of simplicity, 'Lt' has been used for them all.

GLOSSARY AND ABBREVIATIONS

ADD	Long-Range Aviation	Panzer Verbindungs Offizier	Tank Liaison Officer
Aufkl.ObdL	C-in-C Luftwaffe's Reconnaissance Group	Para	two aircraft
		PVO	Counter-Air Defence
BAO	airfield maintenance battalion	RAB	Air Base Region
DBA	Long-Range Bomber Aviation	Rasputiza	the rainy season (literally 'time without roads')
Erg	Training and replacement flight		
Einsatzbereit	operationally ready	Ratas	Polikarpov I-16 single-seat fighters
Flakkorps	Anti-aircraft Artillery Corps		
Flieger-Division	Air Division	Rotte	pair of aircraft
Fliegerkorps	Air Corps	Schlacht	Ground attack
Flivo	Air liaison officer	Schwarm	section of four aircraft
Geschwader(n)	Air Wing(s)	Schwerpunkt	centre of gravity of an attack
Gruppe	Basic Luftwaffe flying unit	Seenotbereichskommando	air-sea-rescue Staffel
JG	Fighter Group	Shturmovik	ground attack
KG	Bomber Group	SKG	High-speed Bomber Group
Kette	three-aircraft formation	Stab	HQ Staff Flight
Koluft	Luftwaffe commanders attached to army HQs	Staffel(n)	Squadron(s)
		Stavka	Soviet High Command
KuFlGr	Coastal Air Group	StG	Stuka Group
Luftflotte(n)	Air Fleet(s)	Störkampfstaffel	harassment bomber Staffel
Luftgau	Regional organisations responsible for the training, administration, maintenance, supply and field defence of Luftwaffe airfields.	TB	heavy bomber
		TBA	Heavy Bomber Command
		VA	Air Army
		VVS	military air forces
Nachtschlachtgruppen	Night ground-attack Gruppen	Zavod	Factory
Nahkampfführer	Close-Support Leader	ZG	Destroyer Group
OKH	Army High Command	Zveno	flight of aircraft. Usually compromised of two *para*
OKL	Luftwaffe High Command		
OKW	Wehrmacht High Command	Zerstörer	destroyers
Panzerjagdkommando	Anti-tank Air Command		

INTRODUCTION

'Of what use is decisive victory in battle if we bleed to death as a result of it?'
Winston Churchill

Nations look at World War 2 through different prisms. The turning point for the British came in November 1942, with Gen Bernard Montgomery's defeat of four German divisions at El Alamein. Yet during the previous 12 months, over nine million troops on both sides had been engaged in a life and death struggle in the East, and in the same month as 60,000 German and Italians losses were inflicted at El Alamein, the Soviets removed 50 divisions and over 300,000 men from the Axis order of battle around Stalingrad. When the war ended, the British had suffered 306,770 military casualties killed or missing, whereas total German armed losses amounted to 13,488,000, of whom 10,758,000 fell or were taken prisoner in the East.[1] Soviet war dead are put at 27 million, with 8,668,000 Red Army officers and soldiers being killed in action.[2]

The German assault on Russia in June 1941 was a massive endeavour, and its impact approximated to a German occupation of the US from the East Coast to the Mississippi River and into the eastern Great Plains. And over the vast expanses of Russian land and water was the air, wherein stupendous battles were fought. Lord Tennyson wrote of 'nations' airy navies grappling in the central blue', an apt description of an air war over Russia that accounted for no fewer than 77,000 German aircraft. Set against 1,733 German aircraft lost between 10 July and 31 October 1940, the Battle of Britain was a flesh wound.[3]

That the Soviets eventually prevailed in a bitterly fought war owed much to air power. This book recounts the story of the air war over Russia between 1941 and 1945 using interviews, diaries, letters, official histories, operational record books and archives, many of which have surfaced since the ending of the Cold War. Throughout, it is clear that the exploitation of air power over Russia was inextricably linked to the ground battle, and victory came to those who integrated their air assets for all meaningful intents and purposes. It is to be hoped that we will never see the like of the air war over Russia again, but the campaign still offers many pointers to what air power can and cannot do in lesser conflicts today.

AIRWAY TO WAR

'In starting and waging a war, it is not right that matters, but victory.'
Adolf Hitler

At the end of World War 1, Germany had approximately 20,000 military aircraft of which some 2,400 were operational bombers, fighters or reconnaissance types. They all had to go under the terms of the Treaty of Versailles, which obliged Weimar Germany to have no airmen among the 100,000 men permitted in the Reichswehr. The German Flying Corps was formally disbanded in May 1920, and even seven air squadrons belonging to the police were obliged to surrender their aircraft.

However, Versailles allowed the retention of a German Defence Ministry and within it the Chief of the Army Command, Gen Hans von Seeckt, retained an 'air advisor' because he was convinced that military aviation would eventually revive in Germany. Seeckt's small cadre of ex-fliers, spread around the Defence Ministry, were encouraged by growing ties with the USSR. The communist Soviet Union was the other great pariah state in the eyes of the victorious powers after 1918, and when the Western Allies arbitrarily extended the veto on German aircraft manufacture in 1922, and announced severe restrictions on the performance of any German aircraft designed in the future, the Germans signed a separate agreement with the Soviet Union at Rapallo. This ended Moscow's isolation and started Germany on the road to becoming the USSR's most important trading partner. Collaboration allowed Germany to build and test weapons prohibited after 1918, including aircraft and tanks, and carry out training and exercises in Soviet airspace. Hitler's Luftwaffe adjutant, Klaus von Below, was one of 120 fighter pilots trained at Lipetz near Voronezh between 1925-33. A further 100 reconnaissance observer pilots were trained at Lipetz between 1928-31, while a test unit evaluating prototype military aircraft and weapons grew from 50 to 200 German personnel. Many Lipetz men were subsequently to command Luftwaffe forces in Russia.[4]

In return, 120 Soviet senior officers went to Germany to attend a secret General Staff course. The Russians also tapped into German military experience and aviation technology, with Junkers establishing an aircraft factory near Moscow. The Paris Air Agreement of 1926 removed all remaining restrictions on the German manufacture of civil aircraft, and Lufthansa became the best equipped airline in Europe with its crews capable of a high standard of day, night and blind flying. When Hitler came to power on 30 January 1933, former World War 1 fighter ace Hermann Göring — credited with 20 'kills' and the last commander of the Richthofen *Geschwader* — was appointed Reich Commissioner for Aviation, with the much more administratively able Erhard Milch, head of Lufthansa and another ex-wartime fighter pilot, as his deputy.

Expansion of the still illicit German Air Force (Luftwaffe) gathered apace, based on 'amateur' sport flying and state flying schools. Gen von Blomberg, the Defence Minister, was selfless in giving up some of his best army officers to boost the secret force, while Milch aimed for a target of 4,021 aircraft by 30 September 1935, of which 2,168 were to be trainers.[5] When the Luftwaffe came out of the closet in March 1935, its strength stood at 1,888 aircraft of all types supported by some 20,000 officers and men. Before Hitler came to power, the entire German aircraft industry employed less than 4,000 workers; by 1937 it was employing 230,000, of whom 121,000 were manufacturing airframes and 73,000 manufacturing engines.[6] In 1938, the Luftwaffe's share of a much increased defence budget had risen to 39.4%.[7]

When the Bolsheviks came to power in November 1917, the Imperial Army and Navy had over 2,000 aircraft and an extensive aircraft industry. These resources were lost or ignored in the new regime's fight for survival but by the middle of 1920, the Operational Air Directorate could concentrate 210 aircraft in 51 flights to support Gen Tukhachevsky's drive on Warsaw.

Soviet Air Forces were not an independent air arm like the RAF or Luftwaffe. Operational control of the *Voyenno-Vozdushnye Sily* (VVS), which simply means 'military air forces', remained firmly in the hands of the Red Army Command and was exercised through the tactical authority of Military District Commanders. But whatever the tactical differences, fascist Germany and communist Russia both saw military aviation as a futuristic and exciting embodiment of their vibrant regimes. During Stalin's first two Five-Year Plans, the number of VVS aircraft rose from under a thousand to over 5,500 by 1938. The proportion of reconnaissance machines dropped from 82% in 1929 to 9.5% by 1938, while the bomber complement rose to about half the combat total and fighter percentages grew from 25% to 39%.[8] During the second Five-Year Plan, defence industries expanded twice as rapidly as Soviet industry as a whole.

Trade and military co-operation between the USSR and Germany reached its peak in the early 1930s, and Stalin would have been happy for this to continue. It was Hitler who pulled the plug, but when the longstanding co-operation between Reichswehr and Red Army was closed down in 1933, it was with expressions of mutual esteem. Few took seriously Hitler's statement in *Mein Kampf* that his aim was 'to cut a road for expansion to the East by fire and sword... and enslave the Soviet people.'

In 1938 the VVS had over 5,500 aircraft and 100,000 personnel. Its Special Purpose Aviation Army of nearly 900 aircraft in the western USSR was regarded by many as both the biggest and the only real multi-engined bomber force in the world. Particularly with the I-15 biplane and I-16 monoplane fighters, and the SB-2 and SB-2bis (*bis* meant modified) twin-engined fast bombers, the VVS was among the world's Premier League air forces.

The Luftwaffe and VVS first came up against each other in the Spanish Civil War.

By 1937, around 1,000 I-15 and I-16 fighters, 200 SB-2 light bombers and some R-5 reconnaissance aircraft made up 90% of the Spanish Republican air arm. Under the command of the able Gen Yakov Smushkevich, the Soviets held air superiority until late 1937.

But just as the Soviet air commitment was reaching full stride, the Germans introduced the next generation of aircraft — Bf109 fighters, Ju87 Stukas and He111 and Do17 bombers — into the theatre. Outclassed at every level, Soviet airmen never clawed back the initiative. Both Germans and Russians learned much from their Spanish combat experience.

The VVS suffered along with the rest of the Soviet military when Stalin started his purges in May 1937. Like many other tyrants he saw the officer corps as potentially the most dangerous threat to his power, but it was precisely those men who had contributed most to the development of a modern and professional Soviet air-land machine who were eliminated. Virtually a new command of all three armed services — at least 1,000 senior officers — had to be created just as the threat of war with

Germany and/or Japan was becoming worrying.

In 1938 the Soviet Air Force was still the largest in the world, and on 28 September the Minister of Defence reported to the Politburo that, if it was necessary to send aircraft to Czechoslovakia, 246 high-speed bombers and 320 fighters could deploy within two days.[9] It would have meant transitting through Polish or Romanian airspace, but the Romanian government let it be known that it would look the other way provided the aircraft stayed above 3,000m.

After Munich, Hitler called for production of 20,000-30,000 Luftwaffe aircraft per year, including 2,000 heavy bombers capable of reaching Britain, the USSR and even the USA by 1944. It was pie-in-the-sky because Hitler's goals for all three services far exceeded German resources in raw materials and skilled workers, and he failed to lay down any clear set of priorities. But the Führer could still play a mean diplomatic game. The most consistent theme in Hitler's foreign policy thinking was the conquest of *Lebensraum* (living space) in the East to solve Germany's economic and social problems.[10] But first, Hitler had to satisfy two conditions he had laid down in *Mein Kampf* — to eliminate the military power of France and conclude alliances with Italy and Britain. To make time for this

Below:
The Tupolev SB-2B bomber, of which 6,831 were built between 1936-41.
Author's collection

before embarking on his mission to extend the Reich eastwards, Hitler came up with a masterstroke in the shape of the Nazi-Soviet Pact of 1939.

On the other side of Asia, a series of incidents between the USSR and Japan escalated to the point where Moscow feared that the Japanese Kwantung Army was aiming to cut the Trans-Siberian Railway. At Khalkhin-Gol, a river near the border of Outer Mongolia and Manchuria, the Soviet 1st Army Group had 500 new T34 tanks and was supported by 500 aircraft. Overall command was given to a rising star, Gen Grigori Zhukov, with Yakov Smushkevich heading the VVS contingent. The Soviets claimed 320 Japanese aircraft downed in aerial combat before Zhukov launched a massive surprise offensive on 20 August. Tanks, artillery, aircraft and infantry were integrated with as much surprise and effect as was achieved at the Battle of Cambrai in 1917. Large-scale air attacks were mounted, and as many as 250 aircraft were noted battling over the 76km front. VSS aircraft fired rockets and 20mm cannon for the first time at Khalkhin-Gol, and Soviet air power was particularly useful in hindering Japanese battlefield reinforcement. At least 15,000 Japanese were killed and by 15 September the Japanese had been expelled. Yakov Smushkevich received his second Hero of the Soviet Union medal, making him one of only three pilots at the time to have been so honoured.

By autumn 1939, the German armed forces had grown from an army of 100,000 (seven divisions) without a military air force to 2,750,000 men mobilised in 103 divisions. Six of these divisions were armoured and four fully motorised, while Luftwaffe strength stood at 3,750 aircraft, of which 1,270 were twin-engined bombers (including 20 of the latest Ju88s). There were small air reserves, varying between 10% and 25% depending on type, backed up by 2,500–3,000 trainers and some 500 aircraft used for operational training.[11] Hitler understood the coercive value of air power. After occupying all of Czechoslovakia, he threatened the Lithuanians with an air attack on their capital unless Memel — a free city like Danzig — was restored to Germany.

On the other hand, the USSR was much weaker relatively in 1939 than it had been four years earlier. Stalin's purge of the Red Army, the replacement of intelligent and thoughtful leaders by mediocre Stalinist cronies and the poor showing made against the Finns in the Winter War in 1939-40 combined to make Hitler believe that the Soviet military lacked any staying power. This miscalculation led him to plan on defeating the Red Army in a single campaign. No provision was made for fighting into winter, or exploiting discontent with Stalin's regime in any occupied territories.

By 1940 British, USA and USSR aircraft production combined was twice that of Germany.[12] The Americans built bombers using the mass production, shift working and parts standardisation techniques pioneered by Henry Ford, whereas the Ju88 medium bomber was designed with 4,000 different types of screw and bolt, and had to be riveted by hand rather than with automatic machine tools. None of this seemed to matter in Berlin, especially when rapid German successes in the Low Countries and France reinforced the impression that any victory was attainable quickly.

The German 'Conduct of Air Warfare' manual saw the Luftwaffe's goal as 'to defeat the enemy armed forces' in combination with the other services. German air power was to be used first to destroy an enemy air force and establish air superiority over the campaign area, before giving direct support to the land campaign. Direct support meant providing a protective umbrella over German armies, attacking targets near the front line and bombing rear areas where reserve and replacement troops, communication links and supply dumps were located. Only in the event of stalemate or a long, drawn out war would the Luftwaffe be sent to bomb strategically vital centres such as cities.

It was understandable why German air planners linked air doctrine and tactics to current technology. Given the range and payload limitations of aircraft in the late 1930s, the Luftwaffe concentrated on fast fighters, medium and dive-bombers that were best suited to combined air-land operations. Emphasis was placed on front-line communications and the most advanced radios. In 1940 the Luftwaffe had three signal regiments, 63 signal companies and 115 special signal units to facilitate timely air-ground co-ordination between panzer and Luftwaffe units to ensure attack cohesion and accuracy.

The use of radios and rapidly-laid land lines to align air power with the main weight of the army, and in particular with its mobile panzer spearhead, became known as *Blitzkrieg* ('lightning war'). The doctrine of concentrating effort at the vital point at the right time worked like a dream against the Poles and the French, but the seemingly unstoppable nature of the German military machine masked two vital lessons from 1939-40. First, even against the Polish Air Force the Luftwaffe lost 285 aircraft to 333 Polish.[13] Second, it was German tank tracks and boots on the ground that broke an opponent's will. The best an air force could aspire to was to keep the opposition off its own troops' backs and ease the path of advancing forces, rather than venture out decisively on its own. The Battle of Britain showed that overall and lasting air superiority was unattainable against a well-armed and motivated enemy with room for manoeuvre and large economic resources.

Klaus von Below's diary entry for 31 July 1940 had Hitler telling his C-in-Cs that 'he thought it likely that Russia would attack from the autumn of 1941 onwards . . . [and] that his decision to invade the Soviet Union in the spring of 1941 was final.' By September, Below noticed 'again and again how he dwelt on the problem of Russia. As Luftwaffe ADC these were difficult weeks for me. Our bomber squadrons flew the Channel to bomb targets in England every night when weather permitted, while in Berlin all the Führer could think of was how he could overcome the Soviets in the shortest possible time.'[14]

The Luftwaffe's defeat in the Battle of Britain confronted Hitler with two widely differing choices. The first, proposed by Grand Admiral Raeder and backed by Göring, was to concentrate on a naval blockade of the UK and drive towards the Middle East. Deprived of food, oil and access to their Empire, the British would surely crumble. The second was to put Britain 'on hold' and conquer Russia in a single Blitzkrieg campaign. Hitler tried to keep his options open. On 4 November 1940 he told his commanders that everything must be done to get ready for 'a major settling of scores with Russia', but when asked for guidance on priorities his Führer Directive No 18, dated 12 November, simply listed all the options.

That same day, Soviet Foreign Minister Molotov arrived in Berlin to 'clarify Russia's attitude for the coming period'. Hitler wanted a free hand in Europe and he tried to persuade the USSR to focus on the Persian Gulf and Indian Ocean. Molotov would have none of this, insisting that the USSR could not be disinterested in the future of Romania, Hungary, Bulgaria and Turkey. Unused to not having his own way, Hitler left further discussions to Foreign Minister Ribbentrop. Halfway through a banquet that evening, an RAF air raid drove everyone into the underground shelter. Insensitive as ever, Ribbentrop kept insisting that the British were finished. 'If this is so,' replied the dour Molotov, 'why are we in this shelter, and whose are these bombs that are falling?'

Once it became clear that Stalin saw Finland and the Balkans as within his sphere of influence, Hitler lost interest in any further negotiations. Before Molotov even left Berlin, Hitler confided to Göring that he intended to attack the USSR. The Luftwaffe hierarchy fell into line rather easily. The chief of the Luftwaffe General Staff, Gen Hans Jeschonnek, had fought only in the West during World War 1. Like many others, he knew the Soviet Union only as a backward place and he was thirsting for some success. The Battle of Britain had not gone well, and the independent strategic employment of bombers against British industry and morale did not seem to be getting anywhere. From 1 August 1940 to June 1941, the Luftwaffe lost about 6,000 aircraft, as well as

3,700 aircrew killed and 3,000 missing, flying against the UK. While the Luftwaffe had no influence on Hitler's decision to invade the USSR in 1941, the service was up for it and backed Jeschonnek's 'positive attitude' in being 'absolutely for a fight'.[15]

On 5 December 1940 the German Army High Command was ordered to accelerate preparations for an attack in the spring. Unfortunately, a unilateral attack on Greece by Mussolini had gone so badly wrong that by 7 December the Italians were in danger of being completely routed. On 13 December Hitler issued Directive No 20 which called for a German task force of up to 24 divisions to be formed in Romania to move across Bulgaria and into Greece as soon as the weather permitted. Five days later, he signed the most fateful Directive of his career, No 21 for Operation 'Barbarossa'. Named after Frederick I, Barbarossa, who marched to the Holy Land in 1190 and was noted for his red beard, the aim was quite clear:

'German Armed Forces must be prepared to crush Soviet Russia in a quick campaign even before the conclusion of the war against England . . .

Below:
General reference map for German operations in the USSR, 1941-5.

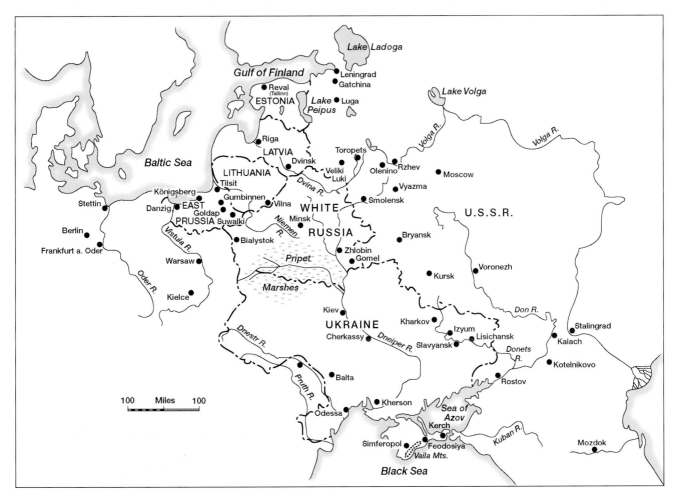

'Preparations requiring more time are to be started now, if this has not yet been done, and are to be completed by 15 May 1941 . . .

'The mass of the Russian Army in Western Russia is to be destroyed by driving forward deep armoured wedges; and the retreat of units capable of combat in the vastness of Russian territory is to be prevented . . .'

Over the next six months, the German General Staff assembled more than three million fighting men on the Soviet frontier. And although it was 1,000km from the German frontier to Moscow, compared with 300km to Paris, planning was based on the same Blitzkrieg tactics that had been employed in May 1940.

The unreal nature of 'Barbarossa' air campaign planning is illustrated by the fact that there was no perceptible increase in German aircraft production in the summer and autumn of 1940. The Luftwaffe High Command (*Oberkommando der Luftwaffe* or OKL) was either not privy to Hitler's thinking or did not take it seriously. As late as 15 October 1940, Gen Tscherersich, the Luftwaffe's chief aircraft procurement planner, was basing his aircraft replacement predictions on a state of peace from 1 April 1941. Bizarrely, his planning figures assumed that a state of war would not resume until 1 April 1947.[16]

During the 1930s the Soviet doctrine of 'All-powerful Defence' centred on a belt of concrete fortifications, field works and natural obstacles on the western edge of Mother Russia known as the Stalin Line. As the USSR absorbed new territories in 1939-40, the Red Army was ordered to desert its fixed defences in White Russia and push forward to around the line of the River Bug. For political reasons the newly acquired territories were to be defended at all costs, which led Stalin to override his General Staff and insist that the new frontier from Finland to Romania be defended, even where it included a number of dangerously exposed salients. This led to Soviet engineers building fortifications in full view of astonished German watchers, right on the frontier itself. Established defences on the Stalin Line were stripped and given up for a hastily constructed affair, often on exposed ground, which still had gaps of 10-80km when the Germans attacked. Only 1,000 out of 2,500 concrete emplacements in the new line were ever fitted with artillery, let alone radios, electricity or air filters. When Stalin belatedly allowed some forces to reoccupy the Kiev Fortified Area, they found it overgrown with weeds and the gun emplacements empty.

Throughout 1940 and the first half of 1941 the VVS was preoccupied with moving into a network of new airfields in Poland, the Baltic republics and Moldavia that had fallen into Stalin's hands after September 1939. A plan to build 190 new airfields in the western expansion zones had been approved in February 1941, but this work together with enlarging existing fields could not be undertaken all at once. From autumn 1940, the runways of more than 250 airfields in the western frontier region of the Soviet Union were extended, and 164 new airfields were built between 8 April and 15 July 1941, especially in eastern Poland and the Baltic States. But many VVS aircraft were based in civilian airports near the border that were poorly defended. It was perhaps for the best that of the 106 new VVS regiments ordered into existence, only 19 were complete by May 1941.

On conclusion of the Nazi-Soviet Pact in 1939, Hitler prohibited any information gathering on the USSR as a matter of principle. After relations with the USSR deteriorated in 1940, eastern intelligence gathering by the Luftwaffe was reactivated. Radio monitoring units were established from Finland to Bulgaria, and their output was supplemented by aircraft photography. Both the British and Germans had used modified civilian spy aircraft to fly over each other's territory before the war, and in 1939 the Luftwaffe set up the *Aufklärungsgruppe Oberbefehlshaber der Luftwaffe* (the Luftwaffe C-in-C's Reconnaissance Gruppe) with its HQ at Werder airfield, 11km east of Potsdam. Reporting directly to Göring and the Luftwaffe High Command, the *Aufkl.ObdL* was commanded by Obstlt Theodore Rowehl, a World War 1 reconnaissance pilot. At the beginning of October 1940, Hitler personally instructed Rowehl to deploy suitable forces to survey European Russia to a depth of 300km, concentrating on airfields, and to do so by 15 May 1941.

The four Staffeln of *Aufkl.ObdL* flew a mix of specially modified, pressurised Heinkel, Dornier and Junkers aircraft fitted with high-altitude engines and the latest cameras. When deployed forward into East Prussia, Hungary and Romania, Rowehl's crews were able to operate, weather permitting, at altitudes above 9,000m. Of some 2,000 identified airfields in western Russia, only 200 were regarded as suitable for Soviet bomber operations. An estimated 180 pre-'Barbarossa' surveys were flown but only one aircraft was lost — a Ju86P, complete with cameras and exposed film of Soviet territory, brought down near Rovno on 15 April 1941 by bad weather. Although the Soviets were well aware of these missions, Stalin refused to allow his air defenders to go after them. That said, the cleaned-up Ju86P with extended outer wings could operate up to 13,000m, way above anything the Soviets could send against it.

On 10 January 1941, Oberst Josef Schmid, chief of the Foreign Air Force department of the Luftwaffe General Staff, was instructed to provide target data out to the Dnieper River, and to reconnoitre Soviet air forces. His staff identified 38 Soviet air divisions and 162 air regiments, though 50 air divisions were believed to exist (in fact, the VVS consisted of 70 air divisions and five brigades). Not that anyone was unduly worried about numerical discrepancies. Luftwaffe intelligence assessed the VVS ground organisation as backward, its supply system poor and the Russians lacking in natural technical gifts. Consequently, VVS combat readiness was assessed at only 50% and hence inadequate. The normally objective chief of Luftwaffe operations, Gen Hoffmann von Waldau, regarded the USSR as a 'state of below-average intelligence' and Hitler felt that 'the Russians will crumple under the massive impact of our tanks and aircraft.'[17]

Although Stalin refused to believe all the intelligence, which shouted out that an invasion was imminent, the Soviets had a defence plan. It called for 171 divisions to be arrayed in three successive belts along the new frontier. The first echelon was a light covering force, and each of the 57 rifle divisions had 70km of front to defend. The next two belts were more powerful, containing most of the 20 mechanised corps in European Russia. The intention was to form a second strategic echelon behind the

A Ju86P high-altitude reconnaissance aircraft of the type flown by Theodore Rowehl's Aufkl.Gr.ObdL over the USSR in preparation for 'Barbarossa'. The Ju86P had three automatic cameras designed to operate from heights around 12,000m, way above the ceiling of any Soviet interceptor in 1941. *Author's collection*

original three belts but as in many other respects, 'Barbarossa' caught the Soviets in transition.[18]

The trouble with the Soviet defence plan was that it assumed that the Red Army would not be taken by surprise, that initial German operations would be conducted with limited forces and that the Red Army would be given time to complete its mobilisation. Stalin was convinced that the main thrust of any German attack would focus on the southwestern front rather than the western, aiming at Ukrainian grain and the coal of the Donbas. Thus fixated, he refused to withdraw strategic reserves east of the Volga for safekeeping — they were left intact and even moved forward into the frontier districts, with no contingency planning in case they were overrun. Stalin, 10 years older than Hitler, had settled on a plan best suited for 1914 rather than 1941.

In his defence, Stalin was not alone in thinking that no sane leader would risk a two-front war or attack the USSR with nothing like the two or three for one numerical advantage that convention demanded. Then the German timetable went awry in the Balkans, with Hitler delaying 'Barbarossa' to drive the British from the Aegean. Both Stalin and Klaus von Below were convinced that it

made no sense to strike east in June with only a few months of combat weather remaining. But Hitler had faith that the Wehrmacht would inflict such catastrophic damage, and that the Soviet leadership and military machine were in such a state, that a short campaign would finish off the USSR. After all, it had only taken 39 days to defeat a major world power like France.

In December 1940 the Luftwaffe ordered the creation of new close-range reconnaissance Staffeln from those already in existence. The army now had 56 close-range reconnaissance Staffeln, as against 30 which had been dedicated to the Western campaign, and from 15 March 1941 all 56 were transferred to army commanders in the East. However, the Luftwaffe did not delegate full tactical control. Short- and long-range reconnaissance units, as well as anti-aircraft artillery (AAA) and air signals units, came under Luftwaffe commanders attached to army and armoured group HQs, who in turn came under Luftwaffe commanders attached to Army Group HQs. These liaison officers were known as Koluft (*Kommandeur der Luftstreitkräfte*).

At airfield level, the modern USAF organisation revolves around an operational wing commander who runs the aircraft, missiles or whatever goes bang, while his base commander looks after the supporting infrastructure. Sixty years ago, the Luftwaffe was run along similar lines. Responsibility for the training, administration, maintenance, supply and field defence of a Luftwaffe airfield was vested in regional organisations known as *Luftgau*. The sharp end would fly in, do its thing and maybe fly off elsewhere, but the base organisation would stay in place ready for the next operational occupants. The eastern *Luftgaukommandos* had to resort to improvisation as few Luftwaffe construction battalions were available and Polish workers could not be employed for security reasons. None the less, 105 airfields were brought into service or enlarged in Luftgau II alone, which encompassed the Warthegau area (Posen and Litzmannstadt) and the northern half of the *Generalgouvernement* of occupied Poland.

Gradually and under conditions of strict secrecy, Luftwaffe units were withdrawn from operations against Britain. Against the backdrop of radio deception and other spoofing measures, fighters were withdrawn first and then the bombers. Movements east took place during the first three weeks of June, with flying units rotated through their home bases for rehabilitation before flying on to their deployment areas. Formations were ordered to be assembled at their airfields, back from the front line, dispersed and camouflaged, by noon on 21 June. Total radio silence was imposed and not until the evening were units allowed to fly, singly or at very low level, to their jumping-off bases near the frontier.

The delayed opening of 'Barbarossa' by the Balkan campaign was not crucial. The snow melted very late that year, and muddy ground conditions, which affected airfields and supply routes, persisted until the end of May. Moreover, Hitler's decision to invade the USSR when he did was not ridiculous. The day after the panzers rolled, the US Secretary of the Navy wrote to President Roosevelt saying 'the best opinion I can get is that it will take anywhere from six weeks to two months for Hitler to clean up on Russia.'[19] Churchill's foremost military strategist, Field Marshal Lord Alanbrooke, wrote after the war that 'My own opinion at the time, and an opinion shared by most people, was that Russia would not last long, possibly three or four months.'[20] These were polite versions of Hitler's words to the head of the Wehrmacht operations staff, Gen Alfred Jodl: 'We have only to kick in the door and the whole rotten structure will come crashing down.'

Below:
An Hs126, the standard army co-operation tactical reconnaissance aircraft in the early years of the war. *Author's collection*

SUNDAY, 22 JUNE 1941

'At last, a proper war.'
Generaloberst Hans Jeschonnek

By mid-June 1941, the Germans had amassed 152 divisions between the Carpathians and the Baltic, of which 19 were panzer and 15 motorised.[21] Together with allies such as 14 brigade-sized Romanian divisions in the south, these forces were divided into Army Group Far North, Army Group North, Army Group Centre and Army Group South. Assigned to each were Air Fleets (*Luftflotten*) through which the Luftwaffe, with Slovak and Romanian air elements in the south, would cover an offensive front stretching 1,600km from the Baltic to the Black Sea.

'Barbarossa's' strategic aim was to destroy the military power of the Soviet Union in six to eight weeks at best, or in three to four months at most. The Luftwaffe's role was outlined in Führer Directive No 21:

'The Luftwaffe will make available for this Eastern campaign supporting forces of such strength that the army will be able to bring land operations to a speedy conclusion and Eastern Germany will be as little damaged as possible by enemy air attack.

'The final objective of the operation is to erect a barrier against Asiatic Russia on the general line Volga-Arkhangelsk. The last surviving industrial areas of Russia in the Urals can then, if necessary, be eliminated by the air force.

'It will be the Luftwaffe's duty to paralyse and eliminate the effectiveness of the Russian Air Force as far as possible. It will also support the main operations of the army, ie those of Army Group Centre and of the vital flank of Army Group South. Russian railways and bridges will either be destroyed or captured.

'In order that we may concentrate all our strength against the enemy air force and for the immediate support of land operations, the Russian armaments industry will not be attacked during the main operations. Such attacks will be made only after the conclusion of mobile warfare, and they will be concentrated first on the Urals area.'

Section IIIB of the Directive listed the goals of the Luftwaffe as (i) to eliminate Soviet air forces, (ii) to support German ground operation, (iii) to interrupt Soviet communications, and (iv) to provide paratroops and airborne personnel if the occasion should require.[22]

The Army Groups and their conjoint Air Fleets were ordered to co-ordinate a surprise attack on the Soviet Union at 03.30hrs (dawn) on 22 June 1941. Directive 21 laid down that German armoured forces would shatter the Russian front defences north and south of the Pripet marshes, after which isolated Soviet forces were to be attacked individually and destroyed. All this was to take place as close to the border as possible — withdrawal of Soviet forces into the interior of the USSR was to be prevented at all costs.

It was left to Hans Jeschonnek, his operations chief Hoffmann von Waldau, and their subordinate staffs to put the detailed meat on these bones. In the Far North, the post of Luftwaffe Commander Kirkenes was established within Gen Hans-Jürgen Stumpff's Luftflotte 5 to support the ground force advance against Murmansk and the Murmansk railway. Alongside Army Group North, Gen Alfred Keller's Luftflotte 1 operated out of its HQ at Insterburg to assist the army advance from East Prussia towards the Dvina River and Leningrad. Luftflotte 1 had only one Air Corps — Gen Helmuth Förster's Fliegerkorps I — with its HQ in the grammar school at Gumbinnen. This Air Corps was to co-operate with the Sixteenth and Eighteenth Armies and, in particular, with Fourth Panzer Group. The initial Army Group North front was about 200km wide, but the distance from Königsberg to Leningrad through Lithuania, Latvia and Estonia, was just under 850km. The other air formation in Luftflotte 1 was Luftwaffe Commander Baltic with its HQ at Metgethen, Samland district. Luftwaffe Commander Baltic was expected to guard the coastal flank by attacking Soviet naval vessels and supporting ground assaults on Baltic islands.

The most crucial point along the entire Eastern Front was the assembly area of Field Marshal Fedor von Bock's Army Group Centre. Army Group Centre had the task of 'bursting forward with particularly strong panzer and motorised formations from the area around and north of Warsaw and of smashing the enemy forces in Byelorussia.' This would create 'the prerequisite' for Army Group Centre to co-operate with Army Group North to 'annihilate enemy forces fighting in the Baltic' and capture Leningrad. Hitler decreed that 'only after the accomplishment of this priority task . . . are offensive operations to be continued with a view to the seizure of the important communications and armaments centre of Moscow.'

Field Marshal Albert Kesselring's Luftflotte 2 was responsible for air power in the centre. With its HQ in a former sports school at Bielany, 7km northwest of Warsaw, Luftflotte 2 had two subordinated Air Corps. Fliegerkorps II, on the right, operated under Gen Bruno Lörzer from his command post at the casino in Otwock. This Air Corps was to support the Fourth Army and, most importantly, Gen Heinz Guderian's Second Panzer Group. On the left wing, Gen Wolfram Freiherr von

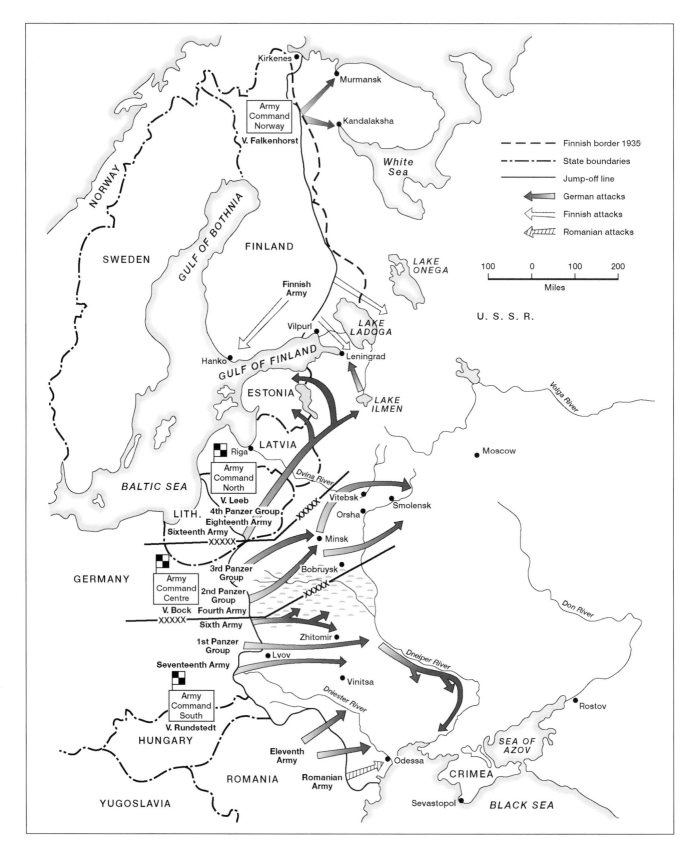

Richthofen's Fliegerkorps VIII, with its command post on the north shore of Lake Wigry, east of Suwalki, was to co-operate with the Ninth Army and its Third Panzer Group. Reinforced by the vitally important anti-aircraft artillery (AAA) batteries of I Flakkorps under Gen Walter von Axthelm, Luftflotte 2's air striking power was to support Army Group Centre's initial drive east on a 300km-wide front between the Baltic States and the largest swamp on the European continent, the Pripet Marshes.[23]

Army Group South covered the area from the Pripet Marshes to Romania, supported by Gen Alexander Löhr's Luftflotte 4 with its HQ just north of Rzeszów. On the Air Fleet's right wing, Gen Kurt Pflugbeil's Fliegerkorps IV was deployed in eastern Romania with its command post at Iaşi. The left wing — Lublin-Zamość in southern Poland — was the responsibility of Gen Robert Ritter von Greim's Fliegerkorps V with its command post at Lipsko, just south of Zamość. Also in southern Poland was Gen Otto Dessloch's II Flakkorps.

Opposite:
The final plan for Operation 'Barbarossa'.

Left:
Deployment of Luftflotten and Fliegerkorps for 'Barbarossa', 22 June 1941.

Luftwaffe Order of Battle, Operation 'Barbarossa', 22 June 1941

Luftflotte 1 (Generaloberst Keller)

2.(F)/ObdL	Do215B
Wekusta 1 (weather observation)	He111, Ju86P
KGrzbV (air transport Gruppe) 106	Ju52/3m
5 liaison squadrons with Fi156 *Storch*	

Fliegerführer Ostsee (Oberstleutnant Wolfgang von Wild)

KGr806	Ju88A
KuFlGr125	He60, He114, Ar95
Seenotbereichskommando (air sea rescue Staffel) IX	

Fliegerkorps I (General der Flieger Helmuth Förster)

5.(F)122	Ju88D, Bf110F
Stab, II., III./KG1	Ju88A, He111H
Stab, I., II., III./KG76	Ju88A
Stab, I, II., III./KG77	Ju88A
Stab, I., II., III./JG54	Bf109F
4., 5./JG53	Bf109F

Luftgau 1 (Königsberg)

Erg.²⁴/JG52, JG54	Bf109E

Army Co-operation (Koluft)

4 long-range day/night recce squadrons with Ju88D, Do17P, Bf110C/F
11 close recce squadrons of Hs126

Luftflotte 2 (Generalfeldmarschall Kesselring)

Stab, 2.(F)/122	Ju88A/D
Wekusta 26	Do17Z, He111P
Stab, I., III./JG53	Bf109F
Erg./JG51	Bf109E

6 liaison squadrons with Fi156

Fliegerkorps II (General der Flieger Lörzer)

1.(F)/122	Ju88D, Bf110F
KGrzb102	Ju52
Stab, I., II., III./KG3	Ju88A, Do17Z
Stab, I., II., III./KG53	He111H/P
Stab, I., II., III./StG77	Ju87B
Stab, I., II./SKG210	Bf110E
Stab, I., II., III., IV./JG51	Bf109F

Fliegerkorps VIII (General der Flieger von Richthofen)

2.(F)/11	Do17P
KGrzb1, 50	Ju52
Stab, I., II., III./KG2	Do17Z
Stab, II., III./StG1	Ju87R
Stab, I., III.Erg./StG2	Ju87B/R

II.(*Schlacht*)/LG2	Bf109E
10.(Sch)/LG2	Hs123A
Stab, I., II./ZG26	Bf110C/E
Stab, II., III./JG27	Bf109E
II./JG52	Bf109E/F

Flakkorps I (Generalmajor von Axthelm)
Stab Flak Regt 101; I Battalion (btn) 12 Flak Regt; I Btn 22 Flak Regt; 77 Light AA Btn

Luftgau II (Posen)

Erg./ZG26	Bf110C/D
Erg./JG51	Bf109E

Army Co-operation (Koluft)
4 long-range day/night recce squadrons with Ju88D, Do17P, Bf110F
23 close recce squadrons with Hs126, 1 with Fw189A

Luftflotte 4 (Generaloberst Löhr)

4.(F)/122	Ju88D
Wekusta 76	He111H, Ju88A
KGrzbV 104	Ju52
8 liaison squadrons with Fi156	

Deutsche Luftwaffen-Mission Rumänien (Generalleutnant Speidel)

Stab, III./JG52	Bf109E

Fliegerkorps IV (Generalleutnant Pflugbeil)

3.(F)/121	Ju88D
Stab, I., II., III./KG27	He111H
II./KG4	He111H
Stab, II., III./JG77	Bf109E
I.(Jagd)/LG2	Bf109E

Fliegerkorps V (General der Flieger von Greim)

4.(F)/121	Ju88D
Stab, I., II., III./KG51	Ju88A
Stab, I., II./KG54	Ju88A
Stab, I., II., III./KG55	He111H, Bf110C
Stab, I., II., III./JG3	Bf109F

Flakkorps II (Generalleutnant Dessloch)
Stab, Flak Regt 6; I Btn, 7 Flak Regt; II Btn, 26 Flak Regt; I Btn 24 Flak Regt; 93 Light AA Btn
Stab, I, II and IV Btns Gen Göring Regt; 43 Flak Regt; 74,83 and 84 Light AA Btns

Luftgau VII (Vienna)

Erg./JG77	Bf109E

Luftgau VIII (Breslau)

Erg./JG3, JG27	Bf109E

Army Co-operation (Koluft)

4 long-range day/night recce squadrons with Ju88D, Do17P, Bf110F
14 close recce squadrons with Hs126

Luftflotte 5 (Generaloberst Stumpff)

Wekusta 5	He111, Ju88, Do17, He60, Ar232
1 liaison squadron with Fi156	
Air Leader Kirkenes	
1 Kette of 5.(F)/124	Ju88D
IV.(Stuka)/LG1	Ju87B
6./KG30	Ju88A
1./JG77	Bf109E
Army Co-operation	
1 close recce squadron with Hs126	
Fliegerführer Nord (Ost)	
1.(F)/124	Ju88D
2 Ketten, KuFlGr706	He115, BV138
1 'destroyer' Staffel of JG77	Bf109E

Slovak Air Force

1st Observation Gp	Letov S-328
2nd Fighter Gp	Avia B534

Romanian Air Group

1st Sqn	Bristol Blenheim 1
1st Bomber Flotilla	
1st Bomber Gp	Savoia S.79B
4th Bomber Gp	PZL37
5th Bomber Gp	He111H
1st Fighter Flotilla	
5th Fighter Gp	He112B
7th Fighter Gp	Bf109E
8th Fighter Gp	IAR80
2nd Bomber Flotilla	
2nd Bomber Gp	Potez 63B, Bloch 210B, IAR37
2nd Army Co-operation Flotilla	
11th, 12th, 13th, 14th Sqns	IAR38/39
3rd Romanian Army	
4th Sqn	Bristol Blenheim 1
19th, 20th, 21st Sqns	IAR39
4th Romanian Army	
3rd Sqn	Bristol Blenheim 1
15th, 17th, 22nd Sqns	IAR39

Just as in the 1991 Gulf and 1999 Kosovo conflicts, the initial 'Barbarossa' air effort was aimed at the opposing air forces. Hitler's Directive stated that 'effective intervention by the Russian air force . . . [was to be] prevented from the very beginning of operations by powerful strikes.' Consequently, all Soviet airfields identified by Rowehl's reconnaissance Gruppe and signal intelligence as being operational near the frontier, including the ground support organisations and flying squadrons which were believed to have some 3,000 aircraft, were to be subjected to surprise attacks by all available assets. And these attacks were to continue against VVS air and ground assets until they were considered eliminated

German Army staffs recognised the need to employ the bulk of Luftwaffe combat power against the VVS during the first days of the campaign. Once air superiority, or better still air supremacy, was achieved over western Russia, the German Army could undertake its offensive without any meaningful interference from Soviet aircraft.

Hitherto, the Blitzkrieg strategy hinged on massed waves of aircraft striking in formation to maximise impact and minimise losses in time and space. Unfortunately the Luftwaffe's medium bombers were based well back from the Soviet border, while the BF109 fighters, Bf110 Zerstörer (destroyers) and Ju87 Stukas, which were based closer to the USSR, could not fly formation at night. To co-ordinate these disparate air elements to best effect, the Luftwaffe High Command would have preferred to attack Soviet airfields *after* the artillery bombardment began at dawn. But the Army objected on the grounds that Soviet air forces, forewarned by the ground assault, would get airborne in the early dawn and either throw themselves against advancing Axis troops or escape to airfields in the rear to fight another day.

In effect, the German Army insisted on attacking at dawn while demanding a guarantee that the Russians would be confined to their airfields. The OKL's argument that neither men nor technology were up to delivering a knockout blow in darkness, and that the Army should delay its advance to allow the Luftwaffe to deliver a shattering, pre-emptive blow at first light, was rejected. The Army line, supported by Hitler, meant that a sizeable medium bomber force would have to get airborne and transit for up to an hour at night without alerting the opposition.

Luftflotte 2 staffs compromised by gathering 30 handpicked crews experienced in night operations, and launching them during the early hours of 22 June. Flying in *Ketten* — three-aircraft Vic formation — these Do17s, Ju88s and He111s flew at maximum altitude over unsettled marsh and forest areas to avoid detection to strike 10 major Soviet air bases precisely at 03.15hrs. 'At 02.11hrs we took off on our first mission against the East,' recalled Hptm Gerhard Backer of III./KG1. 'It was a clear night and the horizon was bright from the midnight sun in the far north.' Backer could see the *Ratas* ('Rats' — the Spanish Civil War nickname for Polikarpov I-16 single-seat fighters) at Libau airfield, Lithuania, parked in nice tight rows, 'offering us a good target in the bright night'.[25]

At lower altitude, a far greater number of German bomber, dive-bomber and fighter formations went for targets closer to the front line. A host of German aircrews had been brought to readiness at 22.00hrs the previous evening. The first wave was

Left:
Bombing up an
He111 of 9./KG53.
*Bauer via Goss/
Rauchbach Archive*

Below and right:
He111s of 9./KG53 flying in formation
en route to the target. *Bauer via
Goss/Rauchbach Archive*

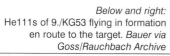

Opposite:
Polikarpov I-16B 'Ratas', capable of firing
1,800 rounds per minute, flying over wooded
Soviet countryside. The stubby I-16 was the
first low-wing, single-seat fighter with
retractable landing gear to enter into service
anywhere in the world. *IWM*

briefed at midnight, whereupon commanders gathered their men about them and read out, often by torchlight, Hitler's message entitled 'Soldiers of the Eastern Front' which called on every man to give his best. BMW, Junkers and Daimler-Benz engines roared into life in East Prussia, Poland and Romania. Gen Guderian, godfather of the Blitzkrieg who had seen the unoccupied Russian defences on the eastern side of the River Bug, was at his command post. His Second Panzer Group watched the Luftwaffe tail-lights vanish east over the frontier. Tanks, artillery and poor bloody infantry waited the last few minutes before their combined force fell upon the Soviet Union.

As the short summer night ended, the first air wave in the early morning of 22 June was directed against 31 airfields, three suspected senior command posts, two barracks, two artillery positions, a bunker system and an oil depot.[26] It was a complete success. Obstlt Paul Deichmann, Chief of Staff at Fliegerkorps II, observed that 'at only one field was a fighter unit met which was just taking off. The bombs fell in the midst of the unit so that the aircraft lay destroyed in take-off formation at the end of the field.'[27] Only two German aircraft failed to return.

The Soviet 15th Fighter Aviation Regt of the 8th Composite Aviation Div had discovered that it was at war a few minutes earlier when Alytus aerodrome, midway between the East Prussian border and Vilnius, was hit by Bf110s of 5./ZG26, led by Hptm Johannes Freiherr von Richthofen, cousin of the Red Baron. But the vast majority of 868 medium bombers, Stukas, Zerstörer and fighter-bombers started bombing and strafing at 03.30hrs, the very moment that German artillery heralded the advance of an *Ostheer* of 3,800,000 men.

For an airman, there is nothing more frustrating than battling to a target only to drop an ineffectual or inappropriate weapon at the very end. A few days after the successful crossing of the Bug at Brest-Litovsk, 45th Infantry Div requested Fliegerkorps II's help to subdue an encircled Red Army commissar school that was stubbornly hindering the forwarding of supplies to Second Panzer Group. Attacks by dive-bombers, which were then able to carry only 500kg (1,102.5lb) bombs, were not up to breaching the school's fortifications. So the Air Corps used a heavy bomber, manned by a specially selected crew and carrying a 1,800kg (3,969lb) bomb that had been brought up from the rear. This SC 1800 bomb tore open the fortifications and the forces in the school capitulated soon afterwards.

All manner of Luftwaffe weapons were dropped on, or fired at, Soviet air and ground forces at the start of 'Barbarossa'. Standard high-explosive (HE) bombs were very effective against concrete runways and permanent buildings, but much less so against Russian border airfields that were often grass strips. HE bombs simply exploded deep in the soft ground, creating visually impressive craters but not much destruction around and about. Incendiary bombs were much better. As they rained down from around 5,000m out of bombers such as the He111s of I./KG53, they set aircraft, accommodation and fuel dumps alight, created panic and mayhem, and acted as beacons to guide subsequent waves of attacking aircraft and to inspire advancing German troops.

The Luftwaffe also unveiled a hitherto secret weapon on 22 June — the SD-2 fragmentation bomb. SD-2 'butterfly bombs' were small 2kg (4.4lb) cylindrical weapons carried in special containers fitted to aircraft attacking at lower level. A Ju88 or a Do17 could carry 360 SD-2s, while a Bf109 or Ju87 could carry up to 96. After being released in rapid succession, each SD-2 bomb casing opened up to form a pair of wings, enabling individual cylinders to spin down to the ground like sycamore seeds. Against minimal opposition, German bomber crews were free to sweep in at low level and plant SD-2s accurately over a wide area. Each 200g explosive charge went off on impact, and the resulting showers of shrapnel proved very effective against 'soft' lines of parked aircraft or troops out in the open.

The SD-2 had its drawbacks. Often, impact detonation from the first bombs to explode blew back to the aircraft not too far above, damaging the release mechanism. Several German aircraft were forced to return with SD-2 bombs hung up on their racks, and some of these detonated on landing, destroying the aircraft and killing or injuring the crew. Not for nothing were SD-2s known to German aircrew as 'the Devil's eggs'.

*   *   *   *

On 22 June 1941, a Luftwaffe force of 500 bombers flew four to six sorties, 270 dive-bombers seven to eight sorties, and 480 fighter/fighter-bombers between five and eight. As the day progressed, their target set expanded to cover 66 Soviet forward airfields where, in the main, no significant effort appeared to have been made either to put VVS fighters on standing patrols or to disperse the large numbers of aircraft deployed on the ground. Russian fighters and bombers were still neatly lined up as they had been on Rowehl's photographs and, as John Erickson put it so aptly, 'not hundreds but thousands of machines were thus displayed in a style best fitted to ensure their destruction.'[28] Only Gen M. V. Zakharov, commander in Odessa, had ordered his aircrews to disperse by dawn on 22 June to their field aerodromes; consequently, only six of his aircraft were destroyed on the ground. Elsewhere, as the telegraph wires went down and operations rooms were blown apart, the chances of any rapid and meaningful dispersal disappeared in the dust.

Dozens of VVS aircraft were turned into scrap before the sun was very high over Lithuania. Maj Hannes Trautloft, Kommodore JG54, gave an air defender's perspective of 22 June in his diary:

'At 02:30, when the stars of the night sky are still shining bright, I arrive at the airfield which awoke a long time ago. In the pens, 45 engines are throttled by the groundcrew, blue-yellow flames thrown brightly out of the exhaust manifolds. The air on the runway is filled with that strange smell, a mixture of soil, flowers, grass, gasoline and oil. In the east the firmament changes colour, shadows and darkness quite quickly. A day of destiny starts, everyone on that airfield knows it. We jump into our machines feeling chilly. The metal in the cockpit is cold, the seat-belts are clammy. My groundcrewman straps me in, shouts "Hals und Beinbruch!" ("good luck" or "break a leg"), then I close the canopy. As before every mission, my throat is dry, though maybe my heart beats a bit faster today than other times.

'All Geschwader of Fliegerkorps I are ordered to cross the border at 03:00. With our flight crossing the border, the front comes alive. I have flown first missions in other theatres, and it is always about the new and the unresolved: What will the Russian do? Will our surprise tactics work? Will Russian fighters join the fight? Are their aircraft better than ours? The first mission gives us a quick answer. The Russians were surprised by our attack. Most of the airfields we attacked were without any defence. In front and below us lie the city and the airfield of Kowno. At exactly this moment the sun rises in the east over the horizon and suddenly we stay in that endless transparent clearness of the morning sky; the bright rays on our aircraft.

'Our bomber units attack Kowno airfield — the hits are falling between the parked aircraft. Suddenly in front of us there are two enemy fighters — as quick as they came, they leave. There is no dogfight between them and us. We return. The Front is burning on many places, large black clouds are rising to the sky. The first mission gave two victories. The Russians were not prepared for this surprise attack. But it changes very quickly during the passage of the day.

'We are in combat all day long. My back is hurting. By the afternoon we have air superiority — Russian fighters can no longer be seen. Escorting bomber groups changes to free hunting and ground attack missions.

'In the evening we cross our infantry and ground troops in a low-level flight. We see the heavy dust clouds marking the direction of each walking column, just as it was in Poland. Everywhere we see fires — complete villages are burning. After the last mission, the day's score is passed to Corps. For just one loss, the Geschwader claimed 45 air victories and 35 ground kills during low-level attacks.

'We are all "dog-tired" and ready for sleep. But we can only sleep at midnight. After two hours we have to be ready for the next mission.'[29]

In Luftflotte 2's area Johannes von Richthofen's older brother, Gen Wolfram von Richthofen, was proving adept at directing Fliegerkorps VIII against the 9th and 11th Composite Aviation Divisions of the VVS. The 9th was based around Bialystok in the path of the Panzergruppe 3 spearhead northeast of Warsaw, and it was commanded by Hero of the Soviet Union Gen Sergei Chernykh. Chernykh had learned his trade in the Spanish Civil War when he was credited with shooting down three Nationalist aircraft, including the first Bf109 lost in air combat. His composite air division — the VVS component of each land army consisted of a mixed division combining fighter, bomber and ground attack regiments in much the same way as a German Fliegerkorps — comprised four fighter regiments equipped with 233 modern MiG3 fighters, and 156 elderly Polikarpovs, plus a regiment with 51 bombers. As the 9th Comp Air Div of the Western Military District was one of the best in the VVS, its destruction was a top Luftwaffe priority. Fliegerkorps VIII and II inflicted heavier losses on the 9th than any other VVS formation on 22 June.

The 10th Composite Air Div, on the right wing of Army Group Centre, was also caught with its pants down. Lt Ernst-Wilhelm Ihrig, Staffelkapitän of 3./KG3, was free to make six low-level passes against Pinsk airfield in the southwestern part of Soviet-occupied Poland. Ihrig claimed to have destroyed 60 aircraft on the ground, while the 39th High-speed Bomber Regt of 10th Comp Air Div recorded the loss of 43 SB bombers and five Pe-2s, but either way it was a hammering. The Bf110s of 1./SKG210 claimed to have taken out around 50 of 10th Comp Air Div's aircraft at Kobrin. Overall, 10th Comp Air Div lost 180 of its 231 aircraft on 22 June, with two of its air regiments being completely wiped out.

It was the same story south of the Pripet Marshes where Gen Löhr's medium bombers and Bf109s went against 29 Soviet airfields all the way down to the Black Sea. KG51 had four Ju88 Gruppen committed to Luftflotte 4 in June 1941. As the far-off artillery thundered out its dawn chorus from horizon to horizon, wave after wave of KG51's bombers rolled with gathering speed off the grass strips at Krosno and Lezany. They set off eastwards towards the rising sun, seeing the roads beneath them filled with unending columns of troops grinding their way forward. KG51's initial strike was against Soviet air bases at Striyski, Buschov II, Tremblovla, Buctsacts, Chodorov and Lisietshe, which were packed with reconnaissance, fighter and bomber aircraft drawn up as if on parade. In some 80 sorties, KG51 claimed to have destroyed about 200 Russian aircraft on the ground. At Kovel airfield in northwest Ukraine, Lt Fyodor Arkhipenko was operations officer of 17 Fighter Regt. 'Beginning at 04.25hrs, about 50 German aircraft bombed our field, coming back four times. Only myself and the duty pilot and the guards, the security forces, were there. Because it was Sunday, the rest had been allowed to go home on leave. The airfield was small, two by three kilometres. You can imagine the kinds of horrors that took place at the airfield.'[30]

But it was not just a great occasion for the Luftwaffe; the Royal Romanian Air Force (*Fortele Aeriene Regale ale Roman* or FARR) also played its part. Gen Wilhelm Spiedel had commanded the Luftwaffe Mission in Romania from his HQ at Ferme Lupescu, immediately north of Bucharest, since October 1940. Just before 'Barbarossa' opened, the Mission was placed under the command of Luftflotte 4 to secure the vitally important Romanian oil fields. Five air defence areas were established around the Ploeşti oil wells and refineries, the oil storage and shipping installations at the Black Sea port of Constanţa, the most vulnerable part of the oil pipeline at the bridge over the Danube at Cernavodă, the oil shipping port of Giurgiu on the Danube, and the airfields of the Mission itself. The only Luftwaffe flying unit in Romania was III./JG52 with its Bf109s. Romanian air force units were not assigned to the Luftwaffe Mission, though the German air defence areas included Romanian AAA units and German and Romanian fighter staffs co-operated at the tactical level. When command staffs, AAA regiments, air raid warning and signals units, and an air defence brigade (including oil fire-fighting units) were taken into account, the total strength of Luftwaffe forces deployed to Romania was about 50,000 men. That is not far short of the size of the Royal Air Force today.

The FARR was equipped with a mishmash of aircraft types varying from the German-made He112B single-engined fighter (a competitor to the Bf109), through Polish PZL P.24E fighters built under licence, to 12 Hawker Hurricane fighters and 40 Bristol Blenheim twin-engined bombers supplied by the British in an effort to counter Axis influence in the Balkans. At 04.30hrs on

22 June, Capitan Aviator Anton Stefanescu's Escadrila 76 and Lt Comador Aviator Stefan Anton's Escadrila 77 bombed Bolgardi and Bulgarica airfields in southern Moldavia from a height of 500m. The Potez 633B-2 bombers attacking Bulgarica were bounced by 30 Soviet I-16s and in the ensuing mêlée, Sublocotenent Aviator Teodor Moscu, flying one of the 12 He112 escorts, claimed two I-16s shot down.

Back over Russia Lt Heinz Knoke was a Bf109 pilot with II./JG52 based at the former Polish Air Force base of Suwalki, alongside Stukas and Bf110s. His diary entry for 22 June showed what was possible when you controlled the skies:

'04.00hrs, general alert for all Staffeln. Every unit on the airfield is buzzing with life. We are only a kilometres from the border.

'04.30hrs, all crews report to the Gruppe operations room for briefing. The commanding officer, Hptm Erich Woitke, reads out the special order for the day from the Führer.

'05.00hrs, the Staffel takes-off and goes into action. In our Schwarm four aircraft, including mine, have been equipped with a bomb release mechanism, and I have done considerable bomb practice in recent weeks. Now there is a rack slung along the belly of my good "Emil", carrying 96 2kg fragmentation bombs. It will be a pleasure to drop them on Ivan's dirty feet.

'Flying low over the broad plains, we notice endless German columns rolling eastwards. The bomber formations overhead and the dreaded Stuka dive-bombers alongside us are all heading in the same direction. We are able to carry out a low-level attack on one of the Russian headquarters, situated in the woods to the west of Druskieniki. Everything appears to be asleep — there is not a Russian soldier in sight. Swooping at one of the huts, I press the bomb release button on the control stick. I feel the aircraft lift as it gets rid of its load. The others drop theirs at the same time. The scene below is like an overturned anthill, as the stepsons of Stalin in their underwear flee for cover in the woods. Light flak guns appear. I set my sights on one of them and open up with machine guns and both cannon. Round again and I let them have it. I never shot as well as this before. I come down to 20m, almost brushing the treetops in the process. I carry out five or six more attacks. We buzz around the camp like a swarm of hornets. Nearly all the huts are in flames.

'05.56hrs, Schwarm landing in formation. Aircraft are refuelled and rearmed at top speed. The Stukas return from their mission in support of our armoured units advancing on the ground. Their crews are jubilant too.

'06.30hrs, we are off again. Our objective is the same headquarters as before. This time considerable quantities of light flak come up to welcome us. I put down my bombs on one of the emplacements. Dirt and dust, the gunsight bust! And that takes care of the Ivans. We land at 07.20hrs. Once again the flight is prepared for action at lightning speed. We pilots help the groundcrews and this time we set a record by being completely ready in 22 minutes.

'There is not much left of the Russian camp by now. I place my bombs on the last building still standing. After 48 minutes in the air, we land again and enjoy our first meal of the day.

'New operation orders have arrived. Russian transport columns have been observed by our reconnaissance aircraft retreating eastward along the Grodno–Szczuczyn highway with our tanks in hot pursuit. We are to support them by bombing and strafing the Russians as they retreat.

'Take-off at 10.07hrs, accompanied by the Stukas. They are to dive-bomb the Russian artillery emplacements in the same area. We soon reach Grodno. The roads are clogged with Russian armies everywhere. We begin to appreciate the full extent of Russian preparations to attack us. We have just forestalled the Russian timetable for an all-out attack against Germany for the mastery of Europe. Thousands of Ivans are in full retreat, which becomes an utter rout as we open up on them. I drop my bombs on a column of heavy artillery drawn by horses. I am thankful not to be down there myself.

'We take-off at 20.00hrs for our sixth mission on this first day. There has been no sign of the Russian Air Force the entire day, and we are able to do our work without encountering opposition.'[31]

The official history of the Soviet Air Force stated that the Germans hit 'more than 66 of our airfields, often several times, on which were based the core of the air forces of the Western border districts.'[32] It is usually difficult for any commander to strike the right balance between sustaining the onslaught on the enemy's air defences while generating sufficient air support for ground or naval forces. But by noon on 22 June this was a no-brainer — Russian air units in the Western Special Military District had already lost 528 aircraft on the ground and 210 in the air.[33] In-place Soviet air divisions were pretty well annihilated within just 24 hours — the 9th Composite Air Div had lost 347 aircraft out of 409 deployed, the 10th had lost 180 out of 231, the 11th, 127 out of 199, and so on. Fliegerkorps IV, operating over the southern flank and up against VVS assets that should have enjoyed most warning time, reported destroying 142 enemy aircraft on the ground and only 16 in the air.

The Soviets lost 890 aircraft on the morning of 22 June, 222 in aerial combat or to AAA fire and 668 on the ground. The Luftwaffe, on the other hand, lost only 18 aircraft. By midnight on the first day of 'Barbarossa', the Germans claimed to have destroyed 1,489 Soviet aircraft on the ground and 322 in the air, as against only 61 of their own.[34] Gen von Waldau, Chief of the Luftwaffe Operations Staff, wrote in his diary on the evening of 22 June that 'the timing of the air attack was a complete success'. The official Soviet Air Force history, written at the height of the Cold War, admitted that 'as a result of these sudden mass attacks at our airfields and intense aerial battles, the air forces of the Western districts in the first day of the war lost around 1,200 aircraft, including 800 that were destroyed on airfields.'[35] The discrepancy between German and Russian figures is explained by the differing definitions of destroyed aircraft — some Soviet aircraft could be salvaged and therefore were not struck off the inventory. There is also doubt about the extent to which 'kills' claimed by AAA and Romanian pilots were included. But on 22 June the Germans were not too worried about precise numbers. They knew that they could never write off every individual VVS aeroplane. What the Luftwaffe had to do was keep as many Soviet aircraft out of the sky as possible, be it by destroying airframes, severing control runs with shrapnel splinters, destroying available aviation fuel supplies or whatever to enable the German Army to finish the job.

The great drawback of air power is that it is transitory: an aircraft delivering mayhem one minute is off over the hill and back to base the next, allowing those with the will to shake off the dust and pick up the pieces. So although the initial Luftwaffe air strikes were designed to generate havoc and confusion at forward Soviet air bases, the pace and tempo of air operations had to be maintained to keep VVS heads down while supporting German troops on the ground. Blessed with high-quality aircraft, experienced personnel and favourable weather, the Luftwaffe was able to launch continuous high-level and low-altitude attacks on Soviet airfields. It also shot down nearly all the hostile VVS aircraft that managed to get airborne to challenge it.

Both the German Army and Air Force understood the need for the early capture of Soviet airfields to maintain the momentum of the 'Barbarossa' assault. There was a comradely synergy in all this. The Air would help the Army advance, whereupon the Army would help the Air to seize the airfields it needed to project its air superiority further eastward.

Another 1,000 Soviet aircraft were destroyed on the second day of 'Barbarossa'. The 66 airfields targeted at the beginning were estimated to contain nearly 75% of Soviet combat aircraft, but within 48 hours, Luftwaffe photo-reconnaissance uncovered a large number of hitherto unknown Soviet airfields, most of which were heavily occupied by VVS aircraft. Hermann Göring, a man well used to putting the best spin on statistics, found reported Soviet losses of around 2,500 for 22-23 June to be exaggerated. He ordered a recount and to his amazement, the reassessment *added* 200-300 Soviet aircraft to the original total. 'Only a few days after the launching of the offensive,' recorded Luftflotte 2 commander Albert Kesselring, 'I was flying solo in my Fw189 (a twin-boom tactical reconnaissance and army co-operation monoplane known as 'The Flying Eye') over the Russian zone: proof of how completely the attacks of the first two days had paralysed the Russian Air Force.'[36] The Luftwaffe had effectively achieved air superiority on the first day of the invasion of Russia, a goal that eluded them throughout the long months of the Battle of Britain.

Left:
Generalfeldmarschall Albert Kesselring, an ever-confident and very able air commander known as 'Smiling Albert' to his troops. Although Kesselring is standing in front of a Storch, he preferred to fly himself around the Eastern Front in his twin-boom, twin-engined Fw189 tactical reconnaissance aircraft. *Author's collection*

THE SKY BELONGED TO THEM

'Through the windscreen I could see 15 German bombers approaching from the west. They were flying low, with provocative insolence, as though our sky belonged to them.'
General I. V. Boldin

That the Soviet Air Force came off second best in the Spanish Civil War was not the end of the world. German ascendancy in equipment and tactics made a deep impression on returning Soviet airmen, who should have been allowed to address the lessons that needed to be learned. The need for a new generation of Soviet aircraft, especially in the fighter and ground-attack roles, was obvious, as were the shortcomings of Soviet engines and armament. Tactically, heavy bombers had to be more effective, fighters had to be employed better in air defence, and there was a pressing need for greater co-operation between air and ground forces. None of this was beyond the wit or comprehension of experienced and thoughtful Soviet airmen, had Stalin not chosen that moment to purge his officer corps of some of his brightest and best talent.

The Red Army placed great emphasis on technology and mechanisation in general, and on air and tank forces in particular. The brain behind this was Marshal Mikhail Tukhachevsky, head of the Army Technology and Armament Dept, and during his time Soviet industry started manufacturing a wide variety of advanced fighter, reconnaissance and bomber aircraft. Tukhachevsky represented the Soviet Union at the funeral of King George V, where this scion of former impoverished gentry impressed foreign dignitaries with his wit, his wide range of languages, his political insight and the originality of his military thinking.

Yet despite Tukhachevsky's thinking on modern warfare, many remained ideologically wedded to the idea that wars were decided by motivated masses rather than by technology and fancy doctrine. Reliance on the tank or the aeroplane, rather than the co-operation of all arms around a strong infantry, was dismissed as 'bourgeois' flummery. It did not help that Stalin viewed the military officer corps with suspicion.

The concept of the 'purge' was rooted in Communist Party theory, not only to prevent backsliding and complacency but also to maintain the spirit of the revolution. The first to go was Marshal Tukhachevsky, who owed nothing to Stalin and was a hero in his own right. He was executed after a secret trial for 'treason' in 11 June 1937, ushering in a purge of great cruelty against the entire military hierarchy from the top down to regimental commanders. Some 35,000 officers out of an officer corps of 80,000 fell victim to the purges. Yakov Alsknis, a veteran of the Imperial Air Force and head of the VVS since 1931, was executed on 31 July 1938. Alsknis' deputy, Vasily Khripin, a

protagonist of the long-range bomber like Tukhachevsky, followed his boss to the firing squad, as did B. V. Troyanker of the Air Force Political Directorate, A. I. Todorsky, head of the Air Force Academy, and most VVS district air commanders. Many victims were ferried for trial from distant regions to Moscow in the 'prison plane' commanded by the unscrupulous Alexander Golovanov, who was destined for wartime command of Long-Range Aviation.

The purges created a debilitating command vacuum in the VVS. The old political commissar system was also restored, adding dual and often disparate founts of authority where there should have been only one. Moreover, Stalin regarded the 'new' Air Force as his special fiefdom, priding himself on his technical knowledge and subjecting designers, engineers and commanders to arbitrary decisions and excessive demands. Failure meant the firing squad or the Gulag, where a number of distinguished aircraft designers including A. N. Tupolev, arrested for allegedly selling the blueprints of the Bf110 to Germany, languished in Beria's prison 'design bureau'.

There were aviation benefits from this carrot-and-stick approach. Nikolai Polikarpov, designer of the I-15 and I-16, had been arrested and imprisoned along with a number of his design staff in 1930 on charges of conspiring to sabotage the aircraft industry after a number of his design prototypes crashed. A special design bureau was then set up for interned designers, named Menzhinsky after the head of the secret police. The first product of this bureau was Polikarpov's successful I-5 fighter; some 800 were delivered between 1931 and 1934, whereupon members of the design team were then set free as a reward for their efforts. V. M. Petlyakov was arrested during the 1937 purge, and while forced to work as an internee he and his team developed a twin-engined, high-altitude, long-range two-seat fighter optimised for combat against long-range, high-altitude bombers. Many novelties such as turbo-superchargers and cabin pressurisation were incorporated in the design, along with all-electric actuation of the undercarriage, supercharger, fuel pump, radiator and wing flap, and trim tabs. This fighter would eventually be transformed into the formidable Pe-2 dive-bomber, which only makes you wonder what Petlyakov would have produced in more congenial circumstances.

Gen Alexander Loktionov, a one-time rifle brigade commander with little experience of air matters, took over the VVS for a brief period until he was replaced by Gen Yakov Smushkevich, hero of Spain and Khalkhin-Gol. This pedigree availed him little. Smushkevich was air commander during the disastrous Winter War with Finland in 1939-40, which was noted for indifferent air gunnery, poor training, neglect of night and bad weather flying, faulty navigation, shortage of radios and lack of personal initiative. As a result, an expanding VVS contingent suffered setback after setback against a Finnish Air Force that could rarely muster more than 100 aircraft, many of them obsolete. By the time massed Soviet firepower and overwhelming numbers pierced the Mannerheim Line — it took 45 rifle divisions, 1,500 tanks and 3,000 aircraft to defeat the Finns — the VVS had lost around 650 aircraft to enemy action and accidents, nearly half of them bombers. Smushkevich was dismissed, leaving Stalin to select the 29-year-old Lt-Gen P. V. Rychagov, who had served as a fighter pilot in China, to take over the VVS.

Under Marshal Voroshilov, a Stalin crony who had introduced a post-purges military career advancement system based on class and political background, changes were made to address the lack of co-ordination between air and ground forces during the early stages of the Winter War. The aviation armies, which had been subordinated directly to the Commissariat for Defence, were disbanded. Henceforward, VVS commanders were subordinated to Army commanders in tactical operations. All *Shturmovik* (ground attack) and many VVS fighter units lost their independence and were put under the direct command of individual Army commanders even though most Army commanders lacked the most basic understanding of how to employ air power effectively and economically.

Voroshilov's successor was Semen Timoshenko, a poor peasant's son who won two St George Crosses as a machine gunner in World War 1. By May 1940 he had been promoted to Marshal of the Soviet Union and Defence Commissar. As Stalin's most professional soldier, Timoshenko was not blind to Soviet military deficiencies. In the autumn of 1940 he reported that 'at all levels we have been operating too simplistically . . . We taught the Army how to die, but not how to win. We taught our forces indiscriminate tactics, based on the idea that we can always oppose force with considerably greater force, send a division to beat a battalion, as we did in the Finnish War.' He criticised Soviet inadequacies in the use of aircraft, pointing out that the VVS Command had no agreed policy or doctrine for planning operations or conducting aerial warfare.

Since Tsarist times, Russian military organisation had centred on Military Districts, with each District theoretically capable of carrying out a range of operations on its own. During World War 1, the Russians had established three Fronts wherein far greater firepower than that from a single Military District was massed. In January 1940, Timoshenko established a North-Western Front against the Finns, with its command HQ at Leningrad made

Below:
Soviet Pe-2s in formation. *IWM*

responsible for organising all land, air, naval and operational reserve forces into one predetermined strategic direction.[37] However, while a new homeland air defence force (PVO)[38] was set up early in 1941, Timoshenko did nothing to correct Voroshilov's mistake in keeping the split between Front and Army Air Forces.

It was not all doom and gloom. In January 1940, the tough-minded and efficient A. I. Shakhurin replaced a party apparatchik as head of the Aviation Industry Commissariat. Shakhurin was to remain in charge of Soviet aircraft production throughout the war, and his arrival heralded a rapid transition to a new generation of military aircraft. Shakhurin was fortunate in that an outstanding bevy of Soviet aircraft designers — Yakovlev, Sukhoi, Lavochkin, Ilyushin, Mikoyan and Gurevich — was demanding to be placed on a par with the likes of Polikarpov and Tupolev. During the first half of 1941, more than 1,900 MiG-3, LaGG-3 and Yak-1 fighters rolled off the production lines while 458 Pe-2 bombers and 249 *Shturmoviki* were delivered to front-line units.

In 1941 Soviet Air Forces consisted of the Long-Range Bomber Aviation (DBA), Front Air Forces and Army Air Forces. The Soviet High Command — the *Stavka* — directly supervised the DBA, which accounted for 13.5% of VVS combat aircraft divided between 13 bomber and five fighter divisions. Front Air Forces (those belonging to the 16 Military Districts and home defence) owned 40.5% of VVS combat aircraft. Army Air Forces, subordinated to the various ground force commanders, had 43.7%, while 2.3% were in Army corps liaison squadrons. Sixty-one aviation divisions (18 fighter, nine bomber and 34 'composite') were subordinate to the ground forces. To add to the disjointed nature of Soviet aviation, each of the Soviet Navy's four fleets had its own air force, while PVO air defence zone commanders controlled their fighter aircraft, AAA guns, searchlights and barrage balloon defences. Naval and PVO assets amounted to about 20% of Soviet aviation.

Below:
An intact MiG-3 captured by the Germans. *Goss/Rauchbach Archive*

The disjointed nature of Soviet air power is shown by the VVS order of battle for 21 June 1941:

FRONT AIR FORCES AND ARMY AIR FORCES[3]

In USSR — 61 air divs (*Aviadiviszii*) and 10 reconnaissance regts (*Aviapolka*)

In western USSR:

VVS-Leningrad Military District (MD)
1 SAD (Composite Air Div), subordinate 14th Army between Murmansk and Kandalaksha
55 Comp Air Div, subordinate 7th Army, Petrozavodsk area
5 Comp Air Div, subordinate 23rd Army, Karelian Isthmus
41 BAD (Bomber Div), subordinate 23rd Army, Siverskaya area
3 and 54 IAD (Fighter Divs), air defence of Leningrad
2 Comp and 39 Ftr Divs, south of Leningrad

Total: 1,270 aircraft

VVS-Baltic Special MD
8 Comp Air Div at Kaunas and Alytus
57 Ftr Div between Vilnius and Daugavpils
7 Comp Air Div, northern Lithuania
6 Comp Air Div between Riga and Liepaya
4 Comp Air Div in Estonia

Total: 1,211 aircraft

VVS-Western Special MD
9 Comp Air Div, subordinate 10th Army, Bialystok border area
10 Comp Air Div, subordinate 4th Army, Brest-Litovsk border area
11 Comp Air Div, subordinate 3rd Army, Grodno-Lida border area
12 Bbr Div, Vitebsk area
43 Ftr Div between Minsk and Smolensk
13 Bbr Div, Bobruysk area

Total: 1,789 aircraft

VVS-Kiev Special MD
14 Comp Air Div, subordinate 5th Army, Lutsk area
62 Bbr Div, subordinate 5th Army, Kiev area
15 Comp Air Div, subordinate 6th Army, Lvov area
16 Comp Air Div, subordinate 6th Army, Ternopol area
63 Comp Air Div, subordinate 26th Army, Stryy area
64 Comp Air Div, subordinate 12th Army, Stanislav area
17 Bbr Div, Proskurov area
36 Ftr Div, Kiev area
19 Bbr Div, Belaya Tserkov area
44 Ftr Div, Vinnitsa area

Total: 1,913 aircraft

VVS-Odessa MD
20 Comp Air Div between Beltsy and Tiraspol
21 Comp Air Div, north Black Sea coast from Bolgrad-Vorms
45 Comp Air Div from Razdelnaya-Fedorovka

Total: 950 aircraft

LONG-RANGE STRATEGIC BOMBER AVIATION (DBA)

In USSR — five BAKs (Bomber Aviation Corps) and three independent *Diviszii* (independent wings of four to six regiments)

In western USSR:

1 BAK, Novgorod area
2 BAK, Kursk area
3 BAK, Smolensk area
4 BAK, Zaporozhye area
18 DBAD at Skomorokhy and Borispol

Total: 1,332 aircraft

NAVAL AIR FORCES

VVS-SF (Northern Fleet)
72 Comp Air Div, 118 Reserve Regt, 49 Independent Recce Aviation Sqn, 24 Liaison Flt

Total: 116 aircraft

VVS-KBF (Red Banner Baltic Fleet)
8 Bbr Aviation Brigade, 10 Comp Aviation Brigade, 61 Fighter Aviation Brigade, 15 Independent Naval Reconnaissance Aviation Regt, plus seven independent aviation squadrons

Total: 707 aircraft

VVS-CHF (Black Sea Fleet)
62 Ftr Aviation Brigade, 63 Bbr Aviation Brigade, 119 Independent Naval Recce Aviation Regt, plus 11 independent aviation squadrons

Total: 624 aircraft

The overall total of Soviet military aircraft stood at 9,912, but numerical superiority has to be employed properly to be effective. Lt Fyodor Arkhipenko of 17 Fighter Aviation Regt wrote that 'around three o'clock that afternoon, the first day of the war, I was able to make one reconnaissance flight from Brest to the region of Lvov along our border. I could see the entire area on our side was on fire. Everything — the towns, the villages, the settlements — everything was burning.'[40] Alexander Yakovlev, the aircraft designer, was not alone in 1941 when, after witnessing the destruction inflicted by the Luftwaffe, he asked, 'Where was our Air Force?'

Part of the answer lay with the diffused Soviet military air organisation which made it impossible to mass Soviet aircraft together quickly to contest air supremacy once the Germans struck. The degree of separation served the diverse requirements of a vast politico-military structure extending from the Baltic to Vladivostok, but it flew in the face of air power logic. As aircraft can straddle the globe speedily, they should never be split into penny packets or one commander could find himself being hammered from the air while his neighbour conserved his aircraft 'just in case'. Command and control in the VVS in 1941 was much too decentralised, which resulted in medium bombers of the Front Air Forces being expected to fly missions unescorted because most fighter units had been divided among the different ground armies to protect the soldiers' backs.

In June 1941 the VVS was in the process of providing three airfields for each regiment — one main, one standby and a field facility. On top of that, the counter-air phase of 'Barbarossa' fell just as the VVS was beginning to re-equip its forward air units with the next generation of combat aircraft. Disruption and bottlenecks abounded as aircrew and groundcrew adapted to the

new MiG3s, Yak-1s, LaGG-3s and Pe-2s, while reporting to higher command that they were keeping a capability in being. Wanting to see for himself, the veteran airman Gen A. V. Nikitin, chief of the VVS Organisation and Manning Directorate, inspected the 12th Bomber Air Div of the Western Military District in April 1941 and found no fewer than 104 crews undergoing conversion training. Fear of flying accidents, with memories still vivid of what happened to those accused during the purges of 'wreckage' or 'sabotage', resulted in retraining at a snail's pace. Nikitin's post-inspection report stimulated an accelerated programme to achieve operational effectiveness, but there was too much still to do and too little time.

In mid-June 1941, VVS airfields in the western border regions were packed with old and new combat aircraft mixed chaotically. Around one-third of some front-line divisions were not up to operating their aircraft effectively, while Moscow strove to create a new air defence network and keep everyone's spirits up. To cope with massive change while taking on the most accomplished and battle-hardened air force in the world was asking too much.

*   *   *   *

Given the state of his forces' unreadiness, Stalin wanted to avoid war in 1941 at all costs. He insisted firmly and persistently that Germany be given no excuse for armed conflict. Notwithstanding all the warning signs, including the increasing intensity of Rowehl's intelligence-gathering flights in June, Stalin could not bring himself to bring his troops into full battle alert until early on 22 June. Timoshenko then signed off the order to the Military Soviets of the Leningrad, Baltic, Western, Kiev and Odessa Military Districts, telling them that 'a surprise attack by the

Above:
Yak-1 fighters, of which 8,721 were built. *IWM*

Germans is possible' but that 'the assignment of our forces' was on no account 'to give way to provocative actions of any kind which might produce major complications'.

Transmission of this uncertain call to arms was completed by 00.30hrs on 22 June.

In the North, three Panzer divisions (about 600 tanks) and 21 infantry divisions faced one weak Russian rifle division on an attack frontage of less than 40km. In the South, two Soviet rifle divisions faced 25 German infantry divisions supported by about 600 tanks. This left Army Group Centre which, in Clausewitz's words, was 'the hub of all power and movement, on which everything depends'. Army Group Centre planned to envelop and destroy the forces that the Soviets had imprudently massed in the Bialystok-Minsk salient through a large-scale pincer movement. Heinz Guderian's Second Panzer Group, with von Kluge's Fourth Army following, was to advance from the Brest-Litovsk area in a flanking movement from the south, while Gen Hoth's Third Panzer Group, backed up by the Ninth Army, was to advance from the Suwalki tip in a flanking movement from the north.

Two Soviet air divisions in the border area, plus seven others to the rear, initially faced Luftflotte 2, and if these had still been in business at the end of 22 June, Army Group Centre would have been up against it. But Luftflotte 2 systematically destroyed all Soviet aircraft on airfields within a 300km radius. The counter-air campaign was so successful that by 29 June the German High Command was able to report the destruction of 4,017 Soviet aircraft, against the loss of only 150 of its own. Consequently, from very early on the Luftwaffe was free to strike at will against defensive fortifications, rail junctions, troop concentrations, barracks and communication nodes. Like the VVS, the Russian Army was caught completely off guard; its response was piecemeal and sluggish, and the net effect was paralysis. Along almost the entire length of the vast front, the German Army achieved tactical surprise. Army Group Centre intercepted a plaintive Russian wireless signal: 'We are being fired upon. What shall we do?' to which the far from helpful reply was: 'You must be insane. And why is your signal not in code?'

Success in 'Barbarossa' relied on the Wehrmacht advancing rapidly through Poland, into White Russia and beyond, whereupon the whole communist edifice was expected to crumble into dust. Such a rapid advance called for the highest degree of mobility, and in the van of Luftflotte 2's close air support effort were the Stukas. Eight hundred tanks of the 2nd Panzergruppe were massed behind the River Bug on 22 June, and the first task of StG77's Ju87s was to go against the Soviet defence works along the opposite bank. Thanks to the Stukas, the ingenious use of underwater tanks and the element of surprise which left the river bridges intact and undefended, the panzers were soon across and racing toward Minsk and Smolensk.

Gen D. C. Pavlov, the son of a lumberjack and a Soviet tank unit commander in the Spanish Civil War, assumed command of the Western Military District in January 1941. Pavlov had the 3rd, 10th and 4th Armies to cover his stretch of frontier, with strong forces by Bialystok and Minsk. At 05.30hrs, just as 4th Army received its copy of Timoshenko's midnight order about the possibility of a surprise blow, Luftwaffe dive-bombers blew Pavlov's Kobrin HQ to pieces. The bombs also ripped into Kobrin

town itself, as Moscow news broadcasts relayed over loudspeakers extolled breezy keep-fit exercises and yet further socialist triumphs in Soviet factories.

Apart from those Ju87s assigned to Luftflotte 5 to help take the vital ports of Murmansk and Arkhangelsk, the only Stukas initially taking part in 'Barbarossa' were those in support of Army Group Centre. Luftflotte 2's Stukas mounted repeated sorties as they moved from one improvised landing strip to another to keep up with the advancing armoured columns. If they were not blasting some heavy fortification, the Ju87s would take it in shifts to loiter over the advancing armour. Whenever an armoured or infantry formation ran into serious opposition, the forward liaison officer would call up the Stukas, which would then smash a way through to let the advance continue.

German close air support was an inter-service science rather than an art. Fliegerkorps VIII commander Wolfram von Richthofen consolidated his reputation as one of the most successful exponents of intensive Army support operations by introducing the post of Tank Liaison Officer (*Panzer Verbindungs Offizier*). As Hptm Helmut Mahlke, commander of III./StG1, recalled:

Below:
Gen Wolfram von Richthofen (left), commander of Fliegerkorps VIII, walking with the commander of I./StG2, Maj Hubertus Hitschhold, in Bulgaria, April 1941. *IWM*

'In Russia we had a large number of UHF radio crews travelling in the same vehicles with the Army. They were a kind of forward air controller group. They moved into the main battle areas as needed and were attached to the Army units fighting in the centre of the battle.

'The personnel were normally Stuka signals men, with sometimes the addition of a Stuka pilot. In my experience, I found the most important part of these units was to get well up in the battle and be as close as possible to the Army commander at all times during the battle.

'We found that our Air Force telecommunications system was far superior to that of the Army. I think that part of the reason for this was the basic necessity for Air Force communications to be brief and precise to avoid giving any delay in targeting location and mission orders.'[41]

Below:
The most famous Stuka pilot of them all — Hans-Ulrich Rudel.
Author's collection

If the Ju87 was the totem of the innovative and awe-inspiring Luftwaffe, no one was to personify the 'new German' air assault ethos better than Hans-Ulrich Rudel. Born the son of a clergyman in Silesia in 1916, Rudel joined the Luftwaffe in 1936. After completing pilot training, he applied for dive-bombing training only to be turned down so he flew long-range reconnaissance missions as an observer during the Polish Campaign. Nothing daunted, he continued to press for dive-bomber training, and his persistence was rewarded in May 1940. After the Stuka Training Wing near Stuttgart, Oblt Rudel was posted to the 1st Staffel of StG2. He flew his first combat dive-bombing mission on 23 June 1941 at 03.00hrs. 'By the evening of the first day I have been over the enemy lines four times in the area between Grodno and Wolkowysk. The Russians have brought up huge masses of tanks together with their supply columns. We bomb tanks, flak artillery, and ammunition supplying the tanks and infantry. Ditto the following day, taking off at 03.00hrs and coming in from our last landing often at 22.00. Every spare minute we stretch out underneath the aeroplane and instantly fall asleep . . . We fly over half-completed airfields; here a concrete runway is being built, there a few aircraft are already standing on an aerodrome. One half-finished airfield is packed with Martin bombers.[42] They must be short either of petrol or crews. Flying in this way over one airfield after another, over one strongpoint after another, one reflects: "It is a good thing we struck".'[43]

The Soviet response on 22 June bordered on farce. In the northwest, although German bombs rained down on signals and communications centres, on naval bases, and in particular on Soviet airfields from Riga to Kronstadt, Soviet fighters standing at one-hour alert were held at their airfields even after the first wave of German bombers had passed. Notwithstanding the thought-bubbles that should have been generated by all the Luftwaffe high-level reconnaissance incursions beforehand, when German bombers hit Brest-Litovsk they found the town fully lit up at night with little sign of any preparations for blackouts.[44]

Baltic Fleet Air Force fighter pilot Igor Alexander Kaberov would complete 476 military sorties between 1941-5, during which time he would shoot down 28 enemy aircraft. He would end up as a Hero of the Soviet Union but in late June 1941 a very green Lt Kaberov was on defensive patrol over the vital Kronstadt naval base. He noticed a reconnaissance aircraft over the Karelian Isthmus heading straight for Kronstadt and so, leaving his comrades to cover the naval dockyard, he climbed in the hope of intercepting the intruder. At about 6,000m he found it difficult to breathe. 'It turned out that there was no oxygen mask in the side pocket. On these flights none of us had flown at a great altitude and the technician had removed the mask because it wasn't needed. The reconnaissance aircraft — there was no mistaking from the long nacelles that it was a Ju88 — passed above me at a height of about 8,000m. It was moving fast and I knew that I could never catch it even with an oxygen mask on. I cannot express the annoyance I felt within me.'[45]

As for the Soviet bombers, they had no authorisation to cross their own frontiers, even though the 11th Army — covering the junction of the Baltic and Western Military Districts — and the 8th — covering the Shauliya–Riga approaches — were losing a

Left:
Soviet DB-3F
medium bombers
in formation. *IWM*

considerable amount of equipment and most of their communication links, courtesy of the Luftwaffe.

On the ground in Minsk, Gen I. V. Boldin — Pavlov's deputy — was told by Marshal Timoshenko 'that no operations against the Germans were to be undertaken without Moscow's express permission.' The *Stavka* clung to the hope that they were witnessing a German provocation by a few isolated firebrands, which Hitler would put a stop to as soon as he heard about it. In vain Boldin argued at least to be allowed to activate the AAA defences. After listening carefully, Timoshenko said: 'Comrade Boldin, take note that you are not to begin any action against the Germans without our knowledge.' Boldin yelled, 'What do you mean? Our troops are retreating, towns are in flames, people are dying.'[46] Eventually, Timoshenko gave permission for the 'red packets' — contingency plans for withdrawal back to the Stalin Line — to be opened. For the 10th Army with its mobility stifled, its radios dead and German bombers hitting its fuel dumps and signals centres with persistent accuracy, the red packets meant nothing. Within a few hours the 10th fell to pieces as a cohesive fighting unit, uncovering Bialystok. The 3rd Army on Pavlov's right flank could offer no succour, finding itself attacked on its front and right flank with no radio sets in use.

Although the Russian military analyst I. V. Timokhovich described the VVS reaction to the Luftwaffe assault as 'spontaneous, unco-ordinated and purposeless,'[47] individual Soviet bravery and initiative were in evidence. Notwithstanding the surprise attack, severed communications and that most personnel were stood down on a Sunday, some VVS pilots fought on 22 June. As the first bombs fell on Kurovitsa airfield, southwest of Lvov in the Ukraine, pilots of 164th Fighter Aviation Regt managed to get airborne thanks to a warning message. As the Ju88s of KG51 turned back for the Reich, they found a number of small I-16s and even I-15 biplanes on their tails. Lt P. N. Rubstov machine gunned a Ju88 until it caught fire and crashed within sight of Kurovitsa field. It was probably the first Soviet air victory of the conflict.

The I-15s, now confined to ground-attack duties, and the compact, short-nosed I-16s pursued the Ju88s of KG51 until the Bf109 fighter escort from JG3 appeared. Oblt Robert Oljernik of I./JG3 probably notched up the first German aerial victory when he shot down an I-16. Two more went down by 04.30hrs as Kurovitsa airfield was engulfed in flames 30km to the east, but there was no disguising the fact that seven of the 28 Ju88s originally dispatched had been shot down.

The Russian bomber force largely escaped the Luftwaffe first strike because its bases were set back from the frontier. At 07.15hrs on 22 June, four hours after the first German bomb fell, Red Army Command finally issued new instructions:

'1. With all their strength and means, troops will attack enemy forces and liquidate them in areas where they have violated the Soviet frontier.

'2. Reconnaissance and combat aviation will establish the locations of enemy aviation concentrations and the disposition of his ground forces. With powerful bomber and ground-attack blows, [Soviet] aviation will destroy aircraft on the enemy aerodromes and bomb the basic groupings of enemy ground forces. Aviation blows will be mounted to a depth of 100-150km into German territory. Königsberg and Memel will be bombed.'

Although VVS bomber crews were now committed to an already outdated plan, Soviet SB-2 and DB-3 medium bombers tried to attack several Luftwaffe airfields north of Warsaw around midday on 22 June. When II./JG53 in East Prussia received the first alarm of approaching Soviet bombers, all available Bf109s were scrambled to meet a formation of twin-engined bombers from the 40th High-speed Bomber Aviation Regt. The first was dispatched by Hptm Walter Spies. Over the next few minutes another seven of the vulnerable Soviet bombers — equivalent in looks and age to the British Blenheim — went down. At another airfield, German personnel watched in disbelief as the slow-flying bombers came five times during the day, each time without a fighter escort. German interceptor pilots and flak crews, forewarned and on alert, had a fine old time: of the 25 bombers that came over on one raid, Bf109s accounted for 20.

On 23 June, VVS bombers tried to hit German targets from 3,000m, the attack altitude prescribed in their prewar training. Not surprisingly, the effect on German ground forces was very limited, prompting the decision to bring the bombers down to 800m. Already vulnerable to Luftwaffe fighters, the slow Soviet bombers were now right in the optimum range for the flak batteries. Once ordered to attack a German position, VVS bombers maintained their course despite withering fire. When his airfield was attacked by 27 bombers on 9 July, Maj Günther Lützow took JG3 into the air and shot down an entire VVS regiment in 15 minutes without loss. This massacre of Russian bombers, 'floundering . . . in tactically impossible formations', was likened by Field Marshal Albert Kesselring to 'sheer infanticide'.[48]

Soviet bravery and resourcefulness had nuisance value rather than any significant impact. In the south for instance, Luftwaffe High Command Situation Report No 656 stated that more than 50 Soviet sorties had been flown over Romania up to 26 June, with Constanţa as the principal target. One VVS formation of 20-30 aircraft making a dawn flight against Ploeşti flew towards Constanţa in error, where it was savaged by German Bf109s and lost 17 of its aircraft. On another occasion, some Soviet aircraft dropped 17 demolition bombs on Bucharest from 7,000m, injuring some of the populace. Overall, the impact of desultory Soviet bombing activity on the advancing German war machine was nil.

In their desperate struggle against the Luftwaffe when the Party was not known for handing out tea and medals to any deemed to have shirked their responsibilities, VVS pilots resorted to the *taran*, or ramming technique, used by the Russians in World War 1. The first deliberate ramming of a German aircraft occurred at 04.25hrs on 22 June, less than an hour into the war, when Lt I. I. Ivanov, a flight commander of the 46th Fighter Air Regt, drove his I-16 into the tail of an He111 after his ammunition ran out.

Ivanov was posthumously awarded the gold star, Hero of the Soviet Union. His was the first of over 200 ramming attacks made on the Luftwaffe during the conflict, and it was a good trade-off to sacrifice an obsolescent I-16 for a modern He111. Anybody could ram head on, but the most useful VVS pilots were those who survived to go back against the enemy on the morrow. Russian pilots tried some skilful and daring manoeuvres, including pushing the propeller tip into the opponent's rudder or elevator. If propeller damage was minimal, the pilot could keep control and land safely.

That Soviet aircrew were reduced to ramming the opposition showed the extent to which their air combat tactics were unsuited to the circumstances of June 1941. The VVS was still flying in tight 'V' formations of three aircraft, as the RAF had done up to 1940. These were tactics from the 1920s when firepower from one fighter was insufficient to bring down a bomber, and combat between fighters was a rare event. Very close formation was a distinct advantage when it came to penetrating cloud, and the leader and his wingman attacked the enemy while the third pilot protected them. Three-aircraft 'Vic' formations also looked great on military parades, but during heavy manoeuvring there was a constant danger that aircraft would collide. More often than not, the flight (*zveno*) of three aircraft simply 'disintegrated' in combat. Thereafter, Soviet aircraft fought individually or in pairs with little co-operation with other pilots, and lack of radios reduced combat effectiveness still further.

The basic Luftwaffe fighter unit was the *Rotte* or pair. On the approach to combat, the two flew in staggered line abreast about 200m apart, each covering the other's blind areas. In combat, the leader did the fighting while his wingman guarded his tail. Two *Rotten* made up a *Schwarm* or flight, and a Staffel flew three *Schwarme* stepped up in line astern. This arrangement was loose to allow individual pilots to concentrate on searching for the opposition rather than holding close formation, and it allowed individual *Rotte* leaders considerable room for initiative. The RAF was wise enough to change over to something similar before the height of the Battle of Britain, and the Soviets would adapt accordingly. However, while they were stuck with elderly fighters that had only high manoeuvrability going for them, those VVS pilots that did not flee on the arrival of Luftwaffe fighters tried to push the combat down to low level before pulling high 'g' to go head-to-head in what can only be likened to an aerial knife fight in a telephone box.

Set against the 1,811 Soviet aircraft destroyed on the first day of 'Barbarossa', the Luftwaffe lost 21 Ju88s, 11 He111s, 1 Do17, 2 Ju87s, 14 Bf109s, six Bf110s and six miscellaneous aircraft from enemy action. To these 61 should be added 50 German aircraft damaged in action and 11 Romanian aircraft shot down.[49] These figures were insignificant when compared to Soviet losses, but they matched the Luftwaffe's worst day in the Battle of Britain. After the last landing on 22 June, the Kommodore of KG51, Obstlt Schulz-Heyn, found that 60 of his Ju88 aircrew (15 crews) had been killed or were reported missing. 'Skilful and aggressive attacks by Russian fighter units,' wrote the KG51 war book, 'ensured that the struggle for air supremacy was no easy game.' But in the euphoric aftermath of 22 June, few up the chain took these thought-provoking words to heart.

*   *   *   *   *

On the invasion of Russia, the Luftwaffe in the East consisted of 29$\frac{1}{3}$ Gruppen, 9$\frac{1}{3}$ dive-bomber Gruppen, 20 fighter Gruppen,

two twin-engined fighter Gruppen, two ground-attack Gruppen and 12 long-range reconnaissance Staffeln, five air transport Gruppen and eight Army liaison Staffeln. Gen Hermann Plocher, in his admirable postwar study of the German-Russian air campaign, put Luftwaffe combat aircraft strength and dispositions on 22 June 1941 as 190 for Reich defence, 370 in the Mediterranean, 660 in the West, 120 in Norway (excluding 'Barbarossa' units) and 2,000 in the East.[50] On the other hand, the British Air Ministry's postwar evaluation assessed that the Luftwaffe allocated some 2,770 aircraft to the opening phase of 'Barbarossa' out of a total aircraft strength at 4,300.[51] Finally, the official Soviet Air Force history of the war positioned 3,950 German aircraft on the western frontier of the USSR in June 1941.[52]

Why the variations? Plocher, Fliegerkorps V Chief of Staff in 1941, omitted transport, liaison and all Koluft reconnaissance aircraft from his totals, and he assumed 10 aircraft per Staffel and 30 per Gruppe. The Soviets on the other hand included all types of aircraft and assumed that all Luftwaffe units were at full strength, ie 12 per Staffel and 40 per Gruppe. The British total figure of 2,770 is a reasonable compromise, and it is closest to the German General Staff return of 21 June which gave the following effective strength and combat readiness states:

Role	Effective Strength	Combat Ready
Strategic Recce (ObdL)	61	39
Maritime/weather	168	125
Bombers	952	757
Dive-bombers	465	360
'Destroyers'	102	64
Fighters	965	735
Transports	292	175
Under Army control (Koluft)		
Long-range recce	146	111
Short-range recce	416	358
Courier/liaison	107	91
Total	3,674	2,815[53]

The gulf between establishment strength and combat readiness came about because the Luftwaffe in June 1941 was battle-worn as well as battle-hardened. For instance, the Luftwaffe's premier close air-support force, von Richthofen's Fliegerkorps VIII, had been working solidly since March 1941 when it was thrown into the Greek and Yugoslav campaigns. Straight after that it took part in the airborne assault on Crete, and the Corps' subsequent transfer north to prepare for 'Barbarossa' was rushed to the point of chaos. Further south, only the 22 Ju88s of I./KG51 within Fliegerkorps V were 100% serviceable. II Gruppe had 29 serviceable aircraft out of an established strength of 36, III Gruppe had 28 out of 32 and IV Gruppe 12 out of 15. Whatever the Luftwaffe's exact combat aircraft strength on the Eastern Front, no more than 60-70% were serviceable at the start of 'Barbarossa'.[54] And these rates would fall rapidly once aircraft were flown intensively for any length of time.

To the Luftwaffe numbers must be added the 504 Romanian front-line aircraft, 61 Slovak and 368 Hungarian after Budapest declared war on 27 June. The Luftwaffe and its allies combined to make an awesome aerial fighting force, but their efforts were spread over an initial deployment area extending from Sevastopol to Leningrad and Kronstadt by way of Rostov-on-the-Don and Moscow. When the Finns under Field Marshal Mannerheim attacked towards Leningrad and into Karelia, 550 Finnish aircraft were added to the Axis air order of battle but the Karelian front extended the combat zone by nearly 350km.

There was no gainsaying that Axis airmen were greatly outnumbered. Working from an estimate of 80 aircraft per air regiment and three to five regiments per division, German intelligence estimated that the Soviets had about 7,300 combat aircraft in European Russia on 21 June 1941, backed up by 3,000 in the interior and another 2,000 in the Far East. As it happened, the USSR had around 20,000 aircraft on 22 June 1941. Barely 10% of these were the latest generation of fighter, bomber and ground-attack aircraft, but just under 10,000 aircraft were immediately available to meet the German attack.

German intelligence seriously underestimated the size of the Soviet air order of battle, as it did the strength of the RAF in 1940. It also misread the quality. Analyses made much use of pejorative terms like 'inferior', 'old', 'obsolete' and 'fair game for German fighters', but more seriously they disregarded the significance of Soviet technical advances in aircraft design. It is hard not to conclude that Luftwaffe intelligence reports pandered to Nazi stereotyping of the Slavs as backward and uninspiring. Only two months before the launch of 'Barbarossa', a team of engineers toured Soviet aircraft factories in the company of the German air attaché in Moscow. Among other sights, Luftwaffe experts were shown mass-production facilities for the latest MiG-3 all-metal, single-seat fighter and the Pe-2 twin-engined light bomber. Yet Oberst Josef Schmid of Luftwaffe intelligence dismissed reports that 'the aero-engine facilities at Kuibyshev alone were bigger than Germany's six main assembly factories' as a product of Soviet deception and the visitors' gullibility.

Hitler had defined the Luftwaffe's task as 'to release such powerful forces for the Eastern campaign that a rapid conclusion of ground operations may be anticipated.'[55] While the Soviets massively misread German intentions, the Germans in turn misread the strength of the VVS, the industry supporting it and the blind courage of the Russian soldier. Most of Hitler's commanders had served on the Western Front in World War 1, and Göring and Jeschonnek in particular had no concept of the endlessness of the Russian interior. Some like Field Marshal Erhard Milch knew the Russians and had flown over the steppes, but even he got carried away by euphoria in June 1941.

Of the aircraft allocated to the eastern German Air Fleets in June 1941, Luftflotte 2 had at least 1,500 including more than half the strike force. Luftflotte 4 had half that number while Keller's Luftflotte 1 (379 aircraft) was the weakest of the main trio. Luftflotte 5 in the far north never exceeded 150. Facing them were upwards of 10,000 VVS aircraft and whichever way you looked at it, the Luftflotten were too thinly spread over 22 degrees of latitude to sustain a long campaign. Fifty years later, Coalition forces amassed 2,615 aircraft on the eve of Operation 'Desert Storm' to maintain air supremacy and support ground forces over a theatre of operations barely 480km wide and 320km deep.

When the staffs of Army Group South and Luftflotte 4 set about planning their part of 'Barbarossa' in April 1941, the Army Group representatives understood the Air Fleet's task to be to 'prevent as far as practicable the intervention of the Red Air Force and to support the operations of the Army Group.' The Army staffs presented a whole shopping list of support activities they expected from the airmen, whereupon the Luftflotte representative unequivocally replied: 'Luftflotte 4, faced with a numerically superior opponent, will require a considerable period of time in order to achieve absolute air superiority. In view of the manifold tasks of the Air Fleet, the troops must not count on the same type of support that they have grown accustomed to in previous campaigns. Officers and men must be aware that the Luftwaffe may support the operations of Army Group South only in the immediate *Schwerpunkt* (centre of gravity) of the attack. The tendency to call in a Stuka attack at the first sign of enemy resistance must from now on be resisted at all costs.' In the event, the Luftwaffe was so short of Stukas that it could not afford to allocate any to Luftflotte 4. In the push towards the Dnieper, Luftflotte 4 had to rely on two Ju88 bomber Gruppen and a fighter Gruppe equipped to drop SD-2 anti-personnel fragmentation bombs to provide direct battlefield support for Army Group South.

Not that any of this seemed to matter in late June 1941. As Axis armies motored east along dry, undamaged roads, with the Luftwaffe supreme overhead and Russian defences in disarray, belief in a short, sharp campaign seemed to be well founded.

RIGHT, LEFT AND CENTRE

'Why does the Red Army have such a low fighting efficiency?'
'The reason is Nazi dive-bombers, incompetence of our commanders, their stupid, idiotic actions, because they put their units into the line of fire.'
Lt Yakov Dzhugashvili (eldest son of Joseph Stalin), POW Interrogation, July 1941

Hitler directed the war through the Wehrmacht High Command (OKW), headed by Field Marshal Wilhelm Keitel with Gen Alfred Jodl as Chief of Operations. The day after Hitler launched 'Barbarossa', he boarded his private train for a new *Führerhauptquartier* in East Prussia. The site, known as Wolfsschanze (Wolf's Redoubt), lay in a small wooded area east of Rastenburg. It had been built the previous winter and was well camouflaged against air attack. At the heart of the 10-bunker complex sat the planning staff under Jodl's deputy, Gen Walter Warlimont. The Army High Command (OKH), with Field Marshal Walther von Brauchitsch as C-in-C and Gen Franz Halder as Chief of Staff, was located a few kilometres to the northeast. The forward echelon of the Luftwaffe High Command (OKL), codenamed 'Robinson', which sent operational orders direct to the Luftflotten commanders, was accommodated in trains in sidings near Goldap and in the Johannesburger Heide.

As Field Marshal von Bock's Army Group Centre was the main show in town, it was not surprising that Field Marshal Kesselring's supporting Luftflotte 2 was the strongest Air Fleet on the Eastern Front. Albert Kesselring, a former Bavarian artilleryman who prided himself on keeping a finger on the pulse of any battle, saw his air priorities as (i) the neutralisation of the VVS, (ii) support for panzers and infantry in mopping up local resistance or eliminating Soviet outflanking threats (tasks primarily for the Stukas and ground-strafers), (iii) smashing or holding of Russian forces trying to move up to the front or to withdraw from the battle (Stukas, ground-strafers, fighters, light bombers and 'practically everything else we had'), and (iv) disruption of operational railway movements, and constant reconnaissance.[56] Having cleared the skies, the task of Gen Lörzer's Fliegerkorps II on the Army Group's right flank, and Gen von Richthofen's Fliegerkorps VIII on its left, was primarily to support Second and Third Panzer Groups, and the Fourth and Ninth Armies following in their wakes. Out of the 1,611 front-line, transport, reconnaissance and liaison aircraft assigned to Kesselring, 1,194 were available to cover the 300km-wide jump-off front line between Brest-Litovsk and Suwalki.

Based on his experiences in France, Guderian was not enamoured of single, co-ordinated attacks against known battery positions. So rather than the standard operating procedure of using

dive-bombers in close, concentrated attacks geared to annihilation, Fliegerkorps II kept a few dive-bombers constantly over Brest-Litovsk with orders to immediately attack any battery that opened fire. This worked to the extent that Soviet batteries remained silent throughout the entire period, but it was a waste of limited air assets and it would have been unworkable if the VVS had been able to mount any meaningful opposition. By now it could not. At the end of operations on 25 June, Luftwaffe units reported that it was increasingly difficult to find meaningful numbers of undamaged Soviet aircraft to attack on the ground.

Army Group Centre advanced over 320km in the first week, with Kesselring's command post in a railway train. This almost

Below:
Early German operations in the East, June-July 1941.

suicidal dash created deep, open and weakly protected flanks, which strong Soviet forces attacked time and again. These critical situations were redressed only by swift and versatile Luftwaffe action. On 24 and 25 June, continuous Fliegerkorps VIII bomber and dive-bomber attacks broke up Soviet armoured units in the Kuźnica-Odelsk-Grodno-Dabrowa area. Richthofen wrote in his diary that when strong Soviet tank and cavalry forces attacked the Ninth Army on the afternoon of 24 June 'commitment of the entire Fliegerkorps followed'. By evening the Soviets had lost 105 tanks and their attack was halted. 'All crews had abandoned their tanks in terror during the attack . . . horses without riders, broken loose from the wagons, galloped about the land.' Small wonder that the morale of German ground forces stayed excellent and confident, and that Fliegerkorps VIII's support was 'greatly appreciated'.[57]

Notwithstanding constant Soviet armoured resistance, on 25 June German panzers sealed off Soviet forces in the Bialystok-Wilno-Minsk-Baranovichi area. Luftflotte 2 launched no fewer than 1,072 combat sorties the following day. The ring around Bialystok was closed by the rapid advance of the Fourth and Ninth Armies, whereupon Soviet forces tried to withdraw at night or in very small groups by day. Luftwaffe bombing attacks were often ineffective because Soviet troops, when forewarned by the sight of a reconnaissance aircraft, left congested roads and hid in the forests before any bombers arrived. In response, the Luftwaffe adopted a new operational procedure known as the armed reconnaissance. Flying on a broad front in flights of three aircraft or formations of five or six, the bombers did their own recce and then attacked any targets of opportunity identified.

Close air support aircraft were employed immediately forward of the armoured spearheads to break any resistance that developed. The limited range of close-support aircraft made it essential to move their bases quickly up behind the panzers, for this was the only way to sustain the close co-operation between air and armour. Air-defence fighters also had to be moved forward expeditiously to provide a protective umbrella, since an eventual revival of VVS activity could never be discounted. Each Soviet airstrip occupied by the Luftwaffe was one denied to the enemy. When III./JG53 took over a large airfield on the outskirts of Vilnius in Lithuania, German crews were amazed and relieved to find 56 Soviet aircraft on the ground.

It was not until Guderian's panzers tried to cross the Berezina at Bobruysk that strong Soviet air attacks tried to stop them. To focus Soviet minds on the task in hand, the commander of the Soviet Western Front, Gen Dmitri Pavlov, his Chief of Staff and his Signals Commander were sentenced to death by firing squad on 30 June. Marshal Timoshenko took over and all available bomber units were ordered to attack Guderian's forces 'to the last aircraft'. Hundreds of attack aircraft, including obsolete four-engined TB-3 bombers dragged from training airfields in Central Russia, were launched against the Berezina bridge on 30 June. Coming in at a suicidal 2,000m, the Soviets ran into a wall of fire from the 10th Flakregiment. Those aircraft that got through found their defensive formations torn apart, making them easy prey to the Bf109s of Oberst Werner Mölders' JG51 which had been concentrated over this strategic objective. Large aerial battles raged over Bobruysk, during which the VVS lost 113 aircraft.

Mölders notched up his 82nd victory that day, surpassing the Red Baron's top score of 80 in World War 1. Guderian, watching 60 German aircraft dogfighting overhead, was fulsome in his praise of the support given to his troops by the top German fighter ace and his airmen.

The Bialystok pocket fell on 1 July, and the two Panzer Groups, their wings pushed forward to the front and supported by all Luftflotte 2 flying units in relays, encircled four Soviet armies in a second great pocket just west of Minsk. Continuous Fliegerkorps VIII support for 3 Panzer on the northern wing worked well because the Corps was specifically equipped and organised for the task. On the other hand, the heterogeneous Fliegerkorps II supporting Guderian's Second Panzer on the southern wing was not so blessed. It soon became impossible for Fliegerkorps II to direct its bomber and long-range recce units, which for logistical reasons were based further to the rear, while ensuring seamless co-operation between close air-support units which were often based 100km nearer to the front. Delegation was necessary and after the first few days of the advance, the post of Close Support Leader II was provisionally established and given to Maj-Gen Martin Fiebig. Henceforward, Nahkampfführer II and his *ad hoc* staff, acting under orders from Fliegerkorps II, directed the Bf110s of SKG210 and Bf109s of JG51 in close support of Second Panzer Group.

Although Guderian was grateful for the quality of his air cover, the great tank leader was less than impressed with Fiebig's organisation. This was unfair, given the novelty of the new command arrangements. Kesselring believed that Fiebig developed into a close-support air commander comparable to von Richthofen, and Guderian's gripe showed that German ground troops had become outrageously spoiled by the continuous employment of Luftwaffe units in direct support of the battlefield. Richthofen's diary entry for 5 July noted that 'the Army refused to accept that the Luftwaffe could not be dribbled out to all and sundry. For maximum effectiveness, air power had to be concentrated at major points. Every sortie needed time. Aircraft had to be refuelled, bombs loaded, and then flown to the new objective. Everyone in the Army wanted to take over the Luftwaffe, but the Army was completely unaware of the potentialities of air power.' Richthofen's observations would be echoed by his RAF and USAAF opposite numbers in North Africa in 1942.

During the encirclement battle at Minsk, strong Luftwaffe bomber and dive-bomber forces attacked columns and river crossings. They also undertook interdiction operations in the Soviet rear to seal off the battle area, with rail junctions at Smolensk and Polotsk coming in for particular attention.

Soviet military doctrine relied on the railways. Back in 1918 and 1919, Lenin and his commissar for military affairs, Trotsky, managed to stave off defeat only by using the Tsarist railway network to shuttle their limited reserves from place to place. In 1941, no German air attacks were made against enemy rail or road bridges without agreement from sector Army staff so as not to destroy bridges that the Wehrmacht was depending on for the smooth advancement of German armoured and other ground units. In such cases, air attack was limited to missions against Soviet forces jamming the bridges. But there was no objection to

Above:
The results of a Stuka attack by III./StG2 'Immelmann' on a train near Tuschkovo, 8 July 1941. *IWM*

the destruction of the great railway bridge at Bobruysk, which was crucial to the Soviets' resupply of new forces and matériel. Its breaching was a particular success for the Luftwaffe, but the fact that it was restored to use within 24-36 hours by over 1,000 skilled workmen, 'directed' by the People's Commissar for Communications, said much about Soviet resolve.

Active Soviet airstrips around Minsk, Bryansk, Smolensk and Polotsk were repeatedly attacked, and a major effort was made against airfields around Gomel on 2 July. Luftwaffe interdiction against the vital Soviet rail network behind the front also aided the Army's advance. Gen Halder wrote in his diary that 'the number of track sections occupied with standing trains, (many) loaded with tanks, is increasing satisfactorily.'[58] But the Luftwaffe found that air attacks on scattered villages and road intersections did not have the same impact on a retreating enemy as in western Europe. The Soviet Union was too open and the rubble from flimsy houses too easily circumvented to have any great bottling-up effect. The best results came from attacking bridges over small rivers, especially those in flood.

The Minsk encirclement yielded 287,000 prisoners but, given no time to rest, Second and Third Panzer Groups pushed on towards a new Soviet force that apparently intended to defend the Dnieper-Dvina line. Army Group Centre hoped to thwart this by another encirclement in the Smolensk area, and as everything depended on getting Guderian's Second Panzers across the Dnieper, Fliegerkorps II and VIII were tasked to support the river crossing near Mogilev on 12 July.

During the first days of July, Kesselring's command post was in a motor transport column east of Minsk trying to keep in close contact with his units. A meeting at 2 Panzer HQ decided that most Luftflotte 2 forces be concentrated under the direct control of Fliegerkorps II. However, Luftflotte 2 hung on to its bomber units, which although committed to direct support of the ground forces were also expected to operate in the rear of the attack zone. Guderian's successful crossing of the Dnieper on 11 July showed how strong air forces could provide a sudden concentration of heavy, annihilating firepower at a given point. Guderian later stated that numerous Soviet bombing attacks made crossing operations more difficult for his armour, but he confirmed that the Luftwaffe always secured temporary air superiority where it mattered. 'Whenever Mölders showed himself, the air was soon clear.'[59]

But air defence involved more than just the fighter boys. Heavy and light AAA battalions were attached directly to ground forces under the control of commanders of the Luftwaffe (Koluft) assigned to the ground formations. The AAA heavy mob in Combat Zone Centre was Gen Walter von Axthelm's I Flak Corps, consisting of the 101st and 104th motorised regiments, each with

Above:
Werner Mölders and Hptm Wolf-Dietrich Wilcke, Gruppenkommandeure of III./JG53, showing by their smiles that it was good to be a fighter pilot on 23 July 1941 in the heady summer when 'Barbarossa' was going well. *Schmidt via Goss/Rauchbach Archive*

three heavy and one light battalion. Working in close co-operation with 2 Panzer, I AAA Corps was there to support any break through Soviet border fortifications, to protect the armoured group from air attacks during the advance, and to help break up all enemy resistance.

I AAA Corps helped to keep open the bridge across the Berezina at Borisov in the face of repeated VVS air attacks, but given the general lack of Soviet aircraft to fire at, von Axthelm's men soon found themselves being used primarily against ground targets. The flat trajectory and high rate of fire of their 88mm guns were very potent against fixed-point targets such as bunkers, observation posts, towers and entrenched tanks, and as Soviet air attacks continued to be sporadic, I AAA's tertiary mission soon became its primary task. Whenever ground forces came up against strong pockets of resistance, the call invariably was heard, 'Anti-aircraft artillery to the front!' In severe fighting in the Yelnya salient, I AAA batteries provided the main defence of the Army fighting units for more than four weeks. It was a measure of the effectiveness of German air-land co-operation that the AAA units under control of Koluft Army Group Centre brought down 500 aircraft and destroyed 360 armoured vehicles between 22 August and 9 September 1941.

On 9 July 3rd Panzer Group captured Vitebsk and then pushed on to Yartsevo before wheeling its right wing towards Smolensk.

The tired and footsore infantry of Fourth and Ninth Armies tried to close the circle around Soviet forces west of Smolensk, with Luftflotte II's close-support aircraft giving sterling support as usual. To give some idea of the Luftflotte II's contribution to the ground advance, the twin-engined Bf110s of SKG210 destroyed 915 Soviet aircraft in 1,574 sorties flown between 22 June and 26 July. The fast bomber Geschwader also put out of action or destroyed 165 tanks, 2,136 motor vehicles, 194 cannon, 52 trains and 60 locomotives.[60]

In among the ordnance dropped by dive-bombers on the Smolensk pocket were leaflets encouraging Soviet troops to desert or face certain death, but the Luftwaffe lacked the ability to make good the threat. The Smolensk pocket had not been closed tightly and through a small gap only a few kilometres wide east of Smolensk substantial Soviet forces escaped destruction or capture. After personally inspecting the gap from the air, Kesselring asked Field Marshal von Bock to launch an attack from the north to close the gap, for which he guaranteed air support, but 'unfortunately nothing happened. My proposals by way of the C-in-C Luftwaffe (Göring) were also fruitless.'[61]

Kesselring estimated that over 100,000 Soviet troops escaped from the Smolensk pocket.[62] The Luftwaffe waves could attack by day with great destructive force, but exact target designation was next to impossible at night given the lack of distinctive terrain features. Paratroops could have closed the gap but none was available given the heavy losses sustained in the capture of Crete. Failure to close the Smolensk pocket showed that even when it ruled the skies, the Luftwaffe lacked the all-weather, round-the-clock capability to control ground on its own.

Above:
He111H of KG26 'Lion' on its way to bomb a Russian target. *IWM*

None the less, the OKW reported on 11 July that 328,898 Soviet prisoners, including several senior generals, had been captured, along with 3,322 tanks, 1,809 guns and large quantities of other war matériel. From his vantage point at Fliegerkorps VIII, von Richthofen believed as early as 1 July 1941 that the bulk of the Red Army's attack forces had been annihilated. At the end of fighting in the frontier area 12 days later, it was calculated that 6,857 Soviet aircraft had been destroyed as against 550 lost and 336 damaged on the German side.[63] The following day von Richthofen, who saw no more military obstacles on the road to Moscow, wrote that German forces could reach the Soviet capital in eight days with the Luftwaffe providing triumphal top cover.

By early August 1941, Army Group Centre was two-thirds of the way to Moscow. Von Bock and Kesselring were not alone in seeing the Soviet capital as the next logical objective, and that the Red Army was in no position to stop it being taken. But Hitler's mind was on the northern and southern flanks.

*   *   *   *

At the start of 'Barbarossa', Army Group North set off with the Sixteenth Army on the right (south), Eighteenth Army on the left (north) and Fourth Panzer Group at the join in the middle ready to make a breakthrough. The Army Group was far less powerful then the Red Army it was facing for Gen Erich Höpner commanded the weakest of the Panzer Armies, yet Army Group North had the ambitious task of driving 850km directly for Leningrad.

Gen Alfred Keller's Luftflotte 1 was tasked with (i) destroying VVS forces in Combat Zone North to gain air superiority, (ii) helping Army Group North and especially 4th Panzer advance quickly to Leningrad, and (iii) attacking the Soviet Baltic Fleet in its bases. For these tasks Keller had about 430 aircraft broken down into nine bomber Gruppen (270 aircraft), 3⅔ fighter Gruppen (110 aircraft), 50 long-distance reconnaissance aircraft, one air transport Gruppe and two liaison units. On behalf of the Army, the Luftwaffe operated four long-distance and 11 close-range reconnaissance Staffeln, plus three liaison Staffeln, which totalled 180 aircraft.

After hitting the VVS, Luftflotte 1, which had no large AAA units of its own, supported the ground advance towards the Dvina. The VVS tried to respond — on 23 June, 10 Soviet bombers slightly damaged the gas works and dockyard at Königsberg, and on 25 June eight aircraft left 23 dead and 250 homeless in Memel — but the scything down of an entire formation of 20 Soviet bombers set the tone.

On 29 June a KG1 bomb aimer put a 2,200lb (1,000kg) HE bomb on the lock gate of the White Sea-Baltic Canal, and equally valuable support was given to the German Navy by KuFlGr (Coastal Air Group) 806. By 1 July the Wehrmacht had reached the Dvina on a broad front and captured Riga. Ground forces were particularly grateful to Fliegerkorps I for beating off a Soviet counter-attack, heavily supported by tanks, to the south of Shauliya. Keller's crews destroyed over 250 of these tanks.

Right:
Fi156 Storch at the Imperial War Museum, Duxford, painted in the colours of the aircraft used to fly Gen Erich Höpner over the battlefield when he commanded 4th Panzergruppe during 'Barbarossa' in 1941. *Author's collection*

Below:
German-Finnish theatre of operations, 1941.

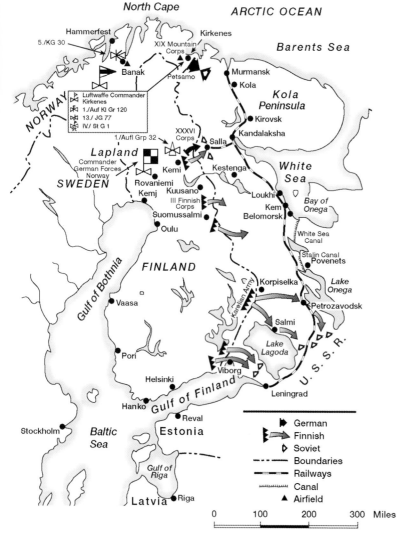

Opposite top:
Precision strike on a road bridge at Volotov, 17 August 1941, by a StG1 Stuka. *IWM*

Opposite bottom:
The Luftwaffe leaves a village burning near Leningrad. *IWM*

The Fliegerkorps reported shooting down 487 Soviet aircraft and destroying another 1,211 on the ground by 13 July. The resulting air superiority was just as well because until the middle of August, Ju52 transport aircraft were temporarily responsible for all resupply of the Sixteenth Army, as the only road from Pskov to Gdov was controlled by Soviet stragglers operating out of the forests.

Meanwhile, the Eighteenth Army on the left wing had pushed forward from Riga to the Gulf of Finland. Excepting targets immediately ahead of 4th Panzer, German bombers interdicted road and rail traffic including the Leningrad-Moscow railway. The rail junction at Bologoe, always heavily occupied by 20-30 locomotives and over 1,500 freight wagons, came in for particular attention. The counter-air effort was maintained against Soviet airfields around Lake Ilmen and Leningrad, while the ground strafers were employed on the laborious task of keeping the remnants of Soviet units in the swampy forests in check. Beyond the coast, Luftwaffe Commander Baltic continued mine laying and operations against Soviet shipping. On 11 August, Luftwaffe bombers severely damaged two Soviet destroyers, sank a 2,000-ton merchant vessel and so damaged a 3,000-ton merchantman that it was a total loss.

Before 'Barbarossa', Berlin had put out feelers to Helsinki to see if the Finns would support an attack on Leningrad. As the Finns were still recovering from the Winter War, Helsinki decided to remain neutral. But Finland allowed German troops going home on leave from Norway to pass through its territory, and German Ju88s used the Finnish Air Force base at Utti to refuel when returning from bombing Leningrad. As Stalin believed that Field Marshal Mannerheim was about to attack towards Leningrad and into Karelia, Soviet artillery and bombers mounted a pre-emptive strike into Finnish territory on 25 June 1941. Fiat G.50 fighters from the Finnish 26th Squadron shot down 13 of the 15 intruding Soviet SB-2 bombers, and the following day Helsinki declared war on the USSR.

At the start of what the Finns termed the Continuation War, the rebuilt Finnish Air Force had six fighter squadrons with about 120 aircraft organised into the 2nd and 3rd Air Regiments, three bomber squadrons (21 aircraft, mainly Blenheims plus some war booty) and five independent squadrons with 58 reconnaissance and liaison aircraft of various types, mainly obsolete. There was no meaningful operational collaboration between the Luftwaffe and the Finnish Air Force, not least because their sectors of responsibility were hundreds of kilometres apart and their missions widely different in character. But although the Finnish Air Force retained its operational independence throughout the campaign, there were close emotional and doctrinal ties — the C-in-C of the Finnish Air Force up to June 1945, Lt-Gen Carl Lundquist, had served in a Prussian fusilier battalion during World War 1.

On 3 August Hitler visited Army Group Centre HQ and reiterated that Leningrad was the primary objective to shut the Russians off from the Baltic and secure the iron ore route to Sweden. His inclination thereafter was to go for the Ukraine, both for its agricultural produce and to neutralise the Soviet air threat to the Ploeşti oil fields. Alan Clark believed that this stemmed from the fact that Hitler 'was determined to resist the temptation of a march on Moscow until he had laid a secure strategic foundation.'[64]

When the order came to 'surround Leningrad and establish contact with the Finnish Army', the Luftwaffe transferred Fliegerkorps VIII from Combat Zone Centre to Luftflotte I. A worrying pointer for the future was the fact that Hitler and Göring decided the move without any reference to the Army C-in-C, and that Hitler was so immersed in tactical decisions that he gave precise instructions to Luftflotte 1 and Fliegerkorps VIII.

At this stage there remained only one position for Stalin's forces to make a stand between the former Estonian frontier and the outskirts of Leningrad itself — the Luga River, running southeast from Narva towards Novgorod at the tip of Lake Ilmen. Höpner dispersed his two Panzer Corps — Reinhardt's on the left at Narva and Manstein's at Luga. Fliegerkorps VIII arrived in the Dno area in time to support their efforts to breach the Luga fortifications.

By 23 August Luftflotte I reported the destruction of 2,514 Soviet aircraft (920 in the air, 1,594 on the ground) and the probable destruction of 433 more. Luftwaffe High Command especially noted the efforts of the Bf110s of ZG26. They carried out two attacks on 19 August against the Soviet air base at Nizino, 28km southwest of Leningrad. The first attack shut down the Soviet AAA while the second wave set 30 VVS fighters on fire, destroyed 15 more and shot down three in combat. This brought ZG26's total bag since 22 June to 854 enemy aircraft destroyed, of which 191 had been shot down.

The Finnish Air Force added to the score. Gen Waldemar Erfurth, assigned by Berlin to the Finnish High Command, reported that Finnish fighter pilots 'can successfully hold their own against a very superior enemy. Numerous aerial combats . . . brought proof of the great flying skills and splendid morale of the Finnish fighters.'[65] Brewster 239s more than coped in a notable dogfight against I-153 and I-16 aircraft over Lahdenpohja on 9 July.

By September, Army Group North had driven the Soviets out of the Baltic States and severed the land connection to Leningrad. But Leningrad did not fall and from 26 September the Germans laid siege to the city. Luftflotte 1, which had supported penetration of the city's outer ring of fortifications with its two Fliegerkorps, was now assigned to attacking important military targets in Leningrad and the Soviet Baltic Fleet in Kronstadt, supporting the Army in containing any attempts to break out of the city, defending the covering front south of Lake Ladoga, and disrupting Soviet supply and evacuation traffic across the lake.

The German failure to capture Leningrad lay in part with Luftflotte I's inability to concentrate its Air Corps on one task at a time. Much of the credit for this lay with the Russians, who refused to allow the Germans to call all the shots. On 7 August, for instance, as Luftflotte I's two Air Corps focused on the final approaches to Leningrad, the Soviets dispatched an air raid against Berlin. Thirteen DB-3T medium bombers from two naval mine-torpedo squadrons left Kagul aerodrome on Ösel Island for a round trip of over 1,750km. Only one bomber appears to have reached the German capital itself, where it was unceremoniously shot down, and a second and much larger raid launched four nights later was no more successful. However, the Berlin raids showed that Soviet airmen had not lost their appetite for brave gestures. 7./JG54's operational record book for 18 August recorded that the Bf109F Staffel 'is involved in daily air combat with numerically superior enemy formations southwest of Leningrad. These engagements frequently last for an hour's time. The manoeuvrability of the Russian fighters makes it hard to shoot them down.'[66] Strong, offensive VVS action distracted Luftflotte I from the direct support of ground forces, and from attacking railways leading from Leningrad as well as the lines south and east of Lake Ilmen. Soviet air attacks forced the Air Fleet to resume its offensive against Soviet airfields, which meant less support for the armies trying to get through the last tenacious defences around Leningrad.

And just as the Russian Luga position was about to collapse, Moscow directed a force round the south shore of Lake Ilmen to attack the right flank of 16th Army. As Novgorod was falling into German hands on 16 August, the Soviet Eleventh and 34th Armies counter-attacked south of Lake Ilmen, at Staraya Russa, supported

by 460 Front and long-range bomber (DBA) sorties. Manstein's armour, which had been moving north to support Reinhardt's surge through the disintegrating Luga front, was ordered to turn about, while the Ju88s of KG77 and the entire Fliegerkorps VIII were immediately sent to fight the fire. Dive-bombers and Bf110 Zerstörer mounted close-support attacks while the Ju88s and Do17s went against troops columns and the railways lines leading to Staraya Russa. All this air effort proved successful, but the

Below:
The 23,000-ton battleship *October Revolution* under Stuka bombardment in Kronstadt, 21-23 September 1941. The *October Revolution* was severely damaged and the battleship *Marat* sunk in the attack. *IWM*

diversion south meant that only one instead of two Air Corps was devoted to the Luga front and Manstein's Panzers wasted five precious days. During the 12 days up to 20 August, Fliegerkorps VIII units flew 4,742 missions and dropped 3,351,350kg (3,300 tons) of bombs. It cost von Richthofen 27 aircraft destroyed and 143 damaged, a high casualty rate for no meaningful gain. If only all of this strike effort could have been used to support the advance of two Panzer Corps, Army Group North might have taken Leningrad before it became exhausted.

On 26 September, with Leningrad completely surrounded apart from a pocket around Lomonosov, the Germans went over to a siege strategy. The plan was to seal off the city 'hermetically, then weaken it by terror (ie air raids and artillery bombardment) and growing starvation. In the spring we shall occupy the town . . . remove the survivors into captivity in the interior of Russia, and level Leningrad to the ground with high explosives.'[67]

To support this operation, the bulk of Luftflotte I assets were placed to the south and southwest of Leningrad, whence they went against targets of military importance and Soviet naval vessels in Kronstadt. The latter effort was particularly directed against two Soviet battleships, the *October Revolution* and *Marat*, which had been under constant surveillance by air reconnaissance. In the face of very heavy AAA fire, the Stukas of StG2 flying in close trail at dive angles between 70° and 80° held their nerve from 15,000ft down to 1,000ft, causing heavy cumulative damage. It was on 22 September that Hans-Ulrich Rudel, ultimately to become the most highly decorated Luftwaffe officer of the war, made a direct hit with a 1,000kg bomb on the 23,000-ton *Marat*. The battleship's entire bow section broke off and the hulk settled on the harbour bottom.

But such success could not of itself win campaigns. The first and overriding principle of war is to select and maintain the aim, something Hitler and Göring never did for long. Notwithstanding Hitler's insistence at the end of July that the capture of Leningrad should be the first priority, the city had not been captured when Fliegerkorps VIII was transferred back to Luftflotte II in Combat Zone Centre at the end of September. Army Group North protested in vain — Berlin had other priorities.

*   *   *   *   *

In contrast to the failure to take Leningrad, German operations in the south were blessed with dazzling success. The 39 divisions of Field Marshal Gerd von Rundstedt's Army Group South were up against two strong Russian groups, fused after 10 July under the command of Marshal Semen Mikhailovich Budenny, a man loyal to Stalin body and soul who declared in 1929 that 'aircraft will not replace the cavalry'. Von Rundstedt opened his offensive by launching the Sixth and Seventeenth Armies, with First Panzer Group on the left flank, between the Pripet Marshes and the Hungarian-Slovakian border. These forces drove east and southeast on 22 June with orders to destroy Soviet forces west of the Dnieper River in Galicia and the western Ukraine, and to establish bridgeheads east of the Dnieper in front of and south of Kiev. The German Eleventh Army was held back with the Romanian Third and Fourth Armies on the Soviet-Romanian border.

Generaloberst Alexander Löhr was a Croatian who flew extensively in World War 1 and became a member of the Austro-Hungarian General Staff. By 1938 he had risen to be C-in-C of the Austrian Air Force, and from 18 March 1939 he commanded the Fourth Air Fleet in Vienna, Poland and the Balkans. The mission of Löhr's Luftflotte 4 was to support Army Group South by (i) attacking Soviet air forces to achieve air superiority and thereby prevent any counter-attack against German units, (ii) rendering direct and indirect support to the Army Group, especially the left flank as the Sixth Army and First Panzer Group advanced to the Dnieper at Kiev, (iii) attacking the Soviet Black Sea Fleet in its bases, and (iv) interdicting Russian merchant shipping on the Black Sea and Sea of Azov.

The main elements of Löhr's Air Fleet on 22 June 1941 were two Air Corps and II Flakkorps. Gen Kurt Pflugbeil's Fliegerkorps IV was tasked with supporting Romanian Air Force and Army operations, protecting the vital oil fields from Russian air attack and attacking Soviet naval bases around the Black Sea. Gen Robert Ritter von Greim's Fliegerkorps V operated on the left flank from the Zamósc-Lublin area, and after securing air superiority against the VVS it was expected to support First Panzer and Sixth Army in their rapid drive on Kiev. II Flakkorps under Gen Otto Dessloch was to provide AAA protection, particularly for First Panzer Group whose ground operations it was expected to support whenever necessary.

Stalin had concentrated his strongest forces and best equipment in the south but the VVS was completely surprised by Luftflotte 4's attack. That was just as well because Löhr's men faced a big task. Pre-invasion reconnaissance had discovered 62 VVS airfields, of which 51 were occupied by 1,270 aircraft concentrated in and around Kiev, Stanislav and Odessa. Despite being up against the best aircrews in the VVS, in the first four days of 'Barbarossa' Fliegerkorps V claimed 774 Soviet aircraft destroyed on the ground and 136 in the air. More than 1,000 aircraft had been destroyed on the ground by 3 July.[68]

A prolonged ridge of high pressure over Southern Russia generated the clear skies similar to those enjoyed by RAF Fighter Command during the Battle of Britain the previous year. By early July, Bf109s of Luftflotte 4 ranged where they willed in small groups on free-ranging hunting missions. Gen Yevgeniy Ptukhin, former 'advisor' to the Republican air forces in Spain who now commanded VVS-Southwestern Front, was relieved of his command on 1 July and eventually faced a firing squad. On 9 August the commander of the Soviet Sixth Army told his German captors that 'the Russian air losses were terrible in the first days and the Russian Air Force has never recovered from this blow.'

On 25 June Fliegerkorps V's main emphasis had shifted from counter-air missions to tactical support of Sixth Army and First Panzer driving for Kiev. Halfway there, First Panzer ran into huge numbers of Soviet tanks. The ensuing tank battle lasted a week, and the Germans were able to hold out only because the Bf109s of JG3 and I.(J)/LG2 shot down over 100 Soviet aircraft, the majority being DB-3 and SB bombers. While supporting ground forces up to 30 June, the Luftflotte claimed to have destroyed 210 tanks, 27 bunkers and two armoured fortifications.[69]

Ever since a rather ineffectual raid by a few German bombers on London back in 1917 sent the British Government into panic, air power has on occasion been able to exert political leverage out of all proportion to any destruction wrought. So it transpired when three P.37 Los bombers from the Romanian 4th Bombardment Group were sent off on 26 June to act as 'Soviet' aircraft. They dropped 30 22kg bombs on the Hungarian town of Kosice, killing 32 and injuring 280. The aim was to provoke Hungary into declaring war on the USSR, and the plot worked. The Hungarian Air Force owned 320 aircraft at the time, of which less than 200 were in the front line.[70] Nothing daunted, early on 27 June the Hungarians sent 35 Ju86K-2s and one squadron of Ca.135s, escorted by nine Fiat CR.42s, to bomb the Soviet city of Stanislav.

Hungarian Air Force, June 1941

1st Fighter Wing
I./I Group   Fiat CR.32
I./II Group   Fiat CR.42

2nd Fighter Wing
2./I Group   Fiat CR.42
2./II Group   Fiat CR.42 (in process of converting to Re.2000s)

3rd Bomber Wing
3./III Group   Ca.135b
3./II Group   Ju86K-2

4th Bomber Wing
Two Groups   Ju86K-2

1st Independent Long-Range Reconnaissance Group
Two squadrons   He170A

Eleven squadrons of short-range reconnaissance He46, Wm21

On 30 June the Soviets pulled back their forces on the Southwestern front to defend Kiev. A Soviet counter-attack against First Panzer on 1 July aimed to cover the withdrawal, but this was thwarted by Fliegerkorps V. The Ju88s and He111s of KG51, KG54 and KG55 reported destroying 220 motor vehicles, including 40 tanks, west of Lvov. KG51 crews found the small SD-2 fragmentation bomb to be very effective against live targets, troop concentrations, moving vehicles and aircraft on the ground.

Given the state of the dirt roads, the mass movement of Soviet troops rearwards was feasible only by rail. So Gen Löhr threw his entire Ju88 and He111 force into an interdiction programme against the rail network west of the Dnieper River. The layout of Soviet railways resulted in two main concentration areas: the first at Kiev and the second, drawing reinforcements from the Crimea and Azov district, further south at Uman. Between these two, Marshal Budenny deployed 1.5 million soldiers, or over half the active strength of the Red Army.

Unlike the trench battles of the Western Front in World War 1, the Russian Civil War had been characterised by large areas defended by relatively small numbers of troops. Consequently, Soviet commanders were forced to integrate all tactical operations into an overall campaign plan, with the aim of hitting objectives deep in an enemy's rear. Victory was to come from concentrating superior forces to overwhelm the enemy at a particular point, followed by rapid flanking or encircling manoeuvres to destroy a thinly spread enemy. All of this depended on a highly mobile offensive force, built around trains and loose horse cavalry formations. The elite of the Red Army, Marshal Budenny's First Cavalry Army, had a passionate belief in the value of mobility and manoeuvre. Unfortunately for Budenny, Stalin gave orders that Kiev was to be held at all cost, and being in receipt of daily Luftwaffe recce reports on the Russian infantry deploying before Kiev, von Rundstedt decided to force his armour south through the gap between the Kiev and Uman concentrations.

The Soviet-Romanian front having stayed static up to now, on 2 July the German Eleventh Army attacked towards the Dniester, covered by Fliegerkorps IV. Romanian and Hungarian armies also crossed the Soviet border, supported by their own air forces. Fliegerkorps IV set about isolating the operational area by attacking road and rail bridges in the Odessa area, on the lower Dnieper at Zaporozhye and Dnepropetrovsk, and on the Dniester at Mogilev Podolskiy, where Moldavia bordered the Ukraine.

The commander of VVS-Southern Front dispatched all his bomber units to try to block Eleventh Army's advance in Moldavia. Reinforcements were brought into the southern combat zone from the Soviet Far East, such that VVS strength rose to over 1,000 operational aircraft. By 9 July, VVS-Southern Front carried out more than 5,000 sorties in the Romanian border area, in the hope that this would result in fighter units being withdrawn from the skies around Uman and Kiev. Although six Soviet bombers raided Romanian oil refineries on 13 July, setting 9,000 tons of oil ablaze, the fact that only two of them made it back to base showed that there was no need to withdraw German or Romanian fighter units from the front line. Between 22 June and 21 October 1941, the Luftwaffe Mission in Romania shot down 143 aircraft, with an almost 50:50 split between fighters and AAA.

It was indicative of the shortage of German aircraft available to cope with the wide Eastern Front that the Stukas of StG77 — the first Ju87s to be made available to Gen Löhr's Soviet campaign — had to be switched from Combat Zone Centre. While Stukas held the Soviet defenders down, the Eleventh Army crossed the Dniester at Mogilev Podolskiy on 17 July. Thereafter, Fliegerkorps IV continuously supported the advancing German and Romanian ground troops.

By 11 July, Luftflotte 4 had closed down the Russian railway system in the rear of the Soviet forces, creating large bottlenecks on the lines south of Kiev and effectively preventing the possibility of any large-scale counter-attack. The next day, Kleist's three Panzer Corps began their drive forward. On 15 July, Sixth Army with First Panzer leading ran into 'the severest fighting' since crossing the border, and much of the credit for holding the line against steady Soviet penetrations into the rear area was given to the Luftwaffe. The close fighter cover of German tank spearheads prevented effective Soviet counter-air measures and eliminated all threats to the flanks.

Budenny should have ordered a strategic withdrawal deep into the Dnieper bend but he stood fast. The great difference between Stalinist and Western military doctrine was that the former was prescriptive — do this in certain circumstances — whereas the latter was descriptive — this is what war is about, make of it what you will. Having been given greater flexibility, the Wehrmacht was able to sweep past Budenny's formations. Worse than that, new men and guns poured into Uman rather than out of it.

Kleist entered Belaya Tserkov on 18 July. First Panzer Group then struck south and southwest, and at the end of the month the leading panzers burst into Kirovgrad, springing the trap on the Sixth and Twelfth Soviet armies in the Uman 'pocket'. As the noose tightened, Luftwaffe bombers and dive-bombers attacked repeatedly to prevent Soviet breakouts and to repel relief attacks launched from outside the ring. As continuous rain and thunderstorms had turned roads into quagmires, it was left to regular low-level sorties by Fliegerkorps V to keep the pressure on. It did so by destroying some 420 motor vehicles and 58 tanks, and putting 22 batteries out of action.

The Sixth and Twelfth Soviet Armies were unified under the command of Maj-Gen P. G. Ponedelin. He was ordered to pull back to escape von Kleist's net but he remained in his parlous positions, much to the rage of his front commander, Gen I. V. Tyulenev. 'We are in contact with Ponedelin by radio, and by aircraft,' reported Tyulenev to Marshal Budenny on 4 August. 'On 3 August a plane took-off from him, sent by us to meet aircraft carrying ammunition to Ponedelin. The pilot reported that in spite of complete concordance of recognition signals on the landing sites for transport aircraft, landing was impossible because of the hurricane of fire opened up by Ponedelin's forces against our own aircraft. One of them was shot down.'[71] Individual Soviet army and aircrew bravery could not offset uninspiring leadership atop an inflexible command structure like this.

It was fortunate that some Soviet commanders played into German hands because the pressure of trying to meet demands in all sectors of the operational area kept the Fliegerkorps' limited resources at full stretch. First Panzer had to be supported in its quick drive southeast, as did Seventeenth Army going east. At the same time, Russian communications in the rear areas and east of the Dnieper had to be attacked. Luftflotte 4, by virtue of the speed and flexibility inherent in air power, found itself cast more and more as the sole means of relieving critical ground situations.

JG3, under the command of Maj Günther Lützow, moved into Belaya Tserkov on 28 July and very quickly established dominance over the Uman pocket, shooting down at least 157 Soviet aircraft. But it proved impossible for the only fighter wing in the entire area, with 125 Bf109s at most on strength and less than half that number serviceable after weeks of combat, to simultaneously protect the Sixth Army driving from Korosten to Kiev, the Seventeenth Army at Uman and the First Panzer Group at Zaporozhye. Although the decisive Uman area took priority, JG3 also had to defend its own large airfield at Belaya Tserkov, which was ceaselessly attacked by VVS aircraft. That did not stop complaints from every other unit, many increasingly under partisan attack out of marsh and woods on their lengthening flanks, and all wanting fighters overhead and bombs dropped ahead of its sector.

First Panzer Group drove on to Dnepropetrovsk and Nikolayev to seize any intact bridge over the Dnieper, with the Eleventh and Seventeenth Armies (right wing and centre of Army Group South respectively) following to mop up any resistance west of the Dnieper.

Fliegerkorps V was expected to support First Panzer while continuing the counter-air and rail interdiction effort. But before they could get under way, the Soviets launched a tank and cavalry attack across the Dnieper at Kanev south of Kiev on 7 August, with the aim of driving through Boguslav to Belaya Tserkov. Eleventh Panzer Division was peeled off from First Panzer Group, but such help was far from the scene. An army bakery company and a veterinary company held out at Boguslav with great courage, but the Russian pressure grew stronger. From the airfield at Belaya Tserkov, itself under heavy attack from VVS waves, light and heavy AAA units were thrown into the breach, platoon by platoon. As the crisis worsened, Fliegerkorps V used its initiative and launched every available aircraft against Soviet tanks and cavalry. There was no time for recce. Each Luftwaffe unit was told to find its own target, with priority given to tanks. Bombers, dive-bombers and fighters took-off singly and in *Ketten* to carry out low-level bombing and strafing in foul weather under 250ft cloud bases. During the first three days, the bombers of KG51, KG54 and KG55 destroyed 148 motor vehicles and 94 tanks.

Once again, the Luftwaffe contained a serious Soviet breakthrough for two long, tense days until major ground reinforcements arrived. On 13 August, Soviet commanders began to withdraw their men back across the Dnieper, whereupon the weather improved and dive-bombers were able to inflict particularly heavy Soviet losses around the congested bridges at Kanev on 15 August.

Diversion of Luftwaffe effort to firefight did not matter while the Germans were on a roll. For as long as superior German panache, tactics and operational expertise was up against stolid and inflexible Soviet leadership, Soviet forces remained on the back foot. Once the Kanev crisis was over, Fliegerkorps V could resume its support for the First Panzer advance to the Dnieper 'without too detrimental a loss of time as a result of the unstinting, unflagging and brave efforts of all the units of Fliegerkorps V.'[72]

Budenny had been massing forces to counter-attack towards Bessarabia and the Romanian oil wells, but in the event 103,000 Red Army soldiers ended up in German confinement. Rolling attacks by Luftflotte 4 bombers on the encircled troops were trumpeted as the first example of a superior air force completely 'surrounding an army from the air'. But that did not do justice to Luftwaffe personnel on the ground, such as the men of Gen Otto Dessloch's II Flakkorps who were integrated with advancing armour and motorised infantry columns up front where Russian air and ground activity was heaviest. A report dated 23 August was proud to note that, during the battle for Uman, II AAA Corps shot down 53 aircraft, destroyed 49 tanks, 93 trucks, 59 machine gun nests and seven observation posts, captured one infantry battalion, one infantry company, three artillery batteries and 140 motor vehicles.

Uman opened the door for the German Eleventh and the Romanian Fourth Armies to advance along the Black Sea coast, towards the mouth of the Dnieper and the port of Odessa. On the other flank of Army Group South, from 17 August the bombers of Fliegerkorps V were sent round the clock against the railway stations, roads and bridges of the traffic hub of Dnepropetrovsk to thwart an orderly retreat of Soviet forces and the establishment of firm defences on the eastern bank of the Dnieper. In parallel, HQ Luftflotte 4 specified that its fighter forces were to concentrate on the Dnepropetrovsk sector. Notwithstanding that there were just 44 fighters left in Fliegerkorps V, 29 DB-3 and SB-3 bombers were destroyed on 17 August alone. But the VVS never lacked spirit. The loss of a crucial timber bridge over the Dnieper at Gornostayploy induced Soviet commanders to make a mighty air effort. VVS bombers and fighters continually attacked the bridge, delivering bombs, machine gun fire and 'Molotov cocktails' from heights as low as 30ft. Although 33 Russian aircraft had been shot down over the bridge at Gornostayploy by 24 August, that did not stop I-16 Rata pilots from dropping petrol drums to try and set the bridge on fire.

*   *   *   *

Things were also warming up in Army Group Centre. On 5 August the encirclement battle of Smolensk was virtually over, and the bulk of Fliegerkorps II dive-bombers and bombers were directed against the railways and roads, especially in the Roslavl-Sukhinichi-Bryansk-Unecha area where air reconnaissance had reported Soviet forces massing.

Constant raids by Soviet ground-attack pilots — usually by a singleton or pair flying at very low level — on the southern wing of Army Group Centre were especially stressful and unwelcome. German air defenders usually arrived too late and, being

unarmoured, dared not pursue the attackers because of strong Soviet ground fire. Shortage of German fighters ruled out defensive air patrols, so ground troops had to strengthen their own defences from strafing attacks with additional machine guns, just as the Soviets had done from the very beginning.

Towards the end of the battle for Smolensk, Guderian was given several armoured and infantry corps to destroy a strong Russian group attacking from the Roslavl area. Ably supported by Fliegerkorps II, Guderian's forces successfully encircled the enemy force and destroyed it, while Luftflotte 2's bombers — mainly under the command of Fliegerkorps II — hammered the Soviet air bases that air reconnaissance and radio intercepts showed were occupied. VVS activity declined markedly after these attacks, thereby easing the pressure on ground forces. By 30 August, Fliegerkorps II had destroyed 2,660 aircraft, including 1,280 taken out on the ground.[73]

Despite pleas to help out around Combat Zone Centre, most Fliegerkorps II flying units remained up in front of the Second Army and Second Panzers facing Soviet forces south and southwest of Bryansk. The Luftwaffe was right to align the Fliegerkorps' main effort in this fashion, especially as it helped eliminate Soviet attempts to drive a deep wedge between Army Groups Centre and South. Ceaseless direct and indirect Fliegerkorps II support of Second Army and Second Panzer Corps contributed decisively to establishing the northern jumping-off point for the greatest battle so far in the Eastern campaign, the encirclement of Kiev.

THE HIGH ROAD TO MOSCOW

'One great "if" of history may be: "If Hitler had been a corporal in the Luftwaffe".'
Roderic Owen

British wartime grand strategy was thrashed out at Chiefs of Staff Committee meetings. There could be fiery debate between Churchill and his military chiefs, but if the Chiefs were united on a course of action, the Prime Minister never overruled them throughout the entire war.

The Chiefs of Staff issued directives on prosecuting the war, and after Pearl Harbor, this mechanism expanded into the Combined Chiefs of Staff. The famous Casablanca Directive of January 1943, which authorised a strategic bomber offensive 'to bring about the progressive destruction and dislocation of the German military, industrial and economic system and the undermining of the morale of the German people to a point where the capacity for armed resistance is fatally weakened,' came from the Combined Chiefs of Staff. Neither Churchill nor Roosevelt issued military strategy directives in their name.

On the other hand, the Germans had got up to Führer Directive No 34 by 18 August 1941. Much heated argument had taken place beforehand, with a host of Army generals plus Field Marshal Kesselring pressing to maintain the aim of destroying Soviet military power. They believed this could be best accomplished by a rapid drive to seize Moscow, which would not only destroy an important industrial and armaments centre but also undermine the prestige of the Soviet Government, just as the advance on Paris in 1940 took the fight out of the French.

However, once the assault on Leningrad went into limbo, Hitler was emphatic that the primary aim before the onset of winter was 'not the capture of Moscow but rather the occupation of the Crimea, of the industrial and coal mining area of the Donets basin, (and) the cutting of the Russian supply routes from the Caucasian oil fields.' The Supreme Commander deflected criticism by declaring that 'my generals know nothing about the economic aspects of war'. Although keen to seize Soviet industrial output and crop fields, Hitler was also anxious to push the VVS beyond bomber range of the vital Romanian oil fields.

With Odessa on a siege footing from 8 August, von Rundstedt's flank was secure enough for him to order his panzers to regroup in a northerly direction. Heinz Guderian was told to forget about Moscow and swing Panzer Group 2 south from the Gomel area, 200km north of Kiev, to join up with Kleist's armour. Their aim, according to Directive 34, was 'not merely to drive the Russian Fifth Army back across the Dnieper . . . but to destroy the enemy before he manages to withdraw.'

It is an article of faith of independent air forces that unity of air effort is best achieved by exercising *command and control* at the highest practicable level. But as no single commander can personally direct the actions of a large number of air units and individuals, decentralised *execution* is essential. Decentralised execution allows subordinate commanders to use their judgement and initiative within the overall pattern of employment laid down by their superiors.

While the German Sixth Army pushed the Red Army towards the Dnieper, action by the bombers of Fliegerkorps V was unremitting. But the troops on the ground were less impressed with their close support, so the posts of Close Air Support Commanders North and South were established to ensure that available Luftwaffe assets were deployed in accord with Army priorities.

Maj Günther Lützow was made Close Air Support Commander North and given operational control of the Stukas of III./StG77 and I and III Gruppen of his own JG3. On 30 August, JG3 shot down its thousandth aircraft in the East. In addition to leading his fighter pilots from the front, Lützow's remit was to help delay the withdrawal of the Soviet Fifth Army over the Dnieper by attacking troop traffic centres and columns on the roads moving eastward.

The post of Close Air Support Commander South was created because First Panzer Group also wanted more effective close air support. The first incumbent was Maj Graf Clemens von Schönborn-Wiesentheid, commander of StG77, who controlled the Stukas of I./StG77 and the fighters of II./JG3 and III./JG52. On 1 September the German Seventeenth Army, effectively supported by the Close Air Support Commander South, established a bridgehead across the Dnieper. Fighter units kept an aerial umbrella over the bridgehead, downing 12 VVS aircraft on the first day. Ju87s and Bf109s attacked Soviet ships, barges and artillery batteries on the east bank of the river. Seventeenth Army subsequently gave von Schönborn's crews the greater part of the credit for protecting the river crossing points.

Army Group South, with Luftflotte 4 support, established bridgeheads at Borislav, Dnepropetrovsk and Kremenchug in the face of superior Soviet air and ground forces. The close interplay between Fliegerkorps IV and V created a swift and flexible force that was often the crucial factor in averting Russian threats to ground operations, and the sole means of converting challenges into victories. German air commanders knew that their declining aircraft numbers and tired aircrew could succeed only if air power was concentrated at key points and employed against strong enemy resistance with the utmost determination. Notwithstanding Army bleats and whinges, Luftwaffe HQs stuck to their guns and allowed no splintering or dissipation of their numerically weak and constantly shrinking front-line combat strength.

Left:
The effects of
a Stuka attack
on a Russian
river bridge.
IWM

The panzers closed the outer ring on no fewer than five Soviet armies on 16 September. In the resulting encirclement battle east of Kiev, northern German Army units were supported by Luftflotte 2 with Fliegerkorps II, and in the southern part by Luftflotte 4 with Fliegerkorps V. It was the first time that two Air Fleets were expected to support the co-ordinated efforts of several armies and panzer units of two Army Groups. Between them, the Air Fleets reconnoitred, established air superiority over, directly attacked and isolated the million-plus Soviet troops and their vast stores of matériel enclosed in the 24,680sq km pocket.

The German fighter boys 'prevented any serious Soviet air interference with German ground forces and protected close support crews as they carried out successful, devastating and virtually undisturbed attacks against Russian troops and matériel in the pocket.'[74] German bomber crews kept any Soviet ground counter-action at bay by continuously attacking the roads and railways leading into the pocket. Not to be outdone, the bombers of Fliegerkorps II (operating from the north of Gomel and Orsha) and Fliegerkorps V (operating from the Kirovograd area in the south) isolated the Kiev pocket. Berlin was particularly impressed with the way in which, between 22 June and 9 September, KG3 destroyed 30 tanks, 488 vehicles, 356 trains (of which seven were armoured) and 14 bridges, interrupting Soviet rail traffic 332 times. The Do17 wing also flew 290 sorties against troop concentrations, barracks, supply depots and artillery positions while shooting down 21 aircraft and destroying another 450 on the ground.[75]

Fliegerkorps V's bombers repeatedly struck at withdrawing Soviet columns, preventing them from reorganising their scattered units and re-establishing their defences such that they continued to retreat in disorder. The VVS brought aircraft forward to try and stop the rot, but continuous bombing of Soviet airfields at Kharkov and Poltava accounted for many of them. Yet the Luftflotte 4 supply chain was stretched so close to breaking point that lack of fuel prevented all but a few bombers from operating on 16 and 17 September.

The Army High Command ordered that Kiev be reduced to 'rubble and ashes', but as usual the Luftwaffe was expected to do 'half of the work'.[76] The Stukas of III./StG77 and the protective Bf109s of III./JG52 were moved to Belaya Tserkov from where the dive-bombers breached the defences to enable the German Sixth Army to capture the fortress. Soviet POWs reported that their fighting morale had been undermined by the Luftwaffe, and Field Marshal von Reichenau, C-in-C Sixth Army, saw for himself the annihilating effects of dive-bomber attacks on closely massed Russian forces while visiting the completely demolished Borispol. Watching the impact of dive-bombing on Soviet positions defending a river, Gen Guderian also noted that although well-aimed bombs did little physical damage, 'the morale effect, which held the Russians down in their foxholes, permitted the river to be crossed almost without losses.'[77]

Fliegerkorps V flew 1,422 sorties and dropped 568,154kg (559 tons) of bombs during the battle for Kiev, for the loss of only 17

Opposite top:
Line up of Ju88s belonging to
4./KG51 in Luftflotte 4. *Ciuraj via
Goss/Rauchbach Archive*

Above:
Sitting pretty on the long-range fuel
tanks of a Ju88. *Goss/Rauchbach
Archive*

Left:
Fw Robert Ciuraj and Lt Bernhard
Sartor of 4./KG51, still wearing their
lifejackets, enjoy a post-attack
cigarette. The bombs behind are for
the next mission. *Goss/Rauchbach
Archive*

of von Greim's aircraft. When the encirclement battle ended around 26 September, the Germans found they had captured 665,000 prisoners, 3,718 guns, 884 tanks and masses of other matériel. It was the greatest battle of annihilation in the entire Russian campaign, and such losses on top of what had gone before would have finished off any other nation.

On the face of it, the Germans were on a high. Leningrad and Odessa were invested, the Pripet Marshes had been cleared, the Dnieper bend occupied, panzer spearheads were driving deep into the Donets basin and the Soviets could no longer draw on the Ukrainian industrial complex. As the battle for Kiev came to a close, the Germans prepared to implement Führer Directive No 35 which ordered that all Army and Luftwaffe forces that could be spared from the flanks be brought together in the Centre to resume the offensive towards Moscow. The attack frontage between Hoth's forces north of Smolensk and Guderian's on the left bank of the Desna was over 240km, and three-quarters of the German Army on the Eastern Front, including all the panzer divisions less one group left to clear the Ukraine, were to be massed against the Soviets under Marshal Timoshenko. But it took time to gather together all the necessary German air and ground elements. Hitler's failure to stick to one clear strategic objective — Moscow *or* the Ukraine had become Moscow *and* the Ukraine — lost many precious campaigning days of firm going and mild temperatures.

Success hinged on Höpner's Fourth Panzer Army breaking the Russian front in two, whereupon the broken formations would polarise around the communications centre of Vyazma and Bryansk. Once the bulk of Army Group Timoshenko was defeated, the way would be clear for Army Group Centre to drive to the Soviet capital. 'You have created the conditions,' declared Hitler's order of the day, 'to strike the last vigorous blows which should break the enemy on the threshold of winter.'

'Smiling Albert' Kesselring wrote after the war that attack preparations were carried out from Luftflotte 2 HQ, in a forest near Smolensk, 'with coldly calculating ardour'.[78] Kesselring talked through requirements with the commanders of the Second, Fourth and Ninth Armies and the interested armoured groups, and out of this came precise tactical tasking of Luftflotte 2 units. II Flakkorps was transferred from Luftflotte 4, and it and I Flakkorps were to provide supporting and artillery assault fire at the main points of effort. Close-support aircraft were tasked with clearing the way for the ground forces, especially the panzers, and to attack Soviet movements on the battlefield. Heavy bombers were expected to close off the battle area to the rear.

At the end of September, Fliegerkorps VIII was transferred from the Leningrad front to the left wing of Army Group Centre where it was to support the Ninth Army in general and 3rd and 4th Panzers in particular. But such was the pressure on the Luftwaffe that there was no opportunity to revamp the Fliegerkorps, and it was therefore much weaker than those planning the drive for Moscow were working on. Some individual Army commanders on the ground were so worried about the lack of air support on offer that they advised against the attack.

Army Group Centre was unable to regroup and renew the offensive, designated Operation 'Typhoon', until 2 October, which gave the Soviets time to move up reinforcements and

Below:
He111 of 9./KG51. *Bauer via Goss/Rauchbach Archive*

prepare their defences. Second Panzer had already launched its attack with support from Fliegerkorps II in order to reach Orel as quickly as possible. From there, the Fliegerkorps regrouped and moved its command post to Shatalovo, a large air base between Smolensk and Roslavl. The Do17s of KG3 and the He111s of KG53 were based at Shatalovo-East and Shatalovo-West, and repeated VVS attacks on these airfields were so strong that a protective fighter unit had to be deployed to an advanced strip east of Shatalovo.

The He111s of KG28, one of several bomber units brought in from the West to boost air strength in the East, were based at Bobruysk, while Kesselring's long-range reconnaissance assets operated from Smolensk-South. Close support was co-ordinated by the II Close Support Air Commander who was given two groups of Stukas from StG1 and three groups of Stukas from StG77, plus two SKG210 groups of Bf110s equipped to carry SD-2 fragmentation bombs. On 1 October, the bulk of the bombers did their bit for the advancing ground forces by successfully attacking Russian troop concentrations and columns of tanks and trucks in the Glokhov-Bryansk-Kursk area.

The rest of Army Group Centre began 'Typhoon' at 05.30hrs the following day and Second Panzer, supported continuously by Fliegerkorps II, reached Orel on 3 October. But the Germans did not have the skies to themselves. Soviet air activity was very lively, with VVS bombers and ground-attack aircraft continuously attacking German assault columns and airstrips in small formations of three to six. Fliegerkorps HQ knew the importance of getting its ground support and fighter aircraft up close behind the attacking columns; immediately after Orel fell, the protective air umbrella was maintained by bringing fighters up to Orel airfield.

'Typhoon' proceeded in the classic manner because, once again, the Soviets contributed to their own destruction by holding rigidly to their lines while the Germans encircled them. On 4 October, OKL statistics recorded that 48 dive-bombers and 32 bombers made successful daylight attacks on rail lines and troop movements in the Sumy-Lgov-Kursk area. Then 202 dive-bombers and 188 bombers, some integrated with panzer units, struck Soviet positions, supply movements, troop concentrations and rail targets in the Bryansk-Spas-Demensk-Sukhinichi area. Next, some 152 dive-bombers and 259 bombers were sent over Belyy-Sychevka-Vyazma to destroy 22 tanks, 450 motor vehicles, 11 horse-drawn limbers, seven tractors, three fuel depots and three AAA emplacements.[79]

On 7 October, Luftwaffe High Command reported that 70 large enemy units in the vicinity of Bryansk and Vyazma would soon be encircled and destroyed. Approximately 800 bombers, most of the available strength, successfully attacked infantry and tank assembly areas, columns of trucks and Red Army accommodation areas. Once Soviet forces were contained in two pockets either side of Bryansk and one west of Vyazma, Fliegerkorps II went after units that escaped and Soviet troops trapped in the pockets. Luftwaffe crews saw thousands of men and vehicles pressed tightly together as they tried to cross rapid streams swollen by rain and snow. Some aircrew reported that it was impossible to miss when bombing such a compact mass of troops and equipment!

And it wasn't all left to the aircrew. In the fighting around Vyazma between 2-13 October, II Flakkorps shot down 29 Soviet aircraft, destroyed 17 bunkers, 18 fortified field positions, 14 armoured cars, 104 artillery pieces, 94 machine guns, five defence posts and a freight train. AAA personnel also thwarted Soviet attempts to break out of the pocket, mopped up a village housing enemy units and took 3,842 prisoners.[80] The Germans eventually captured some 663,000 prisoners from the Vyazma pocket and another 100,000 from Bryansk, and it is clear from reports that the flexibility and responsiveness of all Luftflotte 2 units played a large part in the success of the encirclement operations. Air-land co-operation appeared to have kicked open the door to Moscow.

*   *   *   *

Within a few days of the start of 'Barbarossa', the Luftwaffe had destroyed the greater part of Soviet air forces in the field. Thereafter, the VVS appeared to be paralysed — only small units, appearing at very infrequent intervals, took part in combat actions, most of which were unco-ordinated and unfocused. The chances of Soviet air power halting or even delaying the swift advance of the German Army Groups, or threatening the Reich in retaliation, were almost non-existent. Events seemed to be going so well that Mussolini entered the fray in August 1941 by sending one air corps, consisting of four squadrons of 51 Macchi MC.200s (22nd Fighter Gp), three squadrons of Caproni Ca.311 light reconnaissance bombers (61st Observation Gp) and some Savoia S.81 and Ca.133 transports to support Fliegerkorps V in Romania. The Italians soon moved 1,900 personnel forward to Krivoi Rog on Russian soil, and on their first foray over the front on 27 August the Italians met a large formation of SB-2 bombers and I-16 fighters. Six Russian bombers and two fighters were claimed shot down, without any Italian loss.

The technical superiority of Luftwaffe aircraft, the high level of operational training and experience of their personnel, and their high morale and aggressiveness had enabled the Germans to gain early mastery of the air which was then exploited to support army operations. Co-operation between German land and air forces was outstanding, and the Luftwaffe had succeeded in destroying local Red Army resistance on three fronts while simultaneously delaying or destroying Soviet forces struggling or straggling to and from each battle. However, the scale of German air successes masked some disturbing trends for the future. From the start, the Luftwaffe was asked to do too much. The four Luftflotten allocated to 'Barbarossa' were expected to operate over 22 degrees of latitude, and this was far too wide a remit for a long campaign. Ultimate German success in Russia hinged on achieving its objectives quickly, which turned on whether Berlin had read Soviet military capabilities correctly.

Writing about 'Typhoon' air planning after the war, Field Marshal Kesselring saw his fighter-ground-attack aircraft as being there 'to blast a path for the army divisions' and the role of his heavy bombers 'to seal off the battlefield to the rear'.[81] The trouble was, he lacked the assets in October 1941 'to blast' or 'to seal' anything for very long. The German High Command's first mistake was to go into battle in the East against an opponent who turned out to be far stronger than predicted in numbers and potential. This was a pretty bold gamble given that the Luftwaffe had an air strength of 3,451 in June 1941, and their own intelligence branch estimated that there were 7,000 Soviet combat aircraft in European Russia, plus another 2,000 in Asiatic Russia.[82] The Germans took comfort in their own battle experience, the relatively poor quality of Soviet aircraft and Soviet pilot training, and the belief that the Soviet aircraft industry was small, strategically vulnerable and inefficient. As it happened, not only did the VVS in the west have upwards of 10,000 aircraft, including reserves, but also the Luftwaffe underestimated the replacements in the pipeline. Berlin estimated that some 5,000 aircraft per annum rolled off Soviet production lines in 1939 and 1940, whereas the actual figures were 10,382 in 1939 and 10,565 in 1940.[83]

Kesselring wrote that 'thanks to the tireless, willing effort of the (long-range and tactical reconnaissance) units, it was possible on the strength of the excellent photo-reconnaissance to achieve air superiority within two days.'[84] But if aerial pictures could show quantity, they could not always show quality. A photograph of Orsha taken early in the campaign appeared to show a large number of vehicles drawn up in rows next to a large hangar-like building. On the strength of this photo, HQ Luftflotte 2 received a personal order from Göring that the combat vehicles stored in the 'tank depot' at Orsha were to be attacked immediately by all available forces. Twenty bombers hit the parked vehicles and surrounding buildings on 27 June but when Orsha was subsequently captured, it was found that the 'tank depot' was merely a collecting point for horse-drawn vehicles.

The fact that C-in-C Luftwaffe was directly involving himself in detailed operational planning boded ill for the future. Equally disturbing, the Orsha incident showed that the analysis and evaluation of Luftwaffe reconnaissance reports left much to be desired. By the end of July, Moscow had fielded nearly two dozen armies, double the German intelligence estimate. Advancing units were often held up by Soviet forces whose existence was unknown to the Germans 'until they bumped into them'.[85]

On 29 June, the OKW was pleased to report the destruction of 4,017 Soviet aircraft, for the loss of only 150 German.[86] Maj-Gen Hoffmann von Waldau, Chief of the Luftwaffe Operations Staff, reserved judgement on the strategic air situation until the early dust had settled. On 3 July, when he felt able to make a detailed appraisal of the situation, he expressed surprise that the Soviets still had some 8,000 aircraft ready for action in the western area.[87] After driving from Dubno with the Chief of Staff of Fliegerkorps V on 15 July, von Waldau saw 'hundreds of Russian tanks, many of which [were] super-heavy' and that 'the equipment of the Red Army amazes us again and again'.[88] Most telling was Hitler's admission to Guderian that 'If I had known the true figures for the Russian tank strength, I would not — I believe — ever have started this war.'[89]

Luftwaffe photographic and visual reconnaissance crews did their best but the lack of sufficient strategic reconnaissance aircraft to cover the massive western USSR continuously, the primitive character of the Red Armies, their absence of a heavy 'tail', their ability to move at night and a lack of understanding of what was happening inside Moscow or further east, made it impossible for the Germans to build up an intelligence assessment based on the big picture. Commanders could only rely on local, tactical information, which was no great handicap so long as the

Above:
He111 carrying an SC1000 bomb on its way to a target in Russia. *Price*

Germans retained the initiative and had complete ascendancy over the battlefield. But once their advance was slowed down and tired forces became over-extended, ignorance of real Soviet air capabilities and intentions started to matter. Conversely, the *Rote Kapelle*, a spy cell operating deep inside the German Air Ministry and including a senior Luftwaffe intelligence officer, was particularly valuable in supplying Moscow with information on Luftwaffe dispositions, strengths and objectives for particular operations and even details of individual air raids.

Such was the continuous intensity of Luftwaffe operations over Russia that only a few serviceable reconnaissance aircraft remained available within weeks of the opening of 'Barbarossa'. After discussing air reconnaissance with Field Marshal von Bock on 10 July, Gen Halder noted that the long-range squadrons assigned to Army Group Centre 'have three machines ready to fly on one squadron and none on the others. Only two serviceable aircraft are available for night reconnaissance.'[90] The Luftwaffe proposed combining Army and Air Force reconnaissance to get the best value out of what remained, but the Army was dead set against losing operational control of its assets.

By 5 July 1941, Luftwaffe front-line strength on the Eastern Front was down to 1,888 fighters and bombers, which were far too few to meet all crucial tasks.[91] While the Germans were involved in hard fighting around Smolensk in late July, Göring ordered the transfer of von Richthofen's Fliegerkorps VIII to Combat Zone North. The plan was for the Air Corps to move to the Vitebsk area to re-equip and prepare for the ensuing commitment, leaving only weak close air support forces behind under the CO of StG1, Obstlt Walter Hagen. But when the Soviets suddenly counter-attacked, Fliegerkorps VIII had to be handed back to Luftflotte 2 because it was the only reserve. Fliegerkorps VIII inflicted heavy losses on the Red Army and hindered its advance until newly arrived German troops were able to parry the attack. Only then was the Fliegerkorps released to join Luftflotte 1.

The fact that the Luftwaffe had 200 fewer bombers in the spring of 1941 than a year earlier showed that Hitler went to war in the East before Germany had made good the losses of the Battle of Britain. For all the hype about Teutonic efficiency, while Luftwaffe professionals were fighting for their lives their technical and industrial back-up was often amateurish. Great names such as Professor Willy Messerschmitt gave the impression of being interested only in designing *new* aircraft. His company was working on no fewer than 11 different aircraft types, while of ten Heinkel designs, only one was in mass production. Such inattention to what really mattered helped explain why the strength of Luftflotte 2 dropped from 1,200 aircraft in June 1941 to 549 at the opening of 'Typhoon', of which only 158 were bombers.

The short-termist nature of Luftwaffe planning was illustrated by the fact that despite adding the USSR and the Balkans to their ongoing military commitments, the Germans manufactured fewer aircraft each month in 1941 than they did in 1940.[92]

Anticipating swift victory in the East, Hitler commanded a reduction in Army armaments production and high priority for the procurement of aircraft in preparation for the subsequent fight against Britain. Ever obedient, Göring issued orders for the quadrupling of the Luftwaffe front line and gave his deputy a special commission to carry the new programme through. Two days after the launch of 'Barbarossa', Field Marshal Erhard Milch ordered the rapid construction of three huge aircraft factories. Albert Speer completed them within eight months, by which time hopes of a Blitzkrieg victory over Russia had receded. In January 1942, Hitler cancelled the absolute priority ordered six months earlier to aircraft production, and reverted to rearmament of the Army in depth.

After two years of combat, the Luftwaffe was very capable of maintaining the serviceability and operational effectiveness of its units under field conditions. But the scale and challenge of the Russian operation exceeded anything German logisticians had faced before. The ground situation changed so often that Luftwaffe aircrew generally did not know when they took-off whether they would land back at their old base after the mission. When Milch toured units on the Eastern Front on 21 August, on every airfield he found scores if not hundreds of damaged aircraft immobilised for lack of spares. It was left to Milch to organise squads of engineers to fly from Staffel to Staffel, cannibalising damaged aircraft to get a proportion of fit ones back in the air again.

Too many logistic minuses flowed from adherence to Hitler's view that if German forces struck hard enough, Russia would collapse like a pack of cards. Although German aircrew operating out of Lipetz before the war had continually reported that their motor vehicles were unsuited to the summer sand and winter mud conditions, the Luftwaffe launched into 'Barbarossa' with very inadequate MT support and no tracked vehicles. Had it not been for the Russian *Hiwis*[93], who repaired captured Russian vehicles in improvised workshops that were then organised into *ad hoc* supply columns, the rapidly advancing Germans would have been in serious trouble.

The vast Soviet Union had only 64,000km of hard-surfaced, all-weather roads and 80,000km of railways in 1941, the latter being of broader gauge than the German. As they advanced, German engineers had to convert occupied railbeds to their own gauge but for much of 1941, all supplies moving forward by rail had to be transferred to whatever rolling stock the Germans could capture. To add to their logistic headaches, as German forces moved deeper into Russia the few roads that did exist soon became clogged. Oberst Rudolf Meister, von Richthofen's Chief of Staff at Fliegerkorps VIII, once took 11 hours to cover 80km back to HQ. At times, the Chief of Staff of Fliegerkorps V and his supply officer were reduced to flying over supply routes in a Fieseler Storch, searching for fuel supply columns. They would then land alongside the moving columns of armoured and motorised troops and pull rank to ensure that the vital aviation fuel bowsers were given 'the proper priority'.[94]

After Orel airfield fell to the Germans, it became a forward air transport base into which 132,000 gallons of fuel and other matériel were flown by Ju52s to keep Second Panzer Group on the move. Authority had been given to move Luftwaffe units up close to the Army front along a line Orel-Juchnow-Rzhev, and when II Close Support Air Commander brought dive-bombers up to Orel, the VVS flocked to the large forward-operating base like bees to the honeypot. Capt Georgiy Zimin was one of six fighter pilots covering ground-attack raids on Orel on 11 October. 'As the main group of our aircraft approach the airfield, four Bf109s were scrambled. Our escort fighters attached and destroyed them during take-off. At this moment, I noticed five Ju52s approaching the field from the south at an altitude of 200m. We bounced them and were able to shoot down all five.'[95]

Operational experience after 1939 had taught the OKL that it could not expect more than 70% of combat aircraft to be operational, and generally no more than 60%. Inadequate supplies of fuel and ammunition only complicated Luftwaffe operations through the autumn of 1941. Fliegerkorps V was tasked with mopping-up operations west of the Lower Dnieper but the Luftwaffe in the East never had sufficient range and power to strike targets in any meaningful fashion beyond the Dnieper. The only way to offset the excessive distances that Fliegerkorps V crews were expected to fly to their targets was to move some attack aircraft up to Krivoi Rog airfield, but there was such a stretch of black, sticky Ukrainian mud between Krivoi Rog and the railhead back west that fuel, spare parts and bombs could be ferried in only by Ju52 transports.

The first snow fell on Army Group Centre on the night of 6–7 October. It soon melted but it was followed by the rainy *rasputiza* — literally meaning 'time without roads' — a period of mud that befell Russia every autumn and spring as the seasons changed. Temperatures fell as low as –8°C, followed by upwards of 20cm of snow and more rain. From then on, German mechanised units would use up motor fuel at three times the previous rate and the endless mud off the few paved roads finally curtailed the mobility that had been the Germans' trump card since 22 June.

Between 22 and 25 October, the Luftwaffe committed from 441 to 481 bombers, 123 to 208 fighters and 13 to 23 reconnaissance aircraft every day to the attack against Soviet armoured and infantry concentrations around Kalinin, Mtsensk, Mozhaysk, Tula and Volokolamsk. Two days later, deteriorating weather conditions permitted only one aircraft to be committed east of the battle area.

At the end of October, the impassable nature of what von Waldau described as 'bottomless roads' brought Army Group Centre's operations against Moscow to a standstill. Luftflotte 2's aircraft were equally bogged down at their advanced airfields.

Winter frosts and snow arrived in mid-November. They abruptly ended the muddy season, and the sudden cold snap froze the ground and gave the Germans back their mobility. Besides supporting ground forces, the Luftwaffe attacked airfields and railways and on one occasion Fliegerkorps II bombers destroyed 10 trains loaded with armoured vehicles. One instance of the way in which air power alone kept a route open was the bridge over the Snopot River. Soviet troops holding the bridge were subjected to such intense bombing and strafing over a 90min period that attempts to blow the bridge were delayed long enough for German armour to arrive and capture this important crossing.

On 18 September 1941, Field Marshal Erhard Milch confided to colleagues that 'perhaps we underestimated the Russians earlier, but now they are soft.' It was symptomatic of the overconfidence in high places that, just over a month later on Hitler's instructions, Chief of Luftwaffe operations von Waldau was considering strengthening Reich air defences by bringing back flying and flak units from the Eastern Front. He proposed to the head of the Army General Staff that only eight bomber Gruppen, three dive-bomber Gruppen, 10½ fighter Gruppen, three aerial reconnaissance Staffeln and five anti-aircrew regiments under two Luftflotten need remain in the East on conclusion of military operations.

Three new air districts — Rostov, Kiev and Moscow — were to be designated by 15 November 1941. The post of Air Leader Baltic was to be abolished, and most unworldly of all, the staffs of Luftflotte 2 and Fliegerkorps II with their fleets and overarching reconnaissance, transport and signal elements that ought to have played a crucial role in the capture of Moscow, were *withdrawn* from Army Group Centre. After flying over 40,000 day and night sorties, dropping over 23,159 tons of bombs, destroying 789 tanks and 3,826 VVS aircraft in the air and on the ground, Fliegerkorps II and some other Luftflotte 2 units were transferred to the Mediterranean.[96] Field Marshal Kesselring went shortly afterwards to take over responsibility for operations in Italy, Africa and the Mediterranean. Under his leadership, between 22 June and 30 November Luftflotte 2 had accounted for 6,670 aircraft, 1,900 tanks, 1,950 guns, 26,000 motor vehicles and 2,800 trains.[97]

Given the mild frost, a renewed assault on Moscow was ordered for 17 November. For a few days it was sunny and German troops set out on what they thought would be their last trial of strength though, with the loss of Luftflotte 2, aerial

support for the drive on Moscow was left almost entirely to von Richthofen's Fliegerkorps VIII. This was a serious misjudgement as Oblt Friedrich Lang, Staffelkapitän of I./StG2, recalled. 'We transferred in November 1941 to Böblingen near Stuttgart. We had desert camouflage painted on our Ju87s and we were fitted out for Africa. At the beginning of January we received orders to cancel everything, respray our Stukas white and transfer in the quickest way possible, Gruppe by Gruppe, to Duo (between Pleskau and Ilmensee) as the position at Wolchow and around Demyansk was becoming disastrous. In the transfer 3.Staffel lost two or three aircraft in a snow storm near Elbing.'[98]

As the only Air Corps left in Combat Zone Centre, Fliegerkorps VIII assumed responsibility for the II Close Support Air Commander on 1 December. But by now the deteriorating weather made it impossible to give ground forces the air support they had come to expect. Many of the most advanced German airstrips were so snow- and ice-bound that take-offs and landings became impossible. On the other hand, the VVS was operating from a number of facilities close to Moscow that were built for the winter conditions, and Soviet air commanders were throwing everything available into the defence of their capital city. Strong AAA, situated on all airfields in the Moscow area, made German counter-air operations extremely difficult. But so few German aircraft got airborne in the conditions that concerted attacks against VVS airfields had to give way to the immediate direct and indirect support of ground forces.

In the face of one of the worst winters in memory, when temperatures fell to −30°C, the Luftwaffe had to go back to basics. Groundcrews found exposed skin freezing to metal, and there was a severe shortage of sheltered work areas. Out of 100,000 Luftwaffe vehicles in the East, only 15% were still functioning early in January 1942.[99] The complicated cold-start equipment was not up to Russian conditions, and the Army, SS and Luftwaffe all ignored the simple cold-start technique of thinning oil with a little petrol while an engine was still warm, which the Luftwaffe had itself demonstrated to Hitler during an air display at the Rechlin test centre in 1939.

Field Marshal Erhard Milch had seen enough of Russia in the past to order both urgent winter equipment for the units and the manufacture of extra woollen underwear, five pairs of stockings, big fur boots and sheepskins for all Luftwaffe personnel on the Eastern Front. 'But it will be all over before winter sets in,' protested Gen Otto Rudel, Chief of Air Defence. 'Whoever said that,' retorted Milch, 'must be mad'.[100]

Thanks to Milch's foresight, while the German Army shivered in its summer kit, the Luftwaffe's 800,000 airmen and ground personnel in the East were warmly clothed for the Russian winter. But that did not stop Soviet air units, long accustomed to cold weather operations, from controlling the skies above much of the frozen ground. Stepan Mikoyan, son of a full member of the Soviet Politburo, joined No 11 Fighter Regt in October 1941. They were flying the low-wing monoplane Yak-1, the first of the new generation designed to replace the I-16 fighter. The first 64 production Yak-1s came off the production lines at Zavod (Factory) No 302 in Moscow and Zavod No 292 at Saratov before the end of 1940, but it was only in limited front-line service in June 1941.

Above:
Ju88 of KG30 coming in to land in the winter of 1941-2. *Goss/Rauchbach Archive*

Above:
StG1, Russia, winter 1941-2. *Diekwisch via Goss/Rauchbach Archive*

Yak-1s were pressed into ground attack service in the critical days of the Battle of Moscow. Even No 11 Fighter Regt's two-seat Yak-7V trainer was given an armoured pilot's seatback and sent into combat. Once winter came the Yaks were painted white for camouflage and their wheels replaced with skis that retracted flush to the wings. The fact that Axis rubber tyres became brittle at extreme temperatures was but one reason why, between 15 November and 5 December 1941, the VVS claimed to have flown 15,840 sorties as against 3,500 by the Luftwaffe.[101] Over a town that had fallen to the Germans in late November, Soviet bombers deliberately set out to destroy any shelter that might protect ill-clad German soldiers from the savage and killing cold.

After the June débâcle, Stalin made himself 'Supreme Commander of the Soviet Armed Forces'. This put him on a par with Hitler but, unlike the Führer, Stalin was ready to accept robust professional military advice. That came through the Stavka, a body that could be described as both the Supreme High Command and the General Staff that served it. VVS pilots, in the opinion of Hoffmann von Waldau, distinguished themselves by 'different ideas of the value or otherwise of human life'.[102] The same was true of the Stavka. After some 600 of his aircraft and crews were shot down for minimal effect on the enemy, Lt-Gen I. I. Kopets, air commander Western District, committed suicide on 23 June 1941. Stalin's top airman, the youthful VVS Commander Pavel Rychagov, was sentenced to death for 'treasonable activity', which meant for losing so many aircraft on the ground. Lt-Gen Yakov Smushkevich, hero of Spain and Khalkhin-Gol and now Senior Air Assistant General Staff, was executed at the age of 39. A host of other young, highly educated officers of promise got a bullet too. Against this backdrop, encouragement of Soviet aircrew owed little to 'touchy-feely' management techniques. Stalin, as 'president' of the Stavka, was persuaded to establish a separate Air Force Command, which he entrusted to Lt-Gen P. F. Zhigarev. Simplification was the name of the game. The VVS abolished its Strategic Long-Range Aviation command temporarily, while tactical air units tasked with front support were reorganised into two-regiment divisions with only 30 aircraft, rather than 60 hitherto, to a regiment.

After an initial wobble over whether to leave Moscow or not, Stalin recovered his nerve, imposed martial law upon the city and summoned Grigori Zhukov, the victor at Khalkhin-Gol who had been sent to restore Soviet fortunes at Leningrad, to command Red Army forces in front of Moscow. The leading Germans may have been within 20km of the Kremlin but they were teetering at the end of the precarious supply lines with equipment that was wearing out, and troops who were exhausted. 'Even a powerful air force,' concluded Albert Kesselring, 'could not have helped the frozen and weakened German front decisively against an almost invisible enemy; it was still less to be expected of a weak and overtired air force.'[103]

In October-November, when the Germans were convinced that the Soviets had no reserves, Stalin moved 11 rifle divisions from the Far East. Having been told by Soviet agent Richard Sorge in Tokyo that the Japanese would not invade the USSR, the Stavka was eventually able to transfer some 250,000 troops together with 1,700 tanks and 1,500 aircraft. Just as crucially, while the Luftwaffe was robbing Peter to pay Paul, however desperate the

situation around Moscow for the Soviets, fresh troops and aircrew were not dribbled into battle but were held in the Supreme Command Reserve that was being built up.

On 6 December, Zhukov began a counter-attack using newly arrived, numerically superior and winter-hardened Soviet forces dressed in good winter clothing. It showed the limitations of Luftwaffe air-reconnaissance coverage that the Stavka had, unbeknown to the Germans, gathered 700,000 men together east of Moscow. Army Group Centre put up a fighting withdrawal, supported by attack waves of assets belonging to Fliegerkorps VIII and II Close Support Air Commander in so far as the weather would allow. Hitler's call for 'fanatical resistance' without 'retreating a step' saw light blue ground personnel of the Luftwaffe, AAA and signal service units organised into 'Luftwaffe combat units' and committed in support of the Army.[104]

On 8 December 1941, Hitler issued Directive No 39 that, because of the 'onset of a surprisingly early and severe winter,' ordered an immediate end to offensive action and a shift to defensive positions. The Directive tasked the Luftwaffe primarily with interfering as much as possible with the rehabilitation of Soviet armed forces by launching attacks against training and armament centres, especially those at Moscow, Leningrad, Voronezh, Gorky, Shcherbacov, Stalingrad, Rostov and Krasnodar. Soviet roads and railways, 'by which the enemy lives and by whose use our own front sectors are threatened,' were to be continually interdicted. Along with counter-air operations, the Luftwaffe was to support fully the ground forces against Soviet air and ground attacks. The fact that Luftwaffe strength on the Moscow front was now down to about 500 aircraft, of which fewer than half were serviceable, whereas the VVS was able to keep 1,000 flying in the Moscow sector alone, showed the extent to which the Führer and the OKW were out of touch with air power realities on the Eastern Front.[105]

The Red Army had the potential to field 4.7 million men on European fronts in June 1941. By November, that figure had fallen to 2.3 million, the lowest ever reached throughout the Soviet-German war. In such dire straits and with a shortage of trained staff officers, secure communications and commanders who understood what they were doing, the emphasis was on doing the simple things well. It was not before time, if the diary of the Soviet 15th Infantry Corps was any guide. 'Despite German air supremacy, our marching columns did not use any proper camouflage. Sometimes on narrow roads bottlenecks were formed by troops, artillery, motor vehicles and field kitchens, and then the Nazi planes had the time of their lives . . . Often our troops could not dig in, simply because they did not even have the simplest implements. Occasionally trenches had to be dug with helmets, since there were no spades . . .'

However, what was most remarkable about the first year of the Great Patriotic War was the Soviet air forces' capacity to get back on their feet quickly. JG54, the main Luftwaffe fighter unit on the Leningrad front throughout the entire campaign, was to claim 1,123 Russian aircraft shot down between June-November 1941. Yet just a month after the start of 'Barbarossa', even the elite JG54 reported 37 out of 112 pilots killed or missing with no trend toward lowering losses. By October 1941, more than 70% of the German aircraft that started the war on the Eastern Front had been lost in combat, which meant that the Luftwaffe had lost more aircraft than during the Battle of Britain. Worse than that, Reich industry produced 104 fewer fighters between June and December 1941 than the 1,823 lost up to Christmas.

If Luftwaffe intelligence seriously underestimated VVS numerical strength and dogged determination, it was equally adrift when it came to appreciating what was happening in the Soviet aviation industry. In a speech to the Reichstag on 11 December 1941, Hitler claimed the destruction of no fewer than 17,322 Soviet aircraft over the Eastern Front up to then, but these largely consisted of obsolete types that were already scheduled for retirement. It is arguable that the Luftwaffe simply saved the VVS a disposal problem.

New Soviet aircraft and aero-engine plants had been encouraged since 1937 and while western plants were modernised, new factories were deliberately dispersed eastwards to Tashkent, Irkutsk and Omsk, and further east in Novosibirsk and Komsomolsk.

When the blow fell on 22 June, the State Committee for Defence created a Council for Evacuation to relocate Soviet manufacturing capacity away from major industrial areas such as Leningrad and the eastern Ukraine. This massive undertaking was co-ordinated by N. A. Voznesensky, head of the Soviet industrial planning agency and one of the few senior civilians who dared to tell it like it was to Stalin. While the Red Army engaged in stubborn delaying tactics, workers were moved and buildings and machinery disassembled in the lower Dnieper River and Donbas regions of the Ukraine. Luftwaffe reconnaissance crews were puzzled by the long lines of railway trucks massing in the region. Eight thousand railcars were used to move just one major metallurgy complex to Magnitogorsk in the Urals while a VVS airlift, flown by the 'Special Northern Aviation Group', flew 17,600 workers out of the Leningrad area to the Urals between October and December. This was done on Stalin's authority, as was the airlift of over 1,000 guns and considerable quantities of ammunition from Leningrad into the Moscow defence zone, even though Leningrad desperately needed them itself.

The Luftwaffe launched periodic air raids on western factories and rail lines but by this stage it was so overstretched and Army demands for close air support were so pressing that no concerted action against the relocation effort was possible. And the targets were there aplenty if only the strike aircraft had been available. On the Moscow-Ryazan line, for example, some 80,000 trucks were used to transport 498 factories and industrial facilities from the capital. In the first three months of the war, the trucks that moved two and a half million men to the front returned with 455 plants to the Urals, 210 to Western Siberia, 200 to the Volga and more than 250 to Kazakhstan and central Asia. By mid-November, 914,380 wagons had shifted 38,514 loads for the aviation industry, 20,046 for the ammunition plants and 18,823 for weapons factories.[106]

Artem Mikoyan was Polikarpov's deputy and when Soviet companies were encouraged to create a new generation of aircraft, Mikoyan was part of a Polikarpov team that proposed a high-altitude fighter powered by a liquid-cooled engine. This project appealed to the management of Zavod No 1 at Moscow, who invited Mikoyan to joint the department as its chief. He agreed on condition that a colleague, Mikhail Gurevich, came in as his deputy, and from then on the acronym of MiG, from Mikoyan and Gurevich, became synonymous with Soviet fighter aircraft.

The Soviet Government decreed that aircraft were to be designated by the initial letters of their designer's surnames, followed by odd numbers for fighters and even numbers for bombers and other types. The first MiG-1 soon became the improved MiG-3 to be produced at Zavod No 1. Then Zavod No 1 was moved to Kuibyshev where machinery began operating as the walls of a new aircraft factory went up around it. Just a fortnight after the last trainload from the Moscow factory was unloaded, the first Kuibyshev-built MiG-3 rolled out. Soviet efficiency and ruthlessness made an impressive combination.

Around 100 MiG-3s were delivered to PVO fighter units based around Moscow. But although the high-altitude MiG-3 interceptor could outperform any opposition above 12,000m, the Germans soon learned to lure a MiG-3 pilot down below 4,000m where Bf109Es held the upper hand. The MiG-3 lacked both the armament and the manoeuvrability to mix it at low and medium level, where most fighter-to-fighter combats tended to take place. More importantly, production of its AM-35 engine impacted on the output of Alexander Mikulin's AM-38. This low-altitude modification of the AM-35 was in great demand for Soviet ground-attack aircraft. By edict from Stalin on 23 December 1941, production of the MiG-3 was discontinued and fighter production concentrated on the Yak-1 and LaGG-3, 8,721 and 6,528 of which were produced respectively.

It was small wonder that Stalin wanted to channel all available AM-38 engines towards one of the stars of Soviet aviation — the Il-2. Designed by S. V. Ilyushin, the comparatively crude Il-2 was easy to build with semi-skilled labour using simple jigging and tooling. It could be flown by pilots with relatively little training and although rather sluggish in the air and vulnerable to fighter attack when cornered, it was outstandingly robust and capable of absorbing considerable battle damage from ground fire while remaining airborne. With excellent armour around the engine and pilot's cockpit, two 7.62mm guns and two 20mm cannons in the wings, and underwing capacity for eight rockets or up to 600kg of bombs, it was the Fairchild A-10 Warthog of its day whose liveliness, manoeuvrability and great firepower made it an awesome support weapon for troops in the field. No fewer than 36,163 Il-2 *Shturmoviki* were built, making it both the largest numerical combat aircraft type built during World War 2 and the aircraft that most symbolised the rugged resistance of the Soviet people.

By November 1941, the loss of over 300 factories to the advancing Germans had deprived the VVS of what had hitherto been a monthly production of two million bombs. Aircraft production from the remaining factories that were not moving east dropped from 2,329 in September to 627 two months later. The migration of the aircraft industry had a disastrous impact on output. November's production was about 30% that of September, and Soviet air commanders managed to cope during the winter fighting of 1941-2 only by concentrating their best aircraft on the most decisive sectors of the front.

Yet by the end of 1941, the Soviet aviation industry had turned out 15,735 aircraft, of which 12,516 were combat types. Although two-thirds of these were still of the older types, over 10,000 were produced after the invasion, mostly between July and October.[107] This compared very favourably with the 12,401 aircraft produced by German factories in the whole of 1941, which were not being overrun, dismantled or having many of their skilled workers siphoned off by the army.[108] Soviet output of 5,173 of the latest fighters between July and December far exceeded the 1,619 Luftwaffe fighters rolled out in the same period, or even the 4,408 produced for the RAF.[109] German intelligence had completely underestimated the output and technical expertise of the Soviet aircraft industry, and misread the Russian air force ability to improvise and reorganise both structure and practices while under sudden and devastating attack.

Around 10 million Soviet workers accompanied over 1,500 industrial enterprises beyond the Ural Mountains, and the rebirth of Soviet air power came from this remarkable trek eastward at the height of the German invasion. Not only had the war-sustaining capacity of the Soviet aircraft industry been preserved but also the Soviets had shown an admirable ability to adapt. During 1942, the relocated Soviet facilities would produce nearly 25,000 aircraft. Soviet air power had not been beaten and the foundations were in place for it to fight to the death.

Opposite top:
MiG-3 high-speed, high-altitude interceptors, parked in line during the winter of 1941-2. MiG-3 production stopped in November 1941 after 3,322 had been built. *IWM*

Opposite bottom:
All hands to the pump for the Motherland — rudimentary but none the less effective bomb production somewhere in the Soviet Union. *Society for Co-operation in Russian and Soviet Studies (SCRSS)*

Below:
Il-2s rolling off the line in a factory east of the Urals away from German bombing. *SCRSS*

STRATEGIC BOMBING

Above:
TB-7 under starter's orders. *IWM*

Right:
Soviet paratroops dropping from a Tupolev
TB-3. For its time, the TB-3 was a most
impressive heavy bomber-cum-paratroop
transport. Although 818 were built, they were
obsolescent by 1941. *Author's collection*

'Military thought in the capitalist world has got into a blind alley. Dashing "theories" about a lightning war, or about the air war, which can replace all other military operations — all these theories arise from the bourgeoisie's deathly fear of the proletarian revolution. In its mechanical way, the imperialist bourgeoisie overrates equipment and underrates man.'
Pravda, 6 February 1939

Not content with pulling Luftflotte 2 out of Combat Zone Centre, the OKL compounded its 'Alice in Wonderland' thinking by ordering the staff of Fliegerkorps V to transfer to Brussels on 30 November 1941 in order to organise a new mine-laying air campaign against the UK. Given the withdrawal of Luftflotte 2, Luftwaffe combat flying units in Russia (excluding Luftflotte 5 and air transport units) on 20 December 1941 were as follows:

Luftflotte 1

Weather recce Staffel 1
Fliegerkorps I
Long-range recce: 5.(F)/122; 3.(F)/22; one flight, night recce Staffel 1
Bomber: *Stab*, II., III./KG1; *Stab*, I./KG4; *Stab* KG76
Fighter: I./JG51; I., III., Erg./JG54

Fliegerkorps VIII
Long-range recce: 2.(F) and 4.(F)/11; 1.(F) and 3.(F)/33; 4.(F)/14; Gruppe Gehrken; one night recce flight
Bomber: I., III./KG3; II. in transfer, III./KG76
Dive-bomber: *Stab*, III./StG2; II./StG1; Training Gruppe 2 (Staffeln 4 and 10)
Day fighter: *Stab*, I., II./JG52; Staffel 15./JG27 [110]
Night fighter: I., II./NJG4
II Close Support Leader
Bomber: II.,III. & Staffel 15/KG53; II./KG3; II./KG4; III. (excl Staffel 7)./KG26
High-speed bomber: II./SKG210
Fighter: *Stab*, II., III., IV./JG51

Luftflotte 4

Weather recce Staffel 67
Long-range recce: 4.(F)/122; 2.(F)/22; 3.(F)/10; 3.(F)/11; night recce Staffel 1
Stab/(F)/125 assigned to Air Leader South

Fliegerkorps IV
Long-range recce. 3.(F)/121
Bomber: *Stab*, I., III./KG27; I., II., III./KG51
Dive-bomber: I., II./StG77
Fighter: III./JG77; III., Staffel 15/JG52 [111]

Deutsche Luftwaffen-Mission Rumänien
Fighter: *Erg*./JG77

German assumptions that victory in the East was imminent were dashed when, during the night of 4–5 December, the whole of the 'Northwestern Front' went over to the offensive. The Soviets employed no fewer than 17 armies [112], led by a new generation of commanders. Within days, the main German armoured formations had lost contact with each other and by Christmas Eve Guderian had less than 40 serviceable tanks at his command. It seemed that Bock's entire Army Group would disintegrate.

Once again, the Luftwaffe was expected to make the difference. On 16 December and again on 24 December, Hitler ordered that Fliegerkorps VIII be reinforced without delay by a full bomber Gruppe from the Western Front, three newly activated bomber Gruppen, a twin-engined fighter Gruppe withdrawn from the night-fighter force, four newly activated air transport Gruppen, and one transport Gruppe transferred from Luftflotte 4. All this was valued by Army commanders, but Hitler's intervention into the tactical disposition of forces, the raiding of the Chief of Training's 'last Ju-52s' to make up the new transport Gruppen, the allocation of strategic transports for tactical purposes and serious interference with the training of new aircrews, especially bomber crews, coincided with the Führer assuming command of the German Army after the resignation of Field Marshal von Brauchitsch on 19 December.

The 'Barbarossa' Directive insisted that 'air attacks on England, and especially upon her imports, are not allowed to lapse.' 'Beppo' Schmid of Luftwaffe intelligence was confident enough to tell Dr Goebbels that by autumn 1941 it would be possible to 'have done with the Soviet Union . . . so that the full weight of the German Luftwaffe can once more be thrown against Britain.' But at the beginning of January 1942, half the staff of Fliegerkorps V under Gen von Greim were transferred back to southern Russia as 'special staff Crimea', which put paid to hopes of creating a special mine-laying air corps against Britain.

*　　　*　　　*　　　*

The strategic impact of weakening the last Luftwaffe forces in the West was to leave the RAF free to build up its strength unmolested. This would not have been to the liking of the great prophet of strategic bombing, Gen Giulio Douhet. Born near Naples on 30 May 1869, Douhet was so shocked by the incompetence and unpreparedness when Italy entered the Great War in 1915 that he frequently wrote to his superiors, suggesting both organisational reform and increased use of the aeroplane. Despairing of the offensively orientated ground strategy of the General Staff, he commented ruefully that 'to cast men against concrete is to use them as a hammer'. Douhet saw air power as unhampered by geography, enabling aircraft to fly over surface forces, which then became of secondary importance. In his opinion, aircraft were the only alternative to waging a prolonged war of attrition between mass armies equipped with advanced technology weapons.

Douhet was ahead of others in realising that the key to air power lay in targeting, because although aircraft could strike at virtually anything, they should not try to hit everything. Success in an air campaign lay with identifying the most important centres of gravity and then hitting them most forcefully. Choosing the right objectives would not be easy and would require great insight; it was here that the most successful air commanders would be separated from the also-rans.

Douhet identified five basic centres of gravity as vital to the functioning of a modern country: industry, transportation infrastructure, communication nodes, government buildings and the will of the people. But it was no use expecting generals and admirals to allocate aircraft for these strategic purposes if that meant exposing their armies and fleets. Just as the British realised in 1918 when they amalgamated their Flying Corps and Naval Air Service into an independent RAF, Douhet believed that an air force should not be the 'Cinderella of the family' dependent on the generosity of older sisters. Only a separate air force, looking after its own needs with its own budget, could free air commanders from soldiers and sailors who would otherwise insist on using aircraft in support of tactical operations.[113]

Like all clever people, German military leaders learned more from their defeat in 1918 than their Allied counterparts did from victory. Although Douhet was not published in German until 1935, it appears that Hitler was initially taken with his ideas. But the German leader was not alone. Russian interest in long-range bombers pre-dated the 1917 Revolution. Igor Sikorsky, who later emigrated to the United States, designed the world's first four-engined bomber — named 'Ilya Muromets' after an early national hero — for the Tsar's air force.

The leading Soviet military theorist between 1925 and his fall from grace in 1937 was Marshal Tukhachevsky. In his theory of the 'deep battle', air power prepared the way for the breakthrough of motorised and mechanised troops and then supported the advancing mobile forces deep into enemy territory. Light bomber and ground-attack units would prepare the battlefield and interdict enemy reserves. Aircraft belonging to the Army Group would then isolate the breakthrough sector and interdict the enemy's strategic reserves. Finally, airborne forces would be dropped behind enemy lines to seize headquarters and supply bases.[114]

In 1932 Tukhachevsky declared that future independent air operations, which he defined as strategic bombing and airborne insertions, would prove decisive in war. He predicted that improved aerodynamic design would enable aircraft to fly fast, at great range and at high altitude. He foresaw that in a decade or so, strategic bombing, coupled with paratroop drops, could seize the enemy's rail system and paralyse the mobilisation of enemy forces, thus 'turning precious operational concepts inside out'.[115] VVS Chief of Staff V. V. Khripin echoed this line when he wrote at the beginning of 1935 that modern warfare could not be waged without undertaking 'independent air operations'.

With perhaps a greater understanding of human resilience, Soviet thinkers were not taken with the idea of using strategic bombing to break national will. It also has to be said that the enthusiasm of VVS officers for strategic bombing was based not so much on a rational analysis of the capabilities of air power and aerial technology as a feeling that strategic bombing was somehow more 'modern' and therefore more in accord with that most 'modern and scientific' of all ideologies, Bolshevism.

In 1924 a British company was asked to produce a new Soviet heavy bomber, but its bid price was too high. Instead, the design of a twin-engined heavy bomber (to became the TB-1[116]), was entrusted to A. N. Tupolev. Two hundred were built in 1929-32, followed by a four-engined development to carry up to two tons of bombs. Over 800 of what became known as the TB-3 were

built — an extraordinary production run for the time — and they were to form the basis of the Soviet strategic air arm of the 1930s. No less than 60% of Soviet air strength lay in bombers by November 1935.

In 1934 a specification for a TB-3 replacement was issued based on an operating level of 8,000m rather than 4,000m, plus a much higher performance to evade fighter interception. This became the TB-7 and then, under the new designation system, the Pe-8. But the day of the big bomber-dominated VVS had peaked. There was never any question that the air arm of the huge Red Army would need a great number of tactical aircraft, but the trend away from strategic bombers started when Soviet (and German) experience in the Spanish Civil War showed that Douhet did not have all the answers. On top of that, Tukhachevsky and allies such as Khripin fell in the great purge. By the time the Pe-8 appeared, the emphasis had shifted to lighter aircraft and only 93 Pe-8s were built, not many more than the 'Ilya Muromets'.

The TBA[117] — the Soviet heavy bomber command — was formally organised in 1936. The TBA and the paratroop arm (VDV) were formed into three special-purpose Air Armies directly under the High Command, because the TB-3 was also the primary Soviet paratroop carrier. But the large, independent TBA was downgraded and reorganised in 1940. It was redesignated DBA (Long-Range Bomber Aviation), with its strike forces split into smaller units and orientated more towards tactical duties under army regional command. This was not just a matter of post-purge political correctness. No aviation industry in the world was capable in 1940 of producing the radios, navigation instruments, sophisticated bombsights and other technologically advanced support needed for a long-distance, all-weather strategic bombing campaign. By stripping his bomber forces in the West for his campaign in the East, Hitler gave the British breathing space to work on the problem. The Soviets had no such luxury. As the creation of simple, rugged aircraft to serve as light bombers and fighters was what Soviet industry did best, the Soviets wisely orientated their aircraft production to building attack and light bomber aircraft, plus the fighters to protect them. It was a wise decision.

In the run-up to 1941 and throughout the war, the Soviets maintained a two-tier strategic bomber force: four-engine heavy bombers (TB) and twin-engined long-range bombers (DB[118]). The latter were successors to the TB-1 and carried a lighter bomb load as far as their four-engined brethren, in some cases at higher speed. The RAF enjoyed the same relationship between the Mosquito and the Lancaster, but the Soviets never had the luxury of getting to the Lancaster or USAAF B-17 stage. Circumstances dictated that the DB-3 remained the standard wartime Soviet long-range bomber long after the type attacked Berlin in August 1941.

In May 1941, DBA was formally combined with the long-range transports and some 'frontal' aircraft to form the ADD (Long-Range Aviation). The ADD had five corps and two separate divisions of bombers and transports, but although Long-Range Aviation still reported to the High Command, its bombers were almost wholly involved with the tactical battle. In theory, light bombers were assigned to an army while 'frontal aviation' medium bombers were expected to interdict the battlefield and destroy enemy aircraft on the ground, but the 'mediums' were used for close support when the need arose. In like fashion, the

Above:
Russian and RAF personnel in conversation around a Pe-8, the largest
Soviet bomber developed from the TB-7 of 1937, at RAF Leuchars in
Fife after it brought Soviet Foreign Minister Molotov to the UK on
20 May 1942. *Author's collection*

long-range bomber crews could not sit idly by when Moscow was
threatened. ADD responsiveness was typified by Col N. I.
Novodranov's 8lst Bomber Air Div which, despite being down to
just 40 operational aircraft, was thrown against the airfields
staging the Luftwaffe's air raids on Moscow on the night of
30 September 1941. Soviet airmen may have put Douhet on the
back burner but they underlined the inherent flexibility of air power.

It was a reflection of its importance that the ADD remained an
elite force which received the best equipment, had first priority in
the selection of aircrews and whose personnel received better
rations. After a period under VVS command, the ADD was again
placed directly under the Stavka in March 1942 as an independent
arm until it was absorbed back into the VVS at the end of 1944 as
the 18th Air Army. However, unlike the other 17, it was not attached
to any 'front' and remained directly under the High Command.

Although the German strategic bombing campaign against
Britain in 1917 and 1918 sired the RAF, from Berlin's perspective
the losses in aircrew and aircraft far exceeded the results achieved.
By May 1918, a month after the RAF came into being, the Kaiser's
air service had called off its strategic bombing campaign.

Once Hitler came to power and rearmament was assured,
German airmen prepared to put strategic bombing at the doctrinal
centre of the reborn Luftwaffe. The first chief of staff, Lt-Gen
Walther Wever, was an outspoken supporter of strategic air power
and proposals to create heavy bombers received strong support
throughout the Air Staff. In 1936 the Germans had both the Ju89
and Do19 four-engined prototypes on the drawing board. That the
aim was to produce what Wever portentously called the
Uralbomber showed that the objective was not London or Paris,
but rather industrial targets deep in the USSR.

It was at this point that aspirations ran up against technology.
Long-range four-engined strategic bombers were a step too far in
1936. The prime British hope — the Short Stirling — never lived
up to expectations while the Ju89 and Do19 proved to be
underpowered and unwieldy. Technology would eventually bale out
the heavy bomber mafia, transmuting a barely adequate Avro
Manchester into the superlative Lancaster. But when Wever died in
a flying accident in June 1936, German aero-engine technology was
years away from delivering the range and performance to reach
beyond the Urals. The cancellation of both German four-engined
heavy bomber prototypes in the spring of 1937 reflected the need to
ease pressure on scarce raw materials. When told that industry
could make two and half twin-engined bombers for every four-
engined one, Göring felt he had no option — 'The Führer does not
ask me how big my bombers are, but how many there are.'[119]

Within a year it was realised that the Luftwaffe's existing
bombers could not penetrate further than 700km, and then with
only half a ton of bombs. So in mid-1938 it was decided to order a
different four-engined aircraft with greatly enhanced performance,
the He177. The six-seat He177 was designed around a wingspan

of 31.44m and an all-up-weight of 31,000kg (30.5 tons). The trouble was that the large He177 was to be capable of dive-bombing, which meant coupling the engines in pairs to avoid weakening the wing structures. Enthusiasm for the accuracy conferred by dive-bombing set back German bomber development by years, and forced the redesign of excellent aircraft such as the Ju88 with consequent production delays.

The fourth Chief of the Luftwaffe General Staff, Hans Jeschonnek, had youth on his side but he was not 'Mr Personality' like Wever and Kesselring. It is true that Jeschonnek was infatuated with dive-bombing and gave only minimal priority to the strategic bomber programme and the build-up of transport aviation. But as war loomed, Hitler probably kept Jeschonnek's focus on the here and now rather than the wide blue yonder. Jeschonnek certainly persuaded Göring on 26 October 1938 to authorise at least four Kampfgeschwadern of long-range bombers. The complexity of the design specification meant that this formidable force of 500 30-ton He177s was never going to be ready before autumn 1942 at the earliest, but that was the same year that the Lancaster entered Bomber Command service.

Around the end of June 1941, Hitler stated that Moscow had to be attacked early in the war and, like Leningrad, razed to the ground. On 14 July he justified attacks on Moscow as the 'centre of Bolshevik resistance and to prevent the orderly evacuation of the Russian governmental apparatus.' Führer Directive No 23 of 19 July ordered that Luftflotte 2, temporarily reinforced by bomber forces from the West, bomb Moscow as soon as possible as 'retaliation for Soviet attacks on Bucharest and Helsinki'. The first air raid on the Soviet capital, which apart from housing Stalin's government and the military commands was also the USSR's most important transport junction and a major armaments centre, was launched on the evening of 21 July by Lörzer's Fliegerkorps II and Greim's Fliegerkorps V. Ju88s from KG3 and KG54, He111s from KG53 and KG55, supplemented from the West by KG28 with its two Pathfinder Gruppen (III./KG26 and KGr100), and Do17s from KG2 and KG3 took-off from forward bases around Minsk, Orsha, Vitebsk and Chatalovska bound for Moscow 450-600km away. This force of 195 bombers enjoyed good visibility at altitudes between 2,000-4,000m. They encountered the first searchlights some 30km northwest of Moscow. Soviet air defenders offered heavy resistance, with Lt I. D. Chulkov in his MiG-3 claiming an He111 at 02.10hrs on 22 July. But some Gruppen flew unmolested almost to the Kremlin.

Nearer Moscow, the German bombers were met by heavy AAA fire. 'What was most impressive,' wrote British news correspondent Alexander Werth, 'was the tremendous anti-aircraft barrage, with shrapnel from the anti-aircraft shells clattering down on to the streets like a hailstorm; and dozens of searchlights lighting the sky; I had never seen or heard anything like it in London.' [120] The AAA batteries of 1 Korpus PVO expended 29,000 artillery shells and 130,000 machine gun bullets that night, but they did not stop 104 tons of High Explosive and 46,000 incendiaries from being dropped from the 127 aircraft that reached the target area.

Therein lay the rub: 104 tons of HE and 46,000 incendiaries sounded impressive but its destructive impact was minimised by the fact that the Luftwaffe, like every other air force at that time,

lacked the capability to deliver weaponry at night with any degree of concentration. Not only were the bombs and incendiaries scattered but also they were unsuited to their objectives. II/KG55's target was the Kremlin but although hundreds of incendiaries were scattered on the 17th-century building, its roof was solid and the puny devices just bounced off. Weapon-to-target matching was way out.

The Luftwaffe sent 115 bombers to Moscow the following night, after which the Soviet air defences claimed 15 destroyed and the Germans admitted to five. During the third Moscow raid on the night of 24 July, the attacking force was reduced to 100. Available in-theatre forces were just not sufficient for an effective and sustained heavy bombing operation, and aircraft had to be scraped together from wherever they could be found. In July the attackers were temporarily reinforced from Luftflotte 1 by KG4 (which was normally used to lay mines), KG54 and KG55 from Luftflotte 4, and KG28 from Luftflotte 3 in the West. These Kampfgruppen flew 358 sorties against the Soviet capital during July, briefly forcing Stalin's headquarters below ground into a Metro station.

The first Moscow raids were flown at night because German fighters lacked the range to provide complete protection during the day. That changed as the German Army moved east, and Luftwaffe fighters moved into airfields nearer the capital. Bombing attacks in the late autumn and winter of 1941-2 also became more operational in character as Moscow came within the ambit of the army.

The Luftwaffe attacked Moscow 76 times at night and 11 times during the day, but only the first three attacks were carried out with more than 100 bombers. As it proved impracticable to detach such a large portion of the diminishing German bomber force from the army's growing difficulties at the front, the number of aircraft participating in each strategic raid decreased inexorably. Only half a dozen raids involved 50 bombers each, 19 involved 15-40, and 59 involved 3-10. Eventually, the Luftwaffe 'offensive' against Moscow was reduced to barely nuisance value. It may have given Hitler some solace to know that when Stalin gave his great 'If the Germans want a war of extermination, they can have one,' speech on 6 November, he delivered it to a throng assembled for safety in the marble cavern of the Mayakovsky underground station.

Although these 87 raids killed 1,088 people according to Soviet figures, no strategic effect could have been expected from the limited number of aircraft involved. By 25 October 1941, 59 attacks had deposited just over 1,000 tons of HE bombs, which approximated to the average RAF Bomber Command drop in a *single* night in 1944. The 75th German attack on Moscow took place on 6 December 1941, and the last on 5 April 1942.

Back in 1927 Douhet had written that 'I am against air defence because it detracts means from the Air Force . . . I am against it because I am absolutely convinced that it cannot achieve its aim.' His many followers were equally convinced that expenditure on air defence was money wasted, because 'the bomber would always get through'. The Battle of Britain proved that dictum to be false and Soviet air defence forces around Moscow should have driven the point home. Brig Gen Mikhail Gromadin's Moscow Air Defence District (Moskovskaya Zona PVO) had 585 fighters divided into 29 Fighter Regiments at its disposal, of which more than half (170 MiG-3s, 95 Yak-1s, 75 LaGG-3s) were the most modern types. In addition, Moscow Air Defence District had 1,044 AAA and 336 machine guns in and around the capital.

Yet the Luftwaffe lost only one bomber in each of the first three attacks on Moscow, which showed that fighters and flak blasting away indiscriminately were of limited utility. Radar and effective radio communications would be needed to co-ordinate all this effort and hot metal effectively. The eventual failure of the attacks on Moscow to have any effect on the war in the East owed more to the weakness and inconsistency of the attacking German formations than to the strength of Soviet air defences.

Given the limited Luftwaffe bomber arm, there were more meaningful centres of gravity than Moscow in July 1941. The whole Soviet logistics chain was initially open to attack, and the systematic destruction of Russian aircraft and tank factories would have considerably eased pressure on the German front. The railway lines to and from Siberia, from the Arctic Ocean and the Caspian Sea to the interior of the country, the oil refineries in Tuapse and the oil pipelines in the Caucasus and from Guryev on the Caspian to Orsk, the cracking-plants producing aviation fuel in Ufa and Orsk, and the oil fields of Groznyy and Baku — all these offered worthwhile targets at one time or another.[121]

Professional airmen understood this. The commander of Fliegerkorps V, Gen Robert Ritter von Greim, was credited with 28 'kills' in World War 1, for which he received an hereditary title from the King of Bavaria. Greim helped organise Chiang Kai-shek's Chinese Air Force in the 1920s, and he re-entered military service on 1 April 1934 as a Luftwaffe Major. From 1940-3 he commanded Fliegerkorps V, and few commanders were more popular among German airmen than von Greim. But his suggestions in October 1941 that Fliegerkorps V's bombers would be best employed going for the southern Soviet oil fields fell on deaf ears.

It would be misleading to imply that the German High Command did not think strategically. Hitler understood the importance of securing strategic assets and from the first day of 'Barbarossa', Romania was protected from almost daily Soviet air attacks to safeguard regular fuel deliveries to the German war machine.

The trouble was that the Luftwaffe lacked the air assets to give more than irregular and fleeting priority to targets away from the immediate battlefield. Fliegerkorps V showed glimpses of what might have been achieved, especially during the interdiction of Soviet rail movements around and to the east of Kharkov during the encirclement battle of Kiev. Waves of its bombers attacked the Soviet rail transport system, which was carrying supplies of all kinds and evacuating industrial goods, machines and even food from Kharkov and the Donets basin to the north and east. Severe losses were inflicted on Soviet locomotives and freight cars around Kharkov and when the weather was suitable for hit-and-run raids Luftwaffe daylight attacks were carried out deep in Soviet rear areas as far as the Millerovo-Liski-Voronezh line. Attacks on railways continued whenever there was a bombers' moon.

However, rail interdiction far in the Soviet rear was made possible only by neglecting other air power tasks. It was no use arguing that the interdiction programme gave strong support to the German ground forces, and that such successful air attacks considerably delayed and occasionally prevented the Red Army from resupplying or even mounting major, large-scale attacks or regroupings. Any results achieved by Fliegerkorps V largely went unappreciated by their army brethren who only registered the impact of the strike aircraft they could see.

But the lessons ran deeper than that. For four whole weeks while the encirclement battle of Kiev was raging, the Luftwaffe blocked all reinforcement for Budenny's armies and disrupted all lines of retreat. Yet notwithstanding this immediate and local success, the Russian railway system as a whole came off virtually unscathed. As the Allies showed in the run-up to the D-Day invasion of Normandy, to knock out marshalling yards and major junctions 'for the duration' needed lots of big bombs dropped accurately and in droves. These the Luftwaffe did not possess in 1941, nor the aircraft to carry them *en masse*. And when trains were hit or stretches of line blocked, the Russians proved to be astonishingly skilful at repair and improvisation. Frequently stretches of track, seemingly badly hit in the evening, were in use again by the following night. 'Between June and December 1941 the enemy made 5,939 air attacks on railways adjacent to the front,' recorded the official Soviet war history. 'The average period of disruption to traffic was only five hours and forty-eight minutes.' The Germans now paid the price for letting the OKL off the intellectual hook during 'Barbarossa' planning in the mistaken belief that a war against Russia would be finished quickly.

*   *   *   *

General of the Army V. D. Sokolovsky, one of those to take the German surrender in Berlin on 8 May 1945, attributed the German failure to seize Moscow and the successful Russian stabilisation of the front in late 1941 to the strong Soviet will to resist — probably enhanced by brutal occupation policies of Reich authorities in conquered areas — and the increased output of armaments by Soviet factories. Focusing on the last, by September 1941 the Germans believed that Soviet fighter, bomber and ground-attack forces had all but been wiped out. Yet fresh aircraft kept being thrown into the battle and Soviet sources of supply seemed to be inexhaustible.

We now know why. The man in charge of German military aircraft production was Gen Ernst Udet, the most successful German World War 1 fighter ace after the Red Baron. But for all his boisterous and likeable nature, Udet was not up to the job of co-ordinating the German aviation industry in war. He was not wholly to blame. The basic cause of the Luftwaffe's production problems in 1941 lay in the almost universal dilettantism among the higher Nazi leadership when it came to appreciating the logistic realities inherent in waging total war. In the euphoria after the fall of France, Udet made no effort to enhance the low production outputs from German industry by European integration. During the whole of 1941, the French aircraft industry produced just 62 aircraft for the Luftwaffe, and the Dutch only 16.[122]

By contrast, even while fighting for survival in the second half of 1941, the Soviets quadrupled the mass production of improved aircraft types. Compared with the first half of the year, the production of LaGG-3 fighters rose from 322 to 2,141, of Yak-1 fighters from 335 to 1,019 and of the armour-plated, ground-attack Il-2s from 249 to 1,293. 1,867 bombers were produced at three times the prewar rate, and Soviet industry's total production of all types in 1941 reached 15,735 aircraft.

There were three main reasons why the Luftwaffe did little to prevent this phenomenal resupply activity. First, in the pell-mell Blitzkrieg battle German army priorities took precedence, which conflicted with Anglo-US thinking and experience. On 16 April 1944, ACM Sir John Slessor, the senior British airman in the Italian campaign, wrote to his Chief of Air Staff to say that 'another lesson which I think has been confirmed in recent fighting in Italy is that . . . *the bomber is not a battlefield weapon. . . .* As a general rule I am convinced that bombers of any class should be used on the battlefield only as a last resort in defence. Except in those conditions, even your fighters and light bombers will contribute far more effectively to the Army's battle by paralysing the movement of enemy supply and reserves behind the battlefield than by attacking strongpoints, battery positions etc on the battlefield — that is the job of artillery.'

The Luftwaffe fell into the trap of using bombers in Russia 'as a last resort' all the time, which stemmed from being increasingly at the beck and call of the army. Instead of being under a single command, separate Kampfgeschwadern from different Fliegerkorps were sent here and there on a multitude of individual missions, most of them in a close-support role which was not their own. As the first bomber raid was being launched against Moscow on 21 July, the nearby encirclement battle of Smolensk was under way. Subsequent bomber contributions for Moscow raids were resisted by Fliegerkorps commanders, supported by the Army chiefs, because everyone judged his own sector of operations to be the most important. This was a very wasteful use of air power. In a week of going after individual armour, at great cost to themselves, Luftwaffe bombers succeeded in destroying perhaps one day's output of T34 tanks from the Gorky factory. Though this might have brought joy to soldiers in the front line, it would have been much more efficient and cost-effective to bomb the Gorky factory to prevent any tanks from getting anywhere near the battlefield.

Then there was attrition inflicted by Soviet air forces that refused to play to German rules. In the words of the Soviet history: 'The enemy offensive was decisively halted on the approaches to Moscow by the heroic efforts of our ground and air forces. During the defence of Moscow our air force flew 51,300 sorties, of which 86% were ground support and 14% were in defence of Moscow. The enemy lost about 1,400 aircraft in the Moscow sector, 85% of them the result of the operations of our air force, which made it possible for our air force to claim control of the sky and to disrupt the enemy advance on Moscow.'[123] By 1 November the Luftwaffe in the East, whose average monthly strength was 2,462 aircraft (of which 1,119 were strike), was losing 741 aircraft and 318 aircrew every month. In December, such was the impact of attrition and mental exhaustion that German aircrew losses rose to 371. At this stage the German bomber fleets could achieve little more than a few strategic pinpricks.

Although in an ideal world the Luftwaffe should have gone for the Soviet aviation industry while it was dismantled and on the move eastward, the Germans lacked the aircraft for such a sustained operation while simultaneously supporting the combat on the ground. Given that all significant air operations against Britain had ceased by the start of 'Barbarossa', at least two bomber wings — KG4 and KG28 — could have been pre-deployed to the East for strategic purposes. They were eventually sent east anyway, but by the time they arrived in theatre they were desperately needed for tactical purposes and to fill in the gaps caused by increasing attrition among other Luftwaffe bomber units. Although they had 26-30 aircraft assigned, many bomber Gruppen were down to 10 operational aircraft or less by the end of 1941. But even had they been at full strength and the Germans had neutralised the RAF from Scotland to Cyrenaica before June 1941, the Luftwaffe would still have been spread too thinly to paralyse the Soviet Union strategically.

And by 1942, the German bomber force was rapidly approaching obsolescence. The Ju87 Stuka could only survive where the Luftwaffe enjoyed air superiority, while the primary strike Do17s, He111s and Ju88s had already shown their range and payload limitations during the Battle of Britain. The best of these was the Ju88 *Schnellbomber* (high-speed bomber), but in 1941 the average tactical depth of German bomber penetration, under combat conditions and with only half a bomb load, was 900-1,000km. Destroyers, dive-bombers and fighters, unless fitted with extra fuel tanks, were able to penetrate only about 375km, 200km and 180km respectively into enemy territory.[124] But at least the fighters and dive-bombers were stationed well forward — the depth of penetration by the Ju88s, He111s and Do17s was reduced by their bases being some distance back from the front line. Once the new Soviet aviation industrial centres were up and running in the lower Volga, in the Caucasus and beyond the Urals, they would remain inviolate for all practical purposes. This would act as a sanctuary area in much the same fashion as China sustained the North Vietnamese in the Vietnam War.

According to the United States Strategic Bombing Survey written in 1945, the first factor in the ultimate defeat of the Luftwaffe was that it 'was originally designed for direct support of ground operations, and a lack of a long-range bomber force proved a grave strategic error.' But this statement ignored the unique resilience of Soviet Government and people. It has been calculated that in the first six months of 'Barbarossa', the Soviet Union lost 40% of its population, 63% of its coal, 58% of its steel, 68% of its pig iron, 60% of its aluminium, 38% of its grain, 95% of its ball bearings, and 99% of its rolled, nonferrous metals.[125] Yet not only did the Soviet Union not collapse but it also went on to defeat Germany. It is hard to see how any strategic bomber force could have added meaningfully to Soviet destruction in 1941.

So the Luftwaffe over Russia became the long-range artillery and an auxiliary weapon of the ground forces as much by default as by grand design. Because they could be used swiftly and flexibly, flying units were invariably used to give direct support to increasingly harassed armies. Especially in Combat Zone Centre, the Luftwaffe became the army's 'fire brigade', locked into ground tactical plans and expected to extinguish countless fires.

There was a certain irony in all this. In the few weeks after 22 June, the Luftwaffe was completely tied up with the initial war of movement that made great tactical progress. This dazzling initial success on all fronts took place at perhaps the only time when strategic air power might have achieved anything lasting. In taking their eye off the strategic ball during the first months of 'Barbarossa', the Germans allowed Soviet industrial plants to be evacuated along still-intact railways to safe havens well beyond German bomber range. Thereafter, the VVS started to re-equip massively with new aircraft. Once again, the Germans came up against the hard reality of not beating the Soviets in the first few weeks.

*   *   *   *

By 19 October 1941, the German Eleventh Army had entered the Crimea. In response, the Russians employed their air forces for the first time at a point of main effort — over the narrow, completely level, steppe-like isthmus. The treeless and bush-less terrain offered no cover for the attacking Eleventh Army troops. Gen Erich von Manstein, commander of the Eleventh Army, stated later that the VVS continuously dominated the sky, and very strongly attacked every target sighted. German infantrymen and artillerymen at the front, and even vehicles and horses in the rear, had to be protected by trenches or foxholes.

To meet this threat more effectively, German fighters were placed under the leadership of the General of Fighters Oberst

Left:
Werner Mölders (right) with Hermann Göring in France in 1940.
Author's collection

Werner Mölders, the first German officer to be awarded the Knight's Cross of the Iron Cross with Oak Leaf, Swords, and Diamonds after his 100th aerial victory. In parallel, bomber units of Fliegerkorps IV increasingly attacked VVS airfields in the Crimea while dive-bombers struck the strong ground positions on the isthmus. In Manstein's opinion, only when Mölders and his fighter wing were brought in towards the end of the fighting were the Soviet attackers swept from the sky by day, even though Soviets attacks continued at night.

Then, on 17 November 1941, Gen Ernst Udet shot himself. Bitter at being blamed for the failure to provide enough new aircraft to sustain the advance into Russia, Udet was still accorded a state funeral on Hitler's orders. Göring, whose withdrawal of support had finally pushed Udet over the edge, tried to make public amends by ordering all Luftwaffe dignitaries to be present at Berlin's Invaliden Cemetery to pay their last respects.

One of those expressly summoned to join the guard of honour at Udet's lying in state was fighter ace of aces, Werner Mölders. At the end of difficult air operations over the Lrikin Peninsula, the General of Fighters took-off at once with his adjutant for the long trip back to Berlin in an He111 belonging to a bomber group at Kherson. The pilot was an experienced 'old hand', Oblt Kolbe, who after stopping at Lvov to refuel discovered that Germany lay under a thick layer of cloud. Kolbe was all for waiting until the skies cleared but Mölders insisted on continuing the flight. Popular hero he may have been, but Mölders felt under pressure to comply with Göring's order and arrive at the funeral in time.

Over Poland, a drop in oil pressure forced Kolbe to shut down one engine. Recognising that you can only push against the odds so far, Mölders reluctantly agreed to divert to Breslau-Gandau where he was certain to pick up a rail connection to Berlin. The He111 descended over Silesia through the fog and rain. Kolbe was locked on instruments when, abruptly, the wires of a cable railway leaped into view. He hauled back on the control column but could not prevent a wire strike, which disabled the remaining Junkers Jumo engine. As Kolbe tried vainly to glide in, the He111 stalled. One wing struck a factory chimney and the aircraft spun in a few metres short of the airfield. Mölders, in the nose of the bomber where he was probably trying to use his fighter pilot's vision to pick out the airfield lights, was killed outright.

Eight days after Udet's state funeral, the great and good of the Luftwaffe stood once more round an open grave. Mölders' untimely death, caused by cutting it fine, in a rush, and underestimating what he was up against, was an apt metaphor for the Luftwaffe at the end of 1941. From now on, German airmen would find individual panache and brilliance to be less and less capable of countering an increasingly awesome Soviet air power machine.

BLACK AND BLUE

'The war is extending and becoming harder and longer.'
Maj-Gen Hoffmann von Waldau, 3 December 1941

Four days after Pearl Harbor, Adolf Hitler defiantly declared war on the United States even though his defensive alliance with Tokyo did not require it. 'I was appalled at his unworldliness and innocence as to the industrial potential which just over 20 years previously had been decisive in the Great War,' wrote the Führer's Luftwaffe adjutant, Klaus von Below. 'It exposed the amateurism of his foreign policy and his deficient knowledge of the world beyond Europe.'[126] In the long run the declaration of war on the USA proved to be as fatal for Germany as the 'Barbarossa' invasion in June 1941. Within six months, Germany had gone from undisputed mastery of the European continent to a desperate struggle with the two greatest powers on earth.

At the end of 1941, the Luftwaffe had 5,167 front-line aircraft on all fronts including transports. Of these, only 2,560 were combat-ready aircraft and out of around 1,900 front-line aircraft in the East, only some 960 were combat ready including Ju52 transports. Some Eastern Front units were down to 37% of their bombers and 34% of their long-range recce aircraft. By 10 January 1942, the Luftwaffe order of battle in the East had dropped to 1,713 front-line aircraft of which only 775 were combat ready, but the OKL seemed content that only one-third of its fighting assets were in the East.

By 27 December 1941, the Luftwaffe had lost 2,505 aircraft in the East (327 of which were not due to enemy action), plus 1,895 damaged. When added to attrition on other fronts, the Luftwaffe lost 5,730 aircraft in the second half of 1941. As new German aircraft production (excluding seaplanes, gliders and courier aircraft) over the same period was only 5,141, the Luftwaffe kept going only by recycling around 2,000 repaired aircraft, but many of these were suitable only for training units.

By May 1942 the Luftwaffe had about 15,000 aircraft, of which 6,600 were scattered along the various fronts, 4,300 were in the training schools, 447 in reserve, about 3,000 under repair and 685 'on the way', a euphemism for mislaid in transit.[127] But aircraft were only part of the operational equation. Just before the invasion of Russia, the Luftwaffe numbered 1,269,000 men. Between 22 June and 27 December 1941, human losses in the three branches of the Luftwaffe — flying, AAA and signals — totalled 6,232 killed (including 732 officers), 2,564 (476 officers) missing or captured, and 11,425 (831 officers) wounded. Of these, 3,010 aircrew (including 664 officers) were reported killed, missing or captured in the East, which represented a fifth of the flying personnel lost since September 1939. Yet training hours were not being compromised and as the number of crews undergoing flight training had scarcely declined, the quality and quantity of Luftwaffe aircrew were nowhere near causing concern. Although Soviet aircraft production was giving the VVS numerical superiority in aircraft, the outstanding ability and high morale of German airmen in early 1942 enabled the Luftwaffe to retain air superiority. Soviet air forces still suffered from hastily contrived and sub-standard training, and from a certain mental inertness and standardisation among Soviet commanders and pilots. Courageous acts by some Soviet airmen, especially ground-attack *Shturmovik* pilots, could not offset this deficiency.

* * * *

At the beginning of 1942, Stalin's mood had changed from desperation to believing that the Germans were on their knees. Without waiting to concentrate his forces or eliminate bypassed units, on 7 January he ordered a general offensive along the entire front. As Soviet troops struggled westward, the supporting VVS had to give up its permanent, heated airfields and move to forward airstrips that were just as inhospitable as those occupied by the Luftwaffe. And the Luftwaffe was by no means impotent. At the end of January, the Soviets planned a breakout into the area where von Manstein's Eleventh Army was investing Sevastopol. German aerial reconnaissance followed the Soviet build-up on the Caucasian airfields and in the Black Sea harbours, and such was Teutonic confidence that the Luftwaffe roared over Soviet lines on 23 February dropping leaflets announcing that the offensive would start four days later.

In overestimating his own strength and underestimating the resilience of his enemy, Stalin made the same mistake as Hitler the previous summer. By asking too much of his forces, Stalin failed to eliminate the German forces outside Moscow and made only limited gains elsewhere. The German armies fought continuous delaying actions throughout the winter of 1941-2, some of them of extreme severity, and eventually succeeded in halting the gigantic Soviet winter offensives and in establishing a new, but in places critically thin, defence line. As battles fought over 800km petered out in April 1942, the Soviets found themselves mainly in possession of the impenetrable countryside while the Germans clung fast to cities, villages and key arteries.[128]

The Soviets never wasted anything. The U-2, renamed Po-2 in July 1944 after its designer Polikarpov died, was a two-seat biplane, of which about 14,900 were built for use at flying schools. It would have been kept well out of danger in any Western air force by 1941. But the VVS fitted U-2s with racks for small bombs and sent them to harass German troops after dark. The slow U-2s approached their targets singly, 5-15 minutes apart

Above:
The sturdy Polikarpov U-2 biplane, affectionately known as the 'sewing machine', being used for casualty evacuation. *IWM*

and at altitudes varying from 200m to 1,700m to prevent collisions with each other. There was no way in which a Bf109 pilot could have intercepted them but even in ideal conditions where there were long moonlit or starry nights, flying U-2s in this fashion was a particularly hardy pursuit.

With 200kg (441lb) of bombs on the wing racks and a forward-firing 7.62mm machine gun, the U-2s had a significant impact on German battlefield troops. Often VVS pilots would stop their engines and glide steadily to the target, dropping their bombs by hand. Any German bivouac or campfire sighted became fair game. These seemingly ubiquitous, night attackers, nicknamed 'sewing machines' by German troops because of their noisy engines, forced the Wehrmacht on all fronts to take precautions and lose sleep. Sometimes the only warning of the impending arrival of a fragmentation bomb was the sound of the wind whistling through the wing struts of a gliding U-2 biplane.[129]

Göring, who like Hitler had served on the Western Front in World War 1, was convinced that the USSR would collapse from within 'because the communist system is despised by the masses in Russia'.[130] There were certainly many Soviet citizens who initially welcomed the Germans as liberators, but attacks by Soviet stragglers and then increasingly strong partisan groups

became one of the most important problems facing Luftwaffe ground-support troops, particularly in Combat Zone Centre. Everyone knew what had happened to Oberst von Gerlach who had been shot down while on a cross-country liaison flight from one advance route to another: German troops later discovered his brutally mutilated body. The Luftwaffe learned very quickly about the importance of organising for all-round defence. Oberst Gottlob Müller was praised for his initiative in getting captured Soviet tanks back into use to defend his airfield at Bobruysk.

As Soviet air and partisan activity made rear areas insecure and Red Army breakthroughs encircled forward operating bases, the Luftwaffe became tasked with supplying personnel defending key points. When the boundary between Army Group Centre and Army Group North was ripped open to a width of more than 160km, the whole of General Graf Brockdorff-Ahlefeldt's X Army Corps and parts of XI Army Corps, situated in the Demyansk-Kholm areas southeast of Lake Ilmen, were completely cut off. Rather than withdraw the endangered units, Hitler decided to make them into 'strongholds' in the hope that they would divert Soviet units, which might otherwise have been used to better advantage against Army Group Centre.

Today we take military air transport for granted but back in 1941 a significant percentage of the Luftwaffe's transport aircraft existed only to convert future bomber pilots from single- to multi-engine aircraft. It was during the Spanish Civil War that air transport had first been used to bring an army into the field of battle. For Gen Franco's coup to succeed in July 1936, he had to move his Spanish African army, and in particular the elite foreign legion, from Morocco to southern Spain. Within a few weeks, over 8,000 men, their weapons and kit had been flown into Seville courtesy of Italian Air Force transports and Luftwaffe Ju52s. The Spaniards called it their 'aerial bridge'.

When five Soviet armies were surrounded in September 1941, Marshal Budenny was told that the only way to supply them was by air. 'Such a mass of troops cannot be supplied by air,' declared the Marshal realistically. 'Order at once the most stringent economy in ammunition and supplies.'[131] But if Budenny recognised the limitations of airlift, Hitler did not. In his Directive of 16 December 1941, Hitler plundered the Luftwaffe's Ju52 force as the only effective way of supporting Army Group Centre with new personnel and equipment given the weather and Soviet action. The five air transport Gruppen sent to reinforce Fliegerkorps VIII were placed under the Chief of Air Transport for the Luftwaffe, Oberst Fritz Morzik, in Smolensk.

Responsibility for air supply of the Demyansk and Kholm encirclements was given to Army Group North and its supporting Luftflotte 1. Luftflotte 1's commander at Ostrov, Generaloberst Alfred Keller, now found that his primary mission had altered from attacking Soviet forces to providing combat support and air supply of the Kholm stronghold and what became generally known as the Demyansk fortress. Kholm was the smaller of the two pockets. Completely encircled since 21 January, some 3,500 men were holding out in Kholm under Gen Theodor Scherer. Demyansk was a far bigger prize, after a Soviet advance in mid-February encircled some six divisions numbering 100,000 men. When the gap between them and the yielding German front increased to 120km, Oberst Morzik was ordered on 18 February to move all his flying units to Luftflotte 1's area.

Demyansk needed a daily quota of 300 tons to survive in winter weather against a superior enemy, which Morzik's staff calculated would require a standing force of at least 150 serviceable aircraft. He had only half that number in place, which meant drawing on other fronts and draining the homeland of all available assets. Hitler promised to make 337 transport aircraft available to Luftflotte 1 and within 24 hours, seven air transport Gruppen were available for the airlift. By the end of the month, four more Gruppen and elements of the 105th 'zbV' or 'special purpose' Gruppe had been brought in from Luftflotte 4 in the south. Five further transport Gruppen arrived in early March from the instrument flying and advanced flying training schools back home.

The Ju52s operated out of bases at Pleskau-West and South, Korovye-Solo, Ostrov, Riga and Dünaburg. Morzik, his operations chief, Hptm Wilhelm Metscher, and the rest of the air transport staff had their HQ at Pleskau-South, an airfield they shared with KG4. The Kholm pocket was so small that transports could not land on its single airstrip without being exposed to Soviet ground fire. The one attempt made at the end of February, on the orders of Gen Keller against Morzik's advice, resulted in the loss of five out of the seven participating Ju52s. Thereafter supplies were delivered into Kholm only by airdrop or on 1-ton capacity DFS-230 cargo gliders. Larger Go242 gliders, towed by He111s, brought in heavy items up to 2.5 tons, but as the German-

held pocket contracted under Soviet pressure, eventually only DFS-230 gliders were able to make landings and then only on one street in the village.

By the end of March, two KG4 Gruppen were bombing Soviet forces surrounding Kholm and making supply drops at night. At the third attempt, the German Army relieved Kholm on 5 May. That Gen Scherer's combat group had held out for 103 days against very heavy Soviet attacks owed everything to the courage of the men on the ground, and the combat and air supply missions flown out of Pleskau-South.

There were two airfields within the much larger Demyansk pocket. Demyansk, formerly a Soviet advanced tactical airfield, had a runway 50m wide by 850m long, but it lacked any other installations. Peski's runway of rolled snow, which became available in early March, could be used by only the most capable pilots. Transport aircraft could land at Demyansk and Peski only during the hours of daylight.

The well-organised command system, helped by the availability of combat-seasoned Luftwaffe ground- and aircrews, made it possible to handle up to 600 aircraft daily at the Demyansk airfield. But there was no possibility of stationing even a few fighters inside the pocket, since this would have seriously hampered the supply chain on these small airfields.

At first, small formations of Ju52s flew in at low level. German fighters were assigned roving missions over the approach and return legs and over the landing areas, but they could not fly close escort because the Ju52's cruising speed was too low. On the other hand, the steadily increasing number of Soviet AAA batteries, some of which had highly mobile, self-propelled guns, soon forced the Ju52s to operate in groups of 20-40 aircraft at altitudes ranging from 2,000m-3,000m.

VVS fighters were not particularly aggressive, and they rarely attacked German aircraft flying in formation especially if they defended themselves with all guns. Soviet fighter pilots preferred to attack stragglers or single, unprotected transports. VVS ground-attackers were more of a threat, and surprise Soviet low-level bombing and strafing attacks seriously impaired Ju52 landings and invariably resulted in German personnel and aircraft losses. But the German supply system coped, not least because the Luftwaffe was able to proceed with landing, loading, and take-off operations unmolested at the Ju52 home bases. Energetic Soviet air attacks against these airheads would have seriously jeopardised the entire supply effort to the Demyansk pocket.

Luftwaffe resupply of beleaguered ground forces in the Kholm and Demyansk areas was a German first, but several factors differed from those that would pertain in the Stalingrad relief operation. First, the front stabilised near Kholm and Demyansk, and therefore forward operating fields were only a short distance from the troops they supplied. Second, these forward operating bases were accessible to airfields in the former Baltic countries and were tied directly to the Luftwaffe's infrastructure in Germany, making it relatively easy to move aircraft and supplies forward. And finally, Luftwaffe success in the Kholm and Demyansk operation owed much to the anaemic state of Soviet fighter aviation in the winter of 1941-2.

The relief of Demyansk and Kholm had far-reaching consequences. First, aircraft had to be taken from instrument flying training schools, which seriously interfered with the training of bomber crews. The loss of instructors flying the Ju52s further affected the future training of crews. However, Hitler and the OKW felt that the eventual liberation of encircled ground forces and the holding of the front for future operations fully justified the heavy losses of transport aircraft and crews.

Thereafter, German air transport units, which should have had an essentially strategic function and had already suffered losses well in excess of 100 during the conquest of Crete, were increasingly used for direct ground support. Often, as a result of Hitler's personal intervention, they were detailed to carry fuel, mines and even infantry reserves to the front. As the war dragged on, losses in training resources, particularly in instructor pilots, would become enormous in their cumulative effect. However, in the short term, both the Kholm and Demyansk airlifts succeeded in that the pockets held until relieving forces broke through in May. The Demyansk airlift flew 32,427 missions, moved 64,844 tons of weapons and supplies and 30,500 soldiers into the pocket, and 35,400 (mostly wounded) out. During the entire period from 18 February to 19 May 1942, an average of 302 tons of goods were airlifted daily, just surpassing the aim of 300 tons. But the cost was high. German airlifters consumed 42,155 tons of aviation fuel and 3,242 tons of lubricants. By the time the army relieved the pocket in May, the Luftwaffe had lost 265 transport aircraft, or 30% of the transport force as it stood at the end of February.[132] Only in conjunction with offensive actions on the ground and over territory held by German forces was a prolonged employment of expensive transport aircraft and their crews ever justified.

A wise man would also have noted that in the first six months of 1942, only 235 new Ju52s rolled out to replace the 516 that had been lost on all fronts. But these caveats were overlooked in the belief that the war in the East would soon be over. It did not seem to matter that the only way to build up airlift capability for emergency situations was to strip training establishments of instructors, pupils and aircraft, which made no sense in a long war.

Luftwaffe success at Kholm and Demyansk — once losses were conveniently discounted — served as an illusory model for subsequent German airlift operations. The Führer was therefore only too ready to order similar actions in Stalingrad and in North Africa, even after there was no longer any hope of freeing the encircled army units by land. The Soviets, always keen to perfect their skills at combined-arms operations, recognised the importance of possessing the requisite aircraft, training and battle experience to mount a far more effective aerial blockade the next time around.

*   *   *   *

At the end of March 1942, only eight out of 162 German combat divisions in the East were suitable for full offensive operations, and another 47 could perform only limited offensive tasks. Consequently, there was no more talk of driving forward along three axes as in June 1941. In Directive No 41, issued on 5 April 1942, Hitler ordered that Army Group Centre remain on the defensive while Army Group North undertook a limited offensive against Leningrad to link up with Finland. The main effort would come from Army Group South that would thrust through the economically crucial Donets basin into the bend of the Don River west of Stalingrad and then south into the oil-rich Caucasus.

The primary strategic aim of the easing of Germany's serious oil shortage while denying the oil fields to the Soviets made sense. The southern terrain was well suited to armoured operations, and concerted attacks promised to take out less mobile Soviet forces in repeats of the spectacular encirclements of 1941. In the spirit of hope over experience, Hitler and the OKW believed that once the Red Army's defensive strength had been weakened and the Soviet industrial base undermined, German armies would then break through to Leningrad and perhaps even capture the ultimate prize of Moscow itself. Or then again, the southern advance would continue into oil-rich Iran and Iraq, and thence to the Suez Canal. Either way, German commanders initially regarded the great industrial city of Stalingrad as but a way station en route to the Caucasian oil fields.

Codenamed Operation 'Blau' ('Blue'), even this 'limited' operation would require German troops to advance for a further 800km beyond the farthest German spearhead at Rostov on the Don River. According to a Luftwaffe Intelligence report issued on 7 March 1942, a total of 480 Soviet fighters, 26 reconnaissance aircraft, 149 bombers and 67 other aircraft based on 40 separate airfields faced Luftflotte 4 in Combat Zone South. Aerial reconnaissance recorded the main concentrations on 14 airfields. Luftflotte 4's tasks were to provide air cover for 'Blue', bolster the army's advance and, if the Stavka tried to strengthen defending forces, send bombers to attack the transportation system.

But Moscow was not just waiting passively. On 9 May, while von Manstein was beginning his Crimean offensive to recapture the Kerch peninsula, Soviet ground forces under Marshal Timoshenko suddenly struck near Volchansk and threw back units of the Sixth Army. Preceded by an hour of artillery and air bombardment, another major enemy thrust was made three days later, and what marked this attack out was that, for the first time, the Soviets spearheaded their assault with massed armour. These operations aimed to corner German forces around Kharkov as a basis for a drive across the Dnieper River. The size and shock of the Soviet offensive, and its initial successes on either side of Kharkov, came as a rude surprise to the Germans. By drawing on forces held in readiness for 'Blue', and by calling on Luftflotte 4 for all the help it could muster, the Germans were able to stop the Volchansk drive, but the advance south of Kharkov reached alarming proportions. The OKW therefore took the daring decision to carry out its planned offensive in the form of a single envelopment known as Operation 'Fridericus'. A major tank battle ensued on 17 May, with Kurt Pflugbeil's Fliegerkorps IV heavily reinforced by units of Fliegerkorps VIII, then supporting Eleventh Army operations in the Kerch peninsula. The Luftwaffe focused on the northern area of Soviet penetration west of Izyum where VIII Corps of the German Sixth Army was being hammered by three Russian armies. Attacks by the reinforced Fliegerkorps IV blunted the Soviet drive and were one of the most important factors in preventing the Red Army from enveloping Kharkov.

Despite concentrating powerful armoured units, Soviet forces were unable to counter the attacks mounted by Kleist's First Panzer Army and Seventeenth Army, plus the Sixth Army, largely

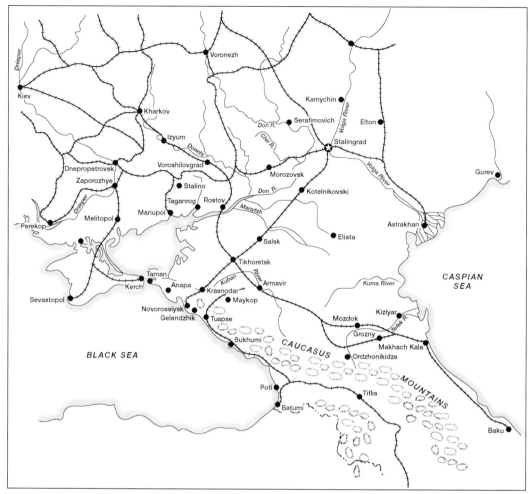

'During battle in the area around Kharkov, the 9th Flak Division destroyed 107 Soviet tanks by 20 May. The 91st Flak Division has registered its 101st tank destroyed in the Eastern Theatre, and the 1st Battalion, 12th Flak Regiment, its 100th tank.

'With a heavy flak gun, Lt Reichwald (who was awarded the Knight's Cross on 7 August 1942) destroyed within a few minutes on 18 May six attacking Soviet tanks, bringing his total up to 27 in the Russian Campaign.'[133]

Although Soviet Southwestern Front Air Forces were reinforced by an additional 233 aircraft before the initial assault, the Luftwaffe still outnumbered the VVS by 1.6:1 in combat aircraft.[134] On top of that, the relatively low quality of many Soviet aircraft, the inexperience of many of their pilots, and poor command, control, communications and tactics, undermined Soviet efforts to blunt the lethal air element that was part of the Blitzkrieg equation. Notwithstanding being taken by surprise, the Luftwaffe had established air superiority over the Kharkov battlefield by 15 May.

The Ju88s of KG51 were heavily committed to the encirclement operation in the area east of Kharkov. A measure of the close support effort flown by the leading long-range bombers in the Luftwaffe was that KG51 aircrews flew three or four sorties a day, dropping large numbers of SD-2 anti-personnel fragmentation bombs which Hitler rated highly.[135] Their difficulty in attacking the area Izyum-Kupyansk-Volchansk was simply that the two armies were so tightly interlocked. All in all the Ju88s of KG51 flew 294 sorties on 20 and 21 May alone. They stayed close to the action, moving up to Kharkov-Voitshenko on 29 May. The Army was very appreciative of the Ju88 crews' efforts:

'To our friends of 9th Staffel, KG51.

'At Ternovaya one of you dropped a mess-tin with some cigarettes and your best wishes. So I should like to write to you and thank you from us all for the dash and courage you have shown in supporting us. The Russians wanted to squeeze us to

Above:
General reference map of the Caucasus.

because of the air support provided by Fliegerkorps IV. Such was the responsiveness of German air power that ground-attackers were often at the scene of action within 20 minutes of the army summoning help.

On 24 May the Sixth Army and Kleist's Army Group sealed the pocket west of Izyum, whereupon Fliegerkorps IV directly assaulted those trapped therein and flew interdiction missions to the east and southeast. The Soviets made frantic efforts to escape the encirclement and two divisions managed to break through and withdraw towards Petrovskaya. Ever flexible, Fliegerkorps HQ brought its dive-bombers to bear on the escaping forces, annihilating both divisions.

No other major groups managed to break out and on 26 May the demoralised Soviet forces capitulated. The Wehrmacht announced that 240,000 Russians had been captured, and that 2,026 guns and 1,249 tanks had been destroyed. Once again, the lack of any serious Soviet air threat enabled the Luftwaffe's 88mm flak guns to be employed in direct fire support. A report submitted by I Flak Corps contained the following:

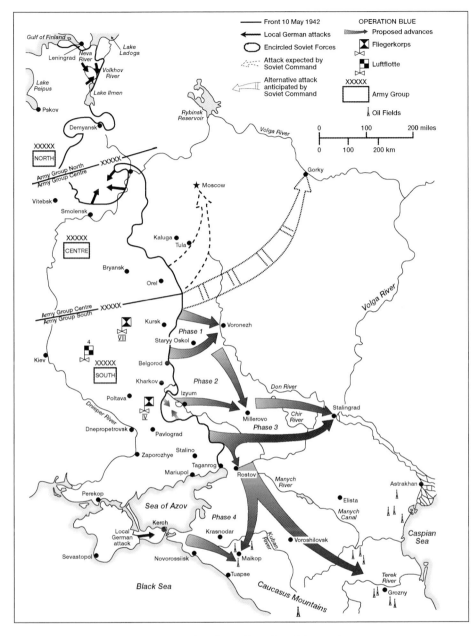

Front 10 May 1942
Local German attacks
Encircled Soviet Forces
Attack expected by
Soviet Command
Alternative attack
anticipated by
Soviet Command

OPERATION BLUE
Proposed advances
Fliegerkorps
Luftflotte

XXXXX Army Group
Oil Fields

0   100   200 miles
0   100   200 km

Gulf of Finland
Leningrad
Neva River
Lake Ladoga
Volkhov River
Lake Peipus
Lake Ilmen
Pskov
Demyansk
Rybinsk Reservoir
Volga River
Gorky
XXXXX
NORTH
Army Group North
Army Group Centre
XXXXX
Vitebsk
Smolensk
Moscow
XXXXX
CENTRE
Kaluga
Tula
Bryansk
Orel
Army Group Centre
Army Group South
XXXXX
Volga River
Kursk
Phase 1
Voronezh
VIII
Staryy Oskol
4
XXXXX
SOUTH
Belgorod
Kiev
Kharkov
Phase 2
Izyum
Don River
Poltava
IV
Millerovo
Chir River
Stalingrad
Dnepropetrovsk
Pavlograd
Phase 3
Stalino
Zaporozhye
Taganrog
Mariupol
Rostov
Manych River
Astrakhan
Perekop
Sea of Azov
Elista
Manych Canal
Local German attack
Kerch
Phase 4
Krasnodar
Kuban River
Voroshilovsk
Caspian Sea
Sevastopol
Novorossiisk
Maikop
Tuapse
Terek River
Black Sea
Caucasus Mountains
Grozny

Left:
The plan for Operation 'Blue'.

Soviet reserves and logistics, and efficient close air support for counter-attacking panzer formations. Increasing German and decreasing VVS daily mission rates told their own story. 'Although German ground forces would probably have achieved victory without dominant air support, German air operations crippled the Soviets' ability to respond effectively to the German counter-stroke. The air dimension only multiplied Soviet pain and the scale of the ensuing disaster.'[137]

The Soviet defeat at Kharkov was followed by a similar disaster in the Crimea. At the end of 1941 the Kerch peninsula had been lost to the German forces. Only by its utmost efforts was the Eleventh Army able to prevent the Red Army from pushing far beyond the juncture of the Kerch and Crimean peninsulas. Thereafter the Wehrmacht was obliged to bolster its defences along the narrows of the Kerch peninsula, west of the Parpach fortifications, and to maintain itself on a constant alert against amphibious landings which might outflank its lines.

The repulse of the last major Soviet attack in the Parpach area in early April 1942 had lent a new impetus to Eleventh Army plans for the recapture of the entire Kerch peninsula. Consequently, Gen von Manstein organised a new offensive, Operation 'Trappenjagd' ('Bustard Hunt'), and assigned to it all of the units he could muster including the Romanian VII Corps plus the German XXX and XXXXII Corps.

death but they didn't succeed. Your bombs really softened them up . . . Your bombs proved to us what the comradeship of arms is really all about, and you kept the pressure on.'[136]

Decentralised control of aircraft and a very limited night capability degraded the Soviet surprise attack. A poor all-weather attack capability also made it impossible for Soviet aviators to hit German operational reserves prior to the initial attack. Once German airmen had control of the skies, the Luftwaffe system of effective control honed over two years of operations enabled commanders to move aircraft rapidly into the Kharkov sector. Thereafter, tried and tested Blitzkrieg tactics resulted in effective engagement of advancing Soviet ground forces, interdiction of

Since January 1942 the Russians had developed the Parpach Line into an exceedingly strong row of reinforced concrete fortifications. The first phase of any German operation had to breach these positions by a frontal attack. Experience had shown that such a difficult task could succeed only with strong air support, and therefore the OKW decided to commit powerful air elements to the operation, particularly in the opening phase.

While the OKL assigned adequate numbers of aircraft to bring the units up to authorised strengths, Luftflotte 4 HQ ensured that its flying organisations, especially the He111 units, did not lack for aircrews by drawing personnel from the fourth (training)

Gruppe of each Geschwader. To add striking power, KG55 was also placed under Luftflotte 4.

Gen von Manstein's insistence on concentrated, powerful air support during the first part of the offensive resulted in Fliegerkorps VIII — the best-equipped close-support corps in the Luftwaffe — being assigned to the job. On 1 May 1942, Fliegerkorps VIII units were transferred to the Crimea where von Richthofen assumed control of all air activities in the area. It was indicative of the fractured nature of Luftwaffe politics that although Fliegerkorps VIII was technically situated within Luftflotte 4's operational area, von Richthofen reported directly to Göring and the OKL, and across to Eleventh Army commander, von Manstein.

'Bustard Hunt' began on 8 May with simultaneous ground assaults and a fearsome dive-bomber and bomber attack on the Parpach positions. It was all too easy once Luftwaffe fighters had driven Soviet aircraft away and established clear air superiority over the field of battle. 'The collapse of Soviet air operations over Kerch had a calamitous effect on ground operations: the Luftwaffe roamed free, smashing up the few control centres, tearing formations and units apart with repeated aerial strikes, mangling the front without respite as it crumbled and finally huddled at the sea.'[138]

A Soviet counter-attack by four divisions stood little chance once forward HQs, exposed and uncamouflaged, were obliterated by German dive-bombers.

Massed attacks by over 2,000 Fliegerkorps VIII sorties helped achieve deep penetrations in the right flank area on the first day of battle, which Eleventh Army expanded into a major breakthrough on the following day. The Wehrmacht announced on 12 May that 29,000 Russians had been captured, along with 220 guns and 170 tanks, in the Kerch peninsula. This was fortunate because that same day, the massive Soviet spoiling attack against Kharkov forced the OKL to redeploy most of von Manstein's air support for the defence of the hard-pressed Sixth Army to the north. It was indicative of the quality and training of Fliegerkorps VIII that it had no difficulty in shifting its focus from Sevastopol to ploughing up Timoshenko's rear to isolate his forces.

By 15 May the harbour and city of Kerch were in German hands and Eleventh Army could turn its attention to the bastion at Sevastopol. The Sevastopol area had been carefully developed as a land and naval fortress by successive generations, and the port of Sevastopol served as a base for the Soviet Black Sea Fleet. From an air standpoint, Soviet airfields within the fortified area were a constant threat to German-held territories along the Black Sea and to the Romanian oil fields.

Sevastopol was described as the strongest land and naval fortress in the world. Its main defences were directed seaward, while the land defences consisted of two converging belts of fortifications, the outer perimeter of which encircled the city at a distance of 15-20km and the inner belt of forts circling at a distance of 5km. Innumerable defence installations of all sorts were distributed throughout the entire fortress area, much of which was rugged, rocky and forested. To the north of Severnaya Bay there were 11 strongpoints, some of which were of modern construction and bore such morale-boosting names as Stalin, Maxim Gorky I, GPU, Cheka, Molotov and Lenin forts.

Sevastopol was defended by the Soviet First Maritime Army,

supported by about 60 aircraft, of which most were obsolete land-based types. On 1 June, Hitler flew to Poltava and laid out his plan for the coming period. Sevastopol was to be attacked on 7 June, the same day as the offensive in the Volchansk area near Kharkov. Assuming these operations went to plan, 'Blue' could proceed as planned about 29 June.

On the evening of 1 June, Fliegerkorps VIII was positioned ready for action at airfields north of Sevastopol. Its aerial forces consisted of a strategic reconnaissance Staffel, two army tactical reconnaissance Staffeln, four fighter Gruppen, three dive-bomber Gruppen and seven bomber Gruppen, making around 600 aircraft in all.[139] It said much about the state of the VVS that these units were allowed to take up their positions unhindered by Soviet air power.

The infantry assault against Sevastopol was to be preceded by five days of artillery fire, during which time the Luftwaffe was expected to soften up any troublesome targets detected within the fortress area. Given that German fighters had established clear air superiority over the Crimea, von Richthofen considered that the best way to support Eleventh Army was to break the morale of the Soviet defenders. From first light on 2 June, hundreds of Fliegerkorps VIII bombers and dive-bombers flew wave after wave to inflict heat and blast on Soviet forces. Dive-bombers maintained a constant series of attacks on Soviet positions in the line of advance of the infantry. Over the following days emphasis was placed upon eliminating the Soviets' chief defensive weapon, their artillery. Destruction of Russian AAA positions allowed the Luftwaffe to support advancing German ground forces with relatively little opposition, and reconnaissance aircraft flew low over the battlefield to make direct reports to air and artillery commanders on any points of stubborn resistance. The few Soviet airmen who, with great courage, went into action with their ground-attack aircraft were immediately pounced upon by German fighters and dispatched in flames.

Fliegerkorps VIII committed 723 combat aircraft on 2 June, 643 on 3 June, 585 on 4 June, 555 on 5 June and 563 on 6 June. In these five days, the air corps delivered 2,264 tons of explosives and 23,800 incendiary bombs on targets in Sevastopol area. In one raid, Stukas of StG77 cut off the city's water supply by destroying pumping installations, water reservoirs and an electric power station, while thousands of propaganda leaflets were dropped to undermine Soviet spirits and morale.[140]

Fliegerkorps VIII's successful aerial assault on Sevastopol owed everything to its commander, von Richthofen. The noted bomber leader, Werner Baumbach, flew in to see him at his HQ. 'Richthofen seemed to be in his element. It was a job after his own heart. He was one of the most striking figures among the Luftwaffe leaders in the war.'[141] Manstein was similarly impressed. 'Fliegerkorps VIII was the most powerful and hard-hitting Luftwaffe formation available for support of military operations. Its Commanding General, von Richthofen, was certainly the most outstanding Luftwaffe leader we had in World War 2. He made immense demands on the units under his command, and he personally supervised every important action in which they were engaged. He was to be found with the foremost Army units at the front . . . I recall von Richthofen's achievements and those of his Air Corps with the utmost admiration and gratitude.'[142]

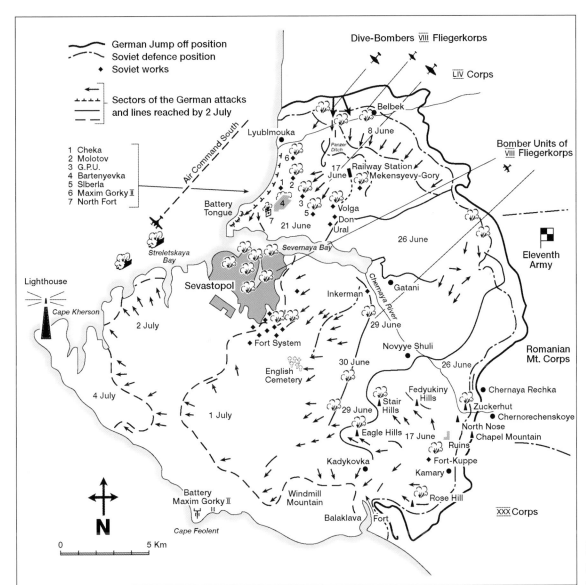

Left:
The conquest of
Sevastopol,
June-July 1942.

Richthofen saw the bombing drama unfolding as he directed air operations from a raised platform. Each dive-bomber and bomber attack, most of which lasted barely 20 minutes, could be followed above the dense brush and forest so that bombing accuracy could be estimated and targeting refinements radioed to units in the air. 'Twelve, 14 and even up to 18 sorties were made daily by individual crews. A Ju88 with fuel tanks full made three or four sorties without the crew stretching their legs.'[143] Fliegerkorps VIII flew up to 1,000 sorties per day and on 19 June Richthofen noted with satisfaction that the city's centre was a sea of flames from air attacks, with smoke columns reaching up 1,500m and stretching to the Sea of Azov and the Kerch peninsula. The strain on Luftwaffe personnel, and Soviet troops who clung tenaciously to their positions under the destructive rain, was enormous.

The effect of highly successful bomber attacks against the scarcely visible Soviet batteries nestled in the ragged terrain, of area bombing against concentrated tactical reserves, and, above all, the results of the annihilating dive-bomber attacks on pinpoint targets in the fortress area were decisive factors in the eventual German victory. The attack by a Luftwaffe lieutenant in which a direct hit was scored on the eastern turret of the heavily armed fort 'Maxim Gorky', thereby putting it out of action, was of momentous importance.

Using the heaviest bombs, German dive-bombers breached the armoured Sevastopol defensive works, opening the way for the infantry to attack the inner defensive perimeter. By 29 June the final assault was made on the inner core of the fortress, von Richthofen having employed all of his air units during the evening hours of the two days preceding the attack against fortified positions in the Sapun Hills. Even reconnaissance aircraft were used to reinforce the strike effort when practicable. Concentrated air attacks allowed German infantry to secure the Sapun heights, enabling the Wehrmacht to lay down massed artillery fire on both the inner fort and the border fortifications. Soviet troops soon became exhausted from the constant bombardment, and all Luftwaffe units were then sent to pursue retreating Russian troops and inflict very heavy losses upon them.

Hptm Herbert Pabst, commander of StG77's operational training Gruppe, flew as many as seven dive-bomber missions a day against Sevastopol. He witnessed the majestic horror of the air-land operation from the ground as well. 'The mountain was terribly ploughed up by the heaviest bombs, craters metres deep, torn armour plating and shattered concrete walls. The dead were lying there, black and mangled in the blazing sun . . . Farther to the east could be heard the shrieking of dive-bombers attacking the firing positions at Inkerman. There, our comrades were hurtling down into the steep valleys. Then flaming explosions rose into the air, together with mushroom-like smoke clouds. Amid fire and smoke the Soviets remained in the rocks, and continued to fire, but their fire was nothing compared to the tremendous impact of thousands of tons of bombs hailing down upon their rocky retreats without let-up.

'Our attacks continued unabated. At times it was hard to decide where to dive in to attack without ramming other aircraft. On low-level missions, where was an aircraft to fly without fear of being rammed by others from higher up, or flying into bursting shells or bombs from friendly artillery or aircraft? In spite of cloudless skies, there was so much smoke and dust over Sevastopol that it was impossible to see even 100m.'[144]

On 1 July 1942, Sevastopol was under German control and in the entire operation, the Wehrmacht captured at least 100,000 prisoners, 622 guns, 26 tanks and 141 aircraft. The Luftwaffe flew 23,751 sorties against the city, port and airfields of Sevastopol, dropping 20,528.9 tons of bombs in the process. German ground-to-air attacks destroyed 611 motor vehicles, 10 tanks, 20 bunkers and 38 guns; silenced 48 artillery batteries, damaged or destroyed 28 barracks and industrial works and detonated 11 ammunition dumps. Off the coast, German aircraft sank four destroyers, one submarine, three E-boats, six coastal ships and four cargo vessels with a total gross register tonnage of 10,800 tons. Axis flak units in the Sevastopol area expended 181,787 rounds of 88mm ammunition, which helped the Germans to destroy 123 Soviet aircraft in the air and 18 on the ground for the loss of 31 Luftwaffe aircraft.[145] The strongest military fortress in the world had fallen in the face of exemplary co-operation between German and Romanian ground and air forces.

There were several lessons from the Sevastopol operation. The effects of even 1,800kg (3,969lb) bombs upon permanent fortifications were usually not sufficient to destroy the positions, even with direct hits. Completely destructive bombing was possible only in attacks upon batteries in open emplacements. The greatest bombing successes came from attacks directly ahead of the spearhead units immediately preceding German infantry and engineer ground assaults. Such air support raised the morale of German assault forces and lowered that of defending Russian forces. The prerequisite for success in combined attack operations lay in detailed daily conferences between participating air and ground commands, covering all aspects of the co-operative effort.

Flying out of Sarabus, Hptm Pabst regarded the air assault on Sevastopol as 'the greatest battle of matériel I ever witnessed'. Yet notwithstanding their seemingly hopeless situation, the Soviet defenders of Sevastopol fought with tenacity. 'Earth, water, rock fragments, steel and cement were intermingled with bleeding corpses. And yet, the Russians clung to their mother earth with unparalleled obstinacy.'[146]

Finally, no struggle for air superiority took place during the battle for Sevastopol. Fliegerkorps VIII enjoyed clear air superiority from the outset, with German fighters driving off the few elderly 'Ratas' that managed to take to the air. Both in quantity and quality, the Soviet air forces within the fortress area were inferior to Fliegerkorps VIII. As for the Soviet air forces from outside areas, sent to support the defensive battle, they followed no established pattern and developed no powerful focus in their attacks against the German airfields at Saki, Sarabus, Eupatoria, Kitay, Simferopol, or the Luftwaffe supply chain. Most Soviet attacks were carried out at night and did little damage.

Below:
A pair of Polikarpov I-153s patrolling the skies over Sevastopol. The I-15 was a highly manoeuvrable fighter dubbed Chato (flat-nosed) when it served in Spain. The ultimate development was the more powerful I-153 Chaika (gull), with retractable wheels or skis folding to the rear. Arriving in service in 1938, some thousands served in the Far East, against Finland and on the Eastern Front. Armed with four 7.62mm machine guns, the I-153 had a top speed of 275mph. *IWM*

By the fall of Sevastopol, the latest Pe-2 bombers, Yak-7b and Yak-9 fighters, Tu-2 bombers and Il-2 *Shturmoviki* were forming over half of the Soviet front-line air strength. But new aircraft would be of little avail if Soviet commanders continued to misemploy them as they had generally done since 22 June 1941.

*   *   *   *

The Soviet hierarchy was seriously caught out in 1941, but for all the bombast and sentencing of unfortunate subordinates to the firing squad, Stalin and the Stavka were not blind to the importance of sound air advice.

The first major changes were made in August 1941 with the establishment of a Commander of VVS Rear Services. Commander of VVS Rear Services was given authority to direct the administrative side of the VVS — logistics, administration, organisation, airfield construction, supplies, aircraft maintenance, petrol-oil lubricants (POL) and munitions — and he worked directly to the C-in-C VVS. The next step was to establish Air Base Regions (RAB[147]), each serving the equivalent of an air corps (three of four two-regiment air divisions) and containing six to eight servicing battalions. Working to the Head of the Engineering Technical service, each RAB had a complete aviation depot, airfield construction battalion, mobile railroad workshop, and road-mobile maintenance battalion.[148] In its new form, the standard airfield maintenance battalion (BAO[149]) could be transferred easily from one airfield to another and readily service any type of aircraft.

These changes re-established centralised control over strengthened yet mobile VVS logistics services without which the future expansion of Soviet air capabilities would have been impossible. This ground organisation would stay basically the same throughout the war and, while considered primitive by the Germans, it was simple, flexible, easily moved and capable of further refinement. In the absence of many permanent airfields, and being constantly on the move, this Soviet approach to maintenance and logistics would meet air commanders' requirements while avoiding the maintenance problems that plagued the Luftwaffe.

Back in January, Army Group North only managed to halt a dangerous Soviet advance by airlifting personnel from Germany, converting men from other arms and services into combat ground fighters and by throwing in the last German reserves. Available personnel were hastily assembled from across the Luftwaffe and organised into Luftwaffe field battalions and field regiments, which were immediately armed and committed as ground forces to help close the numerous dangerous gaps along the Northern Front. The bulk of these units were soon consolidated into the first Luftwaffe Field Division, which helped to defend the threatened Staraya Russa Sector.

What started as operational necessity soon became common practice. Deciding that the Luftwaffe was overmanned with maintenance and support personnel, Göring ordered the establishment of further Luftwaffe field divisions for front-line service. In late February 1942, von Richthofen was forced to order the combing out of 30% of his rear service personnel.[150] Led by officers and NCOs who were largely untrained in ground combat, such units suffered disproportionately heavy casualties, Moreover, this panic measure exchanged first-rate maintenance and support personnel for second-rate riflemen. Thus, just as Milch and his staff in Berlin were preparing for a rapid expansion in aircraft strength and combat aircraft, serviceability rates were dropping through the floor, Göring was squandering the expertise of trained technicians who were already having difficulty in keeping sufficient numbers of Luftwaffe aircraft flying.

As it was, too few existing aircraft were available to the Luftwaffe because of poor servicing and repair. In part this resulted from the Soviets destroying installations so systematically that it was difficult to provide adequate maintenance facilities near the front. But this was not a major drawback. In the course of the Russian campaign, at least 105 airfields were built by II Luftgaukommando alone.

The main problem was organisational. Given the professed short-term nature of the war, Berlin felt no need to invest in a proper Luftwaffe field support structure. Supply and maintenance posts in the Luftgaukommandos were generally given to ex-World War 1 junior officers (*Ergänzungsoffiziere*) brought back into active service in a reserve capacity. Although willing, these E-officers usually had little technical training or aptitude for what proved to be very demanding tasks on the Russian front.[151] Milch tried to bring in skilled engineers but this could only be achieved in 1942 by denuding those aircraft firms in the Reich that were then under pressure to turn out maximum numbers of warplanes and engines. The problems encountered by the Luftwaffe in the winter of 1941-2 were far from solved by the time of the second winter in Russia. At the key Stalino airfield used for supplying Stalingrad, the single vehicle available for warming aircraft engines had to be used repeatedly for thawing out mechanics who, spanner in hand, had literally frozen to their charges.[152] In January 1943, when the VVS Heads of Rear Services and the Engineering Technical Service were well on their way to fulfilling their remit to keep as many Soviet aircraft as possible operational, the Luftwaffe serviceability rate in the East had fallen below 25%.[153] By integrating the RAB organisation into the overall military structure and by giving top priority to those who headed the VVS logistic services, the Soviets avoided losing the initiative through poor aircraft availability and serviceability. Not until much later in the war did the Luftwaffe's repair and maintenance programme in the East receive the same priority it enjoyed with the UK, USA and USSR air forces, by which time it was far too late.

During the initial stages of their winter offensive at the end of 1941, the Soviets learned that the way in which their air forces were organised militated against concentrated air power. Army aviation hung on to 'its' aircraft while 'frontal' was equally possessive, and when the Stavka intervened it tended to squander aircraft on futile gestures. Although air-ground co-operation and fighter operations over Demyansk and the Crimea proved that much still needed to be done, air operations during the battle for Moscow confirmed what should be the basic tenets of Soviet air doctrine: concentration of air power on the major attack zones, proper use of reserves, co-ordination of frontal units with ground operations, and the dovetailing of ADD bomber and PVO air defence units with 'frontal' aviation. The sort of future battles envisaged by the Stavka, involving greater numbers of radio-directed modern aircraft on several fronts, demanded further reorganisation.

In May 1942, Long-Range Aviation (ADD) was placed directly under the Stavka's operational control with Gen A. Ye. Golovanov in command. As a favourite of Stalin, Golovanov was able to make the ADD into an elite, independent bomber force primarily intended to attack strategic and rear area targets. But while such operations were important, the nature of the war on the Eastern Front dictated that the ADD was also extensively employed for interdiction and front-line missions to an extent that would have horrified independent bomber men in the West such as Arthur Harris and 'Tooey' Spaatz. Although eventually numbering 1,500 aircraft in 50 air regiments, the ADD had only limited usefulness during the war due to Soviet emphasis on tactical aviation and the struggle for air superiority over the battlefield. The fact that the Soviets could afford to keep such a luxury as the ADD in being said much for their resources.

On 15 March 1942, VVS C-in-C Gen Zhigarev advised Stalin that the VVS had to be reorganised to establish and command the large air units upon which future offensive air operations would depend. Stalin agreed with the objective but to carry out the changes he replaced Zhigarev on 11 April by the man who would bring continuity, stability and air power professionalism to the leadership of the VVS for the rest of the war, Gen A. A. Novikov.

Alexander Alexandrovich Novikov was born in November 1900 into a poor peasant family. He was attending the Higher Rifle

Below:
The godfather of Soviet military aviation in the Great Patriotic War — Air Chief Marshal Alexander Novikov. *SCRSS*

School for Commanders in 1922 when he won a 15-minute passenger flight from an airfield near Moscow in a lottery draw. Smitten with the aviation bug, Gen Novikov made his name in the grim battle for Leningrad in 1941 by concentrating his assets during a critical battle into aviation 'fists'. The no-nonsense Zhukov found Novikov to be an air commander after his own heart, but more importantly the 'open minded' airman with an attention to detail and brisk efficiency also impressed Stalin. Summoned into the great man's presence on 3 February 1942, Novikov criticised the division into 'Army' and 'Front' aviation that had so plagued his attempts to employ massed air power around Leningrad. Novikov considered the introduction of new and proven aviation techniques to be his 'sacred duty', which must have played a part in Stalin's decision to give him full command of the VVS and make him Deputy Commissar for Aviation.

Like all great leaders, part of Novikov's skill lay in identifying and encouraging talented subordinates, be they gifted administrators or battle-tested combat air commanders. But his first great step was to combine 'front' and army VVS units in large air armies, or VA.[154] These large operational air formations maximised the effective use of 'frontal' aviation, concentrating air strength to best effect in support of ground operations, and co-ordinating independent operations by one or more air armies when necessary to defeat the Luftwaffe. They were similar to the way in which Air Vice-Marshal Arthur Coningham structured British Commonwealth air power in the Western Desert, but the VVS was a much more mobile force. Soviet air armies, which numbered around 1,400 aircraft, had as many as 4,000 trucks, allowing them to advance or retreat as the flow of battle dictated.

The first air armies were formed on the crucial strategic fronts in the west and southwest. On 5 May 1942 the Western Front's VVS units were consolidated into the 1st Air Army under Gen T. F. Kutsevalov. Its initial strength for 'heightening the striking power of aviation and allowing the successful application of massed air strikes'[155] consisted of two fighter air divisions of four regiments each, two mixed air divisions of two fighter and two ground-attack regiments, plus one bomber regiment, a training air regiment, a long-range air reconnaissance squadron, a liaison squadron and a night bomber air regiment equipped with U-2 'sewing machines'.

Other air armies followed suit, beginning with the 2nd, 3rd, 4th and 8th in May; the 5th and 6th in June; the 14th and 15th in July; and the 16th in August. By November 1942, the 7th, 13th and 17th air armies had completed the transformation of Soviet frontal aviation. Except for regimental air units undertaking reconnaissance and liaison work in much the same way as the German *Koluft* units, all Soviet operational aviation was now centred on 13 mobile air armies with tactical aviation removed from the ground armies.

A total of 18 air armies would become operational at one time or another during the war, but the important feature was not the numbers but that an air army would now be assigned to each front, with the VA commander under the front commander and acting as his air advisor. Operational flexibility and concentration of air force was now more than just an aspiration. Instead of dispersing air assets, the VVS could conserve and concentrate its air armies for the main offensive. There was to be no more debilitating lack of effective interaction between Soviet air and ground forces that had so plagued Soviet military efforts since June 1941.

Gone also were the mainly composite units used since 1940, to be replaced by dedicated bomber, ground-attack and fighter air divisions and regiments. Moreover, air regiments concentrated on one type of aircraft such as the Yak-7B or Il-2, which was a great improvement over the previous logistical nightmare whereby a squadron would try to operate several different types. As more aircraft became available in 1942, fighter and attack regiment complements increased from 22 to 32 aircraft, allowing a third squadron to be added. Each regiment was kept to 170-200 personnel, but because it had no organic servicing remit — this was left to the BAO airfield maintenance battalions — it could travel light and therefore redeploy rapidly to wherever VVS power needed to be concentrated.

The transition to integral air divisions simplified operational planning, logistics, training, maintenance, and command and control. Henceforward, only ground-attack air divisions retained a composite structure in that one fighter regiment provided two or three ground-attack regiments with air defence cover. Previously scattered among the combined-arms armies, the ground-attack regiments were now gathered into divisions, greatly increasing their impact and effectiveness. In effect, these were VVS equivalents of Fliegerkorps VIII, and the changes that made VVS air armies into balanced tactical combat organisations of fighter, bomber, ground-attack and reconnaissance units capable of fulfilling the air support demands of the ground armies created Luftflotten by another name. And just like their German equivalents, the strength and composition of VVS air armies could now be altered swiftly and easily to suit shifting frontal requirements.

But if experience had taught him that an aggressive modernisation of the VVS was necessary, Novikov borrowed selectively from the Luftwaffe. During his time in the north, Novikov became the first senior Soviet air officer to command all VVS air assets on two Fronts — Leningrad and Volkhov — and plan and execute massed air operations in support of ground troops. In the process, he came to appreciate the importance of air reserves.

Reserves are not sexy. To those up in the wide blue yonder, there is nothing more useless than the runway behind you, the fuel left in the bowser and the mission that was never flown. But in the fog of war, the good military commander is one who has something in reserve to exploit an opportunity or plug an unforeseen gap. The impact of the sudden appearance of strong, fresh air assets can be entirely different from that if the same squadrons had been in action from the outset.

The British understood this. During the Battle of Britain, Luftwaffe bombers and fighters outnumbered RAF fighters by some 2:1. Yet despite this inferiority, Air Chief Marshal Sir Hugh Dowding kept about one-third of his fighter forces away from the battle zone as an operational reserve. Even at Britain's darkest hour, Dowding's subordinate commanders, Air Vice-Marshals Keith Park and Trafford Leigh-Mallory, maintained their own tactical reserves. Thus, when Göring decided the time was right for the final blow on an apparently beaten RAF on 15 September, German failings were cruelly exposed. The British learned from signal intelligence that the Germans were going for London, and

the air defence radars could see that the German aerial swarm was aiming at one honeypot. With such an inviting target, Dowding used his operational reserve to bring every one of Park's and Leigh-Mallory's fighter units up to strength. In turn, Park committed his tactical reserve of six squadrons and asked that Leigh-Mallory bare his sector to send all his fighters south. With full reserves, RAF Fighter Command was able to hit the Luftwaffe with mass. Within two days, the planned invasion of southern England was cancelled and the Luftwaffe switched from trying to neutralise the RAF to operationally useless night raids on London.

Shrewd German commanders understood the importance of reserves but the lack of fresh, rested divisions — Hitler had thrown all available divisions into the front — meant that the OKW had no reserves worth speaking of. The Russian landmass — it was over 3,000km from Leningrad to Mt Elbrus in the Caucasus — was too big for the German Army and Air Force. Over the winter of 1941-2 this should have become apparent to Hitler, but once its supreme commander insisted that the Luftwaffe take on the RAF *and* the Soviet air forces, the OKL could not afford the luxury of proper air reserves.

For as long as the party line remained that the war in the East was as good as won, every German air asset could be thrown into the breach without qualm because there would be plenty of time and opportunity to rebuild. But the Stavka approached things differently because it knew it was in for the long haul.

In March 1942, the Stavka had 12 reserve air groups (two manoeuvre and 10 strike groups) — each with two to eight air regiments (40-169 aircraft) — operating either independently or attached to a front. On 26 August 1942, approval was given for the formation of additional reserve air groups equipped with the latest aircraft and the creation of the Air Corps of the Stavka Reserve. By November, during the build up for Stalingrad, four of these reserve air corps were formed, which represented more than 30% of available tactical aircraft.

Each reserve air corps normally had two or three air divisions of three regiments, with each fighter and ground-attack regiment having 32 aircraft and each bomber unit 20. In parallel with ground reserves, these air reserves gave the Stavka the wherewithal to concentrate forces to achieve superiority over its Axis opponents at critical times or points on the front. Thus the Stavka was able to reinforce its three frontal aviation air armies at Stalingrad with four reserve air corps in November 1942, giving the VVS numerical advantage over the Luftwaffe that in turn gave the Soviets operational control over the battlefield at the beginning of the decisive counter-offensive.[156] What a change from Kharkov and the Kerch peninsula just six months earlier.

For the remainder of the war, the air corps and independent air divisions of the Stavka Reserve represented between 48% and 63% of the VVS's total frontal air force. As it was now too late for the Germans to build up an aerial reserve, not least because whatever was spare would be needed to counter the upcoming Anglo-US strategic bombing campaign, the Luftwaffe over Russia could cope only by continuing to rob Peter to pay Paul. Such short-termism would suffice for only so long before the Luftwaffe was run ragged.

AIR BRIDGE TO STALINGRAD

'The enemy has broken our front with insignificant force. You have quite enough men at your disposal to destroy enemy units that have broken through. Assemble the aircraft of both fronts and throw them against the enemy . . . J. Stalin'.
Signal to Col Gen Yeremenko, 24 August 1942

Führer Directive No 41 laid down that the second summer offensive — Operation 'Blue' — was to start with a drive by the German Second Army towards Voronezh. Starting from around Kursk, Fourth Panzer Army would execute a curving sweep to the south, and then eastward, linking up with Second Army along the Don River at Voronezh, the aim being to trap an entire Soviet army. Once this had been completed, the second phase of 'Blue' envisaged a bold dash to meet up with the Sixth Army driving northeastward, opening the way for a massive round-up of Soviet units in the bend of the Don River. This would allow German forces to make the long-awaited advance into the Caucasus to seize the oil regions, including Baku and the shores of the Caspian Sea.

It was not a bad plan. Gen Sir Alan Brooke flew from Baku to Moscow on 12 August 1942, keeping below 200ft to avoid any German fighters over one of the main lines of advance from Russia into Persia. 'I had expected to find more than I saw, which consisted of only one half-completed anti-tank ditch, badly revetted and without any covering defences! In fact this back door seemed to be wide open for the Germans to walk through for an attack on the Russian southern supply route, and more importantly still, the vital Middle East oil supplies of Persia and Iraq!'[157]

The Luftwaffe's role in 'Blue' was outlined in Directive No 41 as:

'Besides providing direct support for army operations, to protect the German Army's strategic concentration in Combat Zone South, especially the Dnieper River railway bridges, by assigning additional air defence forces to these areas.

'If the Russians are detected in the process of carrying out concentration movements, their main routes of approach and the rail routes into the operations zone will be interdicted by [air] operations extending far into their rear. The main emphasis will be on destructive attacks against the Don River railway bridges.

'The Luftwaffe will initiate offensive action by concentrated attacks using massed forces against all Soviet air forces and their ground organisations found within the Luftwaffe's attack area.'

The Directive also insisted that 'provisions will be made' to ensure that air units could be transferred rapidly to Combat Zones North and Centre should the need arise.

The Germans had approximately 2,750 aircraft in the East, but major commitments in the Arctic and the need to aid the hard-pressed and equipment-starved Northern and Centre Army Groups meant that only approximately 1,600 aircraft were available to support 'Blue'. Of these, 1,155 were serviceable.

Luftflotte 4 controlled Fliegerkorps IV and VIII, Air Command South and I Flakkorps. The general-purpose Fliegerkorps IV, operating out of Kharkov and commanded by the lanky Kurt Pflugbeil, whom Richthofen regarded as 'composed, sensible and good', was tasked with supporting operations by the German Sixth Army, commanded since January by Generaloberst Friedrich Paulus. The specialist close air support Fliegerkorps VIII was to support Generaloberst Maximilian von Weichs' Second Army. The entire Fliegerkorps VIII, with the exception of a small staff which had been preparing for 'Blue' since the end of April, was heavily engaged in the battle for Sevastopol until 5 July, but it was typical of its 'can-do' spirit that the Fliegerkorps HQ, together with some of its units, were transferred to the Kursk area on 23 June. Richthofen followed the following day, only to move on to take over command of Luftflotte 4 on 19 July. Gen Martin Fiebig who, 16 years earlier, had served as senior advisor and instructor at the Moscow Academy for Air Commanders, succeeded as Fliegerkorps VIII commander. During the heady days of July 1941, Martin Fiebig had controlled the Bf110 destroyers of SKG210 and the Bf109s of JG51 employed in close air support of Panzergruppe 2.

On 19 June, a few days prior to the planned opening of 'Blue', a Storch courier aircraft carrying Maj Joachim Reichel, General Staff officer and Chief of Operations of the German 23rd Panzer Div, apparently lost its way and was shot down close to the front. Contrary to all orders, Reichel had taken a copy of corps' orders for the coming attack. A Soviet infantryman retrieved the briefcase with its 1:100,000 scale map and documents from the wreck, which were soon in Stalin's presence. However, despite confirmatory aerial photographs from VVS reconnaissance aircraft showing sizeable German troop concentrations, Stalin and his Chief of the General Staff, Marshal Boris Shaposhnikov, suspected a German trap. The Stavka was convinced that the 70 Axis divisions deployed within 160km of Moscow still posed a deadly threat to the Soviet capital. Sweeping Maj Reichel's papers aside, Stalin told everyone in no uncertain terms that 'Blue' was a German deception and that the main Axis thrust would be to link up from the south with Army Group Centre. He finished by lashing out at the incompetence of the Soviet intelligence staff.[158]

VVS pilots still did their best to stop the Luftwaffe build-up in the south. Shortly before 'Blue' was launched, Oblt Leonard of I./JG53 reported back to Kursk airfield just before 03.00hrs after a serious goulash supper hosted by a nearby Hungarian unit. No sooner had he arrived at his Bf109F-4 than approaching Soviet aircraft were reported. First came six fighters flying top cover, followed by approximately 20 Il-2s running in low to drop fragmentation bombs.[159]

Army Group South, commanded by Field Marshal von Bock, opened the first phase of 'Blue' at 02.15hrs on 28 June. Co-operating smoothly with Luftwaffe units, the Second and Sixth Armies broke through the Soviet lines near Kursk and Izyum respectively, across a front 290km wide. Dawn VVS

Below:
The furthest extent of the German advance to the Volga and into the Caucasus in late 1942.

reconnaissance brought back pictures of formidable German concentrations already thrusting into the Soviet defences. Precisely at 10.00hrs, Stukas dived down on the forward Soviet positions while German artillery hammered away. Groups of 20-30 Luftwaffe bombers with excellent fighter protection struck into the Bryansk Front rear areas and then deeper, up the River Don. By noon, the Soviet commander was all too well aware that he was facing a major offensive but he had little or no detailed information on actual German movement or concentrations because Soviet reconnaissance aircraft had been hounded out of the battle zone by German fighters. Ground-attack aircraft of Fliegerkorps VIII carried out continuous attacks in advance of the

front-line infantry units, while twin-engine fighters destroyed enemy air power at its source on Soviet airfields. As usual, the German air-land plan of attack had been well prepared right down to details of camouflage and deception.

Fliegerkorps IV bombers led air strikes against Soviet headquarters, command posts, troop reserves and concentrations, and marching columns. They also made heavy strikes on rail links, especially the junctions at the industrial centre of Voronezh, Michurinsk, Svoboda and Valuyki, to thwart the forward movement of Soviet reinforcements and supplies. Large numbers of Soviet bombers were sent into action in a desperate attempt to halt the German advance, but German fighters quickly dispatched them.

'Blue' had been postponed for 24 hours because of heavy rains, and a downpour on the evening of 28 June softened up roads and airfields still further. Nevertheless, Luftwaffe pilots took off on their attack missions where humanly possible, while light and heavy Luftwaffe flak batteries reduced Soviet bunkers and fortifications, and knocked out observation posts and rail installations on behalf of German infantry and armour.

Army Group South, guided and protected by the Luftwaffe, advanced like a giant steamroller on the upper Don. By 2 July it had covered 80km and although the VVS attempted a number of massed raids on German assembly areas in the south, it was

Below:
Ju88 crew of 4./KG51. It must have been summer. *Ciuraj via Goss/Rauchbach Archive*

always too weak to achieve local air superiority. For all the VVS reorganisation, many Soviet reserves remained in the Moscow area rather than redeploying to the south. As late as 5 July, the Stavka still believed that the new offensive was only a prelude to an advance on Moscow, with the attackers wheeling northward once they reached Voronezh. However, although Sixth and Second Armies completed their pincer movement south of Voronezh on 7 July, it closed round very few Russian soldiers. The Stavka had finally absorbed the lessons of the past year; now, when faced with encirclement, it pulled troops back without hesitation.

Besides supporting the eastward drives by the Sixth and Second Armies, Luftwaffe units protected the threatened northern front of the offensive. They struck Soviet railways and road junctions, and, most importantly of all, active VVS tactical airfields. In failing to transfer enough aircraft from their reserves, the Stavka allowed German fighter crews to reap a rich harvest. On 8 July alone, Fliegerkorps VIII fighters operating in the northern part of Combat Zone South shot down 33 enemy aircraft and set another 35 on fire. On 9 July, KG76 successfully attacked Yelets and the rail junctions at Tambov and Povorino. On the same day, German fighters claimed to have shot down 40 Soviet aircraft in this area, and on 10 July, Fliegerkorps VIII fighters dispatched 19 out of an attacking formation of 20 aircraft. Such was the lack of concentrated VVS air activity that, once again, German flak units were free to provide invaluable direct ground fire as well as air defence cover.

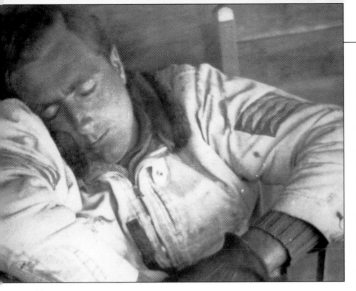

Above:
When you fly many sorties a day, you nap when you can. Bf109 pilot
Ofw Werner Stumpf of 9./JG53. *Goss/Rauchbach Archive*

Given the vast area now to be covered, Army Group South was split in two. Army Group B under von Bock had the northern sector while Army Group A, under Field Marshal List, had responsibility for the southern sector. From the Taganrog-Artemovsk region, Army Group A began its own offensive to push rapidly ahead to the bend of the Don. There it was to cut off retreating Soviet units by linking up with the Sixth Army and Fourth Panzer Army of Army Group B driving along the western side of the Don River towards Stalingrad.

But for all the euphoria, the wheels were staring to come off the German war wagon. On 13 July, after it became clear that large numbers of Soviet troops had lived to fight another day, Hitler sacked von Bock following an argument over how best to encircle the retreating Southwest Front. After appointing von Weichs to command Army Group B, Hitler decided to direct Army Group A in person to add to his other substantial hats as C-in-C of the Wehrmacht, C-in-C of the German Army, political head of state and party leader.

As the Fourth Panzer Army continued its advance and turned toward the southeast, German air units had to shift their bases ever more forward to keep up with the army spearhead. This was especially important for the close air support units, and eventually it became impossible for Fliegerkorps VIII to conduct concurrent operations in the Voronezh area. So a temporary Tactical Air Command North under Oberst Alfred Bülowius was set up, under Luftflotte 4 direction, to support the ground operations of the German Second Army around Voronezh and those of the adjoining Second Panzer Army of Army Group Centre, just to the north. Tactical Air Command North was later required to support the defensive battles of the Hungarian Second and Italian Eighth Armies on the Don, and it was assigned the Ju88s of KG76 (under Obstlt Ernst Bormann), the He111s of KG27 (under Obstlt Hans-Henning Freiherr von Beust), one tactical reconnaissance group, and Bf109 fighters belonging to JG51. Dive-bomber units were added on a temporary basis, as required, but a number of Hungarian and Italian reconnaissance and fighter units were later permanently assigned to Bülowius. It was ironic that the Luftwaffe in the East was being split into penny packets to align

with the demands of widely spreading armies at the very time that the VVS was co-ordinating its air assets so that they could operate mob-handed.

Once Tactical Air Command North was up and running, Fliegerkorps VIII transferred with all haste to the Rossosh area, some 200km away, to support the rapid advance by Hoth's Fourth Panzer Army toward the southeast. German aircrews repeatedly attacked Soviet columns, assembly areas, rail routes and trains leading to the front. Special emphasis was placed on the Don and Donets river bridges but VVS airfields were also important targets. On 13 July, German fighters claimed 12 Soviet bombers as they were taking-off from an airfield east of the Don, while ground-attack aircraft destroyed 20 Soviet aircraft in a single attack on Kamensk airfield. But the number of sorties that German crews could make was seriously reduced by the frequent moves to more advanced airfields, as well as by inadequate communications and the slow arrival of supplies and replacements. Hitler's dreams were close to outreaching German supply lines.

Shortly after the 1918 Armistice, Lord Curzon concluded that 'the Allies have sailed on an ocean of petrol towards victory'. As German armies drove deeper into the USSR, air transportation of fuel became an ever more important factor for the armoured forces as well as the Luftwaffe. On 12 July alone, the Luftwaffe airlifted more than 200 tons of fuel to German panzer units.

On 14 July, Army Groups A and B made contact with each other just as Hitler suddenly abandoned the idea of a combined dash. Determined to fight another great encirclement battle to finish off the Soviets once and for all, he committed the First and Fourth Panzer Armies with the Seventeenth Army to an attack on Rostov. Paulus's Sixth Army was told to press on to Stalingrad without any armoured support.

Richthofen took over the Luftflotte 4 HQ at Mariupol on the Sea of Azov just in time to oversee the assault on Rostov. His I./StG77 Stukas inflicted heavy HE and fragmentation bomb damage on armour, vehicles and troops. By this stage, the long-serving StG77 had clocked up over 30,000 missions on the Eastern Front and had inflicted far more battlefield damage on the Red Army than any other Geschwader.

After Rostov fell on 23 July without any huge encirclement, Hitler become fixated by the industrial and symbolic value of the city that bore Stalin's name. He transferred XXIV Panzer Corps to reinforce Sixth Army's advance towards Stalingrad, which now took first priority for air support and increasingly scarce supplies of petrol, oil and lubricants. No longer deeming it necessary to secure the northern flank and Stalingrad, and *then* head south into the Caucasus, Hitler ordered that both operations be undertaken simultaneously. A German offensive that was already dangerously overstretched was henceforward to operate on two diverging axes, moving east towards Stalingrad and south towards the Caucasus. To much professional consternation, von Manstein's Eleventh Army was also wheeled to the very opposite end of the front, to take part in what was regarded as the relatively simple task of capturing Leningrad.

With scarcely a pause, Fliegerkorps IV attacked Soviet forces retreating into the Caucasus. Masses of Soviet troops were bombed at river-crossing points, while devastating bombing strikes were carried out against congested traffic on the Rostov-Baku railway line. As Army Group A approached the upper reaches of the Kuban River, Bf110 destroyer and bomber units again went into action. Destroyers flew repeated high- and low-level missions in support of the panzers and mountain infantry, then battling to expand their bridgehead over the Kuban, while Luftwaffe bombers struck heavy blows against rear communications networks. 'Scarcely any targets were overlooked . . . The co-operation between the ground troops and the Luftwaffe, guided by the *Flivo* [air liaison officer] . . . was exceptional.'[160]

Day and night, German airmen repeatedly attacked the Baku-Armavir railway, and by 10 August German and Romanian forces had taken the important centre of Armavir and had firm control of the northern foothills of the Caucasus range. Maikop, the centre of the western Caucasus oil district, fell soon afterwards, although the Soviets had extensively destroyed the oil-producing installations. And there was little chance of going any further because 'supply routes had become so long that the supply columns used up virtually all the fuel they could carry in order to cover the long distances. The paradoxical situation came about that camel caravans had to be pressed into service for the transportation of fuel supplies . . .'[161]

Between 20 June and 20 July, Luftflotte 4's complement dropped from 1,610 aircraft to 1,359, while operational readiness fell from 71% to 56%. With this relatively weak air strength, Luftflotte 4 was tasked with covering a zone three times the size of prewar Germany.[162] From now on the Air Fleet would wage three separate campaigns. In the north of von Richthofen's combat zone, there was still a need to support Second Army in its defensive battles in the Voronezh sector. These had become so pressing in recent weeks that it was planned to replace Bülowius's relatively small Tactical Air Command North with Fliegerkorps I. Gen Günther Korten, Chief of Staff of Luftflotte 4 and then aged 44, had just assumed command of Fliegerkorps I from Gen Helmuth Förster. At the end of July, Fliegerkorps I was withdrawn from the northern sector of Combat Zone South and transferred to become Air Command Don with its HQ at Kharkov, with one bomber and two fighter Gruppen assigned.

Operating south of Air Command Don in support of diverging Army Groups A and B, Fiebig's Fliegerkorps VIII was assigned to the Stalingrad effort and Pflugbeil's Fliegerkorps IV to the Caucasus operation. Fliegerkorps IV bomber forces varied between one and three Gruppen, which were tasked by the command post at Kerch and the main forward command post at Maikop. As the crucial battle for Stalingrad developed, Luftflotte 4 bomber units were increasingly re-tasked to supplement Fliegerkorps VIII. This left only weak tactical air assets to support Army operations in the Terek area and for the drive on Tuapse. And after the battle for Stalingrad, von Richthofen had to pull all bombers, dive-bombers and ground-attack aircraft out of the Caucasus to support the Don River front. Only six working Ju88s of 4.(F)/122, two tactical recce units with 6-12 Bf110s and Fw189s apiece, and 37 out of 52 operational Bf109s belonging to III./JG52 and its 13th (Slovak) Staffel were left to guard an area the size of Great Britain. Suffice to say that these were insufficient to protect the army and navy from increasingly merciless VVS fighter and bomber attacks. From November 1942, there would be no effective air support for German forces in the Caucasus.

In truth, Army Group A never had the manpower and skills to hold and exploit the Caucasian oil fields even if it had managed to battle the 865km from Maikop to Baku. So with no credible strategic goals east of the Don, all attention now focused on Stalingrad. With German forces moving unmistakably southeast, Stalin was forced to trundle his reserve armies out of the Moscow region to build up a new Stalingrad Front. Gen T. T. Khryukin's 8th Air Army attached to the Front could put up 454 aircraft, of which 172 were fighter types. As Stalingrad was not put on a war footing until 14 July, it is not surprising that the military cupboard was bare. The three armies to the west, the 62nd, 63rd and 64th, had exactly four anti-aircraft guns between them, while the city's own AAA guns were moved in part to cover crucial river crossings. Novikov ordered the crack 102nd Fighter Air Division with its 85 fighters to move south from Moscow to take over the aerial defence of the burgeoning industrial city of half a million people on the Volga.

By 2 August, the German Sixth Army's drive toward Stalingrad began to falter in the face of problems with replacement personnel and matériel, and steadily stiffening Soviet resistance. Fliegerkorps VIII concentrated on the railways and Volga traffic near Stalingrad, and on Soviet supply columns in transit that could thwart the Sixth Army. The 11 heavy and 19 light batteries belonging to Generalmajor Pickert's 9th Flak Div smashed field fortifications and enemy armoured vehicles, while generally keeping the airspace above the most advanced Sixth Army elements free of any VVS fighters and ground-attackers that eluded Fiebig's Bf109s. On 8 August, Pickert personally received Paulus's 'praise . . . for the close co-operation between the army and the flak teams'.[163] Richthofen credited the rapid advance of German panzer spearheads to the fine support given by his flak artillery units.

Fliegerkorps VIII's dive-bombers and ground-attack units faced little meaningful opposition as they went against Soviet troops, vehicles and field positions. Fiebig's bombers, with fighter escorts, were also free to hit railway lines and trains south of Stalingrad and VVS airfields southwest of the city, where 20 aircraft were claimed destroyed on the ground on 10 August alone. A numerically and operationally superior Fliegerkorps VIII was mauling Khryukin's 8th Air Army, and although the Stavka sent 447 reinforcement aircraft between 20 July and 17 August, these only matched Khryukin's attrition rate.[164]

On 5 August the Stavka split the 700km-long Stalingrad Front into two separate commands: the Southeastern with 8th Air Army, and a new Stalingrad Front supported by the hastily formed 16th Air Army under Gen Sergei I. Rudenko from 28 September. By 20 August, Gen Golovanov had moved five of his ADD divisions from Moscow to the Stalingrad area from where they went after targets in the German rear. Both 8th and 16th Air Armies received a steady flow of the latest aircraft types and air regiments drawn from the Stavka reserve, but many units arrived at the front well below strength. The 228th Shturmovik Air Div for example began combat operations with only one third of its prescribed complement.[165] Given that most aircrew were inexperienced and still hindered by poor logistic back-up and dismal air-ground communications, the two Air Armies were initially no match for Luftflotte 4. Fliegerkorps VIII suffered no losses while claiming 25 out of the 26 VVS aircraft destroyed that attacked German airfields on 12 August, and 35 out of 45 destroyed the following day. But Gen Novikov, as both VVS C-in-C and Stavka 'representative', now enjoyed special authority to concentrate all fighter aircraft of the Stalingrad and Southeastern fronts on any sector where they were needed.

On 21 August, with continuous support from Fliegerkorps VIII, Sixth Army launched a new attack and succeeded in establishing a bridgehead across the Don River north of Kalach. Flying overhead, von Richthofen looked down on 'extraordinarily many knocked-out tanks and dead [Russians'. Later that day, the Ju88s of KG76 blew away two reserve divisions caught in the open after just bridging the Volga. 'Blood flowed,' wrote Richthofen approvingly.[166] The loss of 50,000 Soviet troops and 1,100 tanks around Kalach forced Stalin to commit more reserves and to place the Stalingrad and Southeastern Fronts under the authority of one of his most trusted commanders, Col Gen A. Yeremenko.

Once the Don was bridged at Vertyachiy north of Kalach, Gen Hube's 16th Panzer Div, 'the battering ram of the Corps', began to cross. Several hundred aircraft and 9th Flak Div units were assigned to protect bridge construction operations and troop crossings from Soviet air attacks. Only weak Soviet air units tried to interfere with German operations during this phase. Bf109s of JG3 inflicted very heavy losses on them, and the entire period was characterised by continuous and clear German air superiority.

As Hube's armour set off at dawn on 23 August, von Richthofen landed in his Fieseler Storch. On orders from the OKW, Fliegerkorps VIII was to be reinforced with all Fliegerkorps IV assets. 'Make use of today,' Richthofen told Hube. 'You'll be supported by 1,200 aircraft. Tomorrow I can't promise you any more.'

Richthofen was pleased to watch from on high as his air armada 'completely paralysed the Russians and enabled panzer forces to advance 56km practically unopposed'. 'We landed, refuelled, loaded bombs and ammunition, and immediately took off again,' wrote Stuka leader Hptm Pabst. 'It was "all go" and splendid

Above:
Oblt Wolfgang Tonne, Staffelkapitän 3./JG53, during the advance towards Stalingrad. 3. Staffel recorded 391 'kills' in summer 1942, including those by a Schwarm detached to protect army units advancing on Astrakhan in the Volga Delta. Tonne was awarded the Knight's Cross on 6 September 1942 after his 54th victory. *Schultz via Goss/Rauchbach Archive*

advances. As we took off, others landed. And so it went.'[167] It was all done by using the standard operating procedure of one flight attacking, one flight providing cover from above and one protecting the flanks, all in rotation.

In parallel, over 400 Ju88 and He111 aircraft, operating between 2,000m and 4000m, and interspersed with dive-bomber attacks, flew 1,600 sorties by day and night against Stalingrad. They dropped 1,000 tons of bombs, double the tonnage dropped on Coventry on 14 November 1940. In among the HE, incendiary bombs showered down on the wooden houses along the southwestern edge of the city. Huge petroleum storage tanks on the banks of the Volga were hit, sending a ball of flame 500m into the sky and producing columns of black smoke that could be seen over 300km away. Soviet estimates put the loss of life at tens of thousands, compared with an estimated 550 dead and 1,000 injured at Coventry. The Stalingrad destructive effort exceeded that expended on Sevastopol in scope and made the bombing of Guernica, where von Richthofen had honed his bombing expertise, seem mild by comparison. During this time,

Above:
A LaGG-3, the main Soviet fighter alongside the MiG-3, facing the Luftwaffe during the advance towards Stalingrad. *Author's collection*

Fiebig's units downed '91 Soviet aircraft, losing only three German aircraft . . .'[168] Even the Soviet official history, noted for glossing over reverses, acknowledged there was a 'fierce air battle'.[169] At 23.10hrs the reinforced 79th Panzer Regt reached the Volga River.

Normally Fliegerkorps VIII had two or three bomber Geschwadern based at Morozovsk and Tatsinskaya, five or six dive-bomber Gruppen and one or two ground-attack Gruppen operating from tactical airfields, and a twin-engine Bf110 and three or four Bf109 Gruppen situated near the front on both banks of the Don. The Fliegerkorps also employed seven Romanian bomber squadrons equipped with He111 and Italian Savoia aircraft, and eight Romanian fighter squadrons equipped with Bf109s and Romanian-made IAR80 and 81s.[170] Tactical airstrips were constructed on the plains, close behind the front and near the main supply routes, enabling air units to deliver large amounts of supplies close to those in need.

It is worth making the point that the Luftwaffe was involved in serious airlift work long before the siege of Stalingrad. Supplies were transported by rail as far forward as Taganrog, Mariupol, Stalino and Makeyevka, and occasionally even to Kharkov. From there they were transported by air to advanced airfields. Nine Ju52 and one He111 Gruppen airlifted 42,000 tons of supplies to areas immediately behind the front. Out of 33,397 tons of Luftwaffe supplies, 9,492.6 tons were bombs and aircraft ammunition, 20,173 tons aviation fuel, and 3,731.8 spare parts and equipment. Supplies airlifted for the German Army amounted to 9,233.4 tons, including 1,787.8 tons of ammunition, 4,615.6 tons of motor fuel and 2,830 tons of equipment. In addition, the Luftwaffe carried 27,044 troops to the front and evacuated 51,018 casualties.[171] These airlift operations made it possible for Fourth Panzer Army and the Sixth Army to stay engaged in heavy combat.

The plan was for Fourth Panzer Army to meet up with Sixth Army, from where they would drive together into the centre of Stalingrad. Ground-attack and dive-bomber units were committed again and again ahead of the Fourth and motorised units advancing across the plain between the Don and the Volga rivers. But when Hoth reported on 2 September that virtually no enemy forces lay immediately before his army, Weichs ordered the panzer commander to swing east into the city without waiting for Paulus. Richthofen, who had already expressed the fear that his army colleagues were too timid, tasked Fliegerkorps VIII with launching a maximum effort to pound Soviet positions in and around Stalingrad. Fiebig responded with gusto, sending round-the-clock raids against the already shattered city on 3 September. This crushing attack destroyed the Soviet 62nd Army's command centre and almost killed its commander, Gen Vasili Chuikov. Between 5 and 12 September, Luftflotte 4 conducted 7,507 sorties, averaging 938 a day. These sorties inflicted heavy losses on Soviet troops and armour. Gen Zhukov, sent to check on the situation, reported back to Stalin that 'enemy aircraft had superiority in the air and bombed our positions all day'.[172]

But in spite of the co-ordinated air-land effort, Stalingrad did not fall for several reasons. First, Luftflotte 4's effectiveness was declining fast. When 'Blue' started almost three months earlier, the Air Fleet had been capable of mounting 10,750 sorties in a week. After 11 weeks of virtually nonstop operations, and with replacement aircraft and spares in short supply, Luftflotte 4 was down to 950 aircraft of which just 550 were operational.

Richthofen's bomber fleet had been hardest hit. Not only were more spares required to keep larger aircraft serviceable but also 16th Air Army commander Sergei Rudenko had ordered his inexperienced VVS fighter pilots to avoid mixing it with their German counterparts and go for bombers and reconnaissance aircraft instead. The *zasada* or 'ambush' became a new VVS technique as increasingly experienced Soviet pilots lay in wait for fully laden bombers on their flight routes out to Stalingrad.

In June 1942, Luftflotte 4 had 480 bombers of which 323 (67%) were serviceable. By 20 September, it had no more than 232, of which only 129 (56%) were combat ready.[173] And Soviet probing attacks and attempted or threatened offensive activity in the 'quiet' North and Central sectors of the Eastern Front were keeping local Luftwaffe forces so busy in their own right that the OKL was unable to transfer forces south to help out. At a time when the only major Axis *offensive* operations in Russia were taking place at Stalingrad and in the Caucasus, Luftflotte 4 had to make do with only 38% of the aircraft in the East. Everything else was needed to help Army Groups North and Centre meet their *defensive* remits.

On 10 October von Richthofen sent his entire remaining bomber fleet against the Soviet oil refineries in Groznyy. Huge flames leapt from the shattered oil tanks and he was delighted to note in his diary that dense clouds of smoke rose 5,500m high. The raids were repeated two days later but they marked Luftflotte 4's only 'strategic' attacks on Stalin's Caucasian oil facilities. Some have argued that the Luftwaffe should have concentrated more on oil and petroleum rather than rearranging the rubble in Stalingrad, but this criticism ignores three factors. First, although a whole petroleum cycle is very vulnerable to attack, and the Luftwaffe finally crumbled in September 1944 when its ability to produce aviation fuel had fallen by 98%, even if the Luftwaffe could have blown up every Caucasian well and refinery, the Soviet war machine could have survived on its war reserves for months. German air power could not have interdicted the Soviet petroleum chain in time to have any impact on the Stalingrad campaign. Second, the German Army fighting hand-to-hand in Stalingrad needed all the morale-boosting air support it could get. And third, Richthofen no longer had the bombers left to close, and keep closed, the southern Soviet oil fields and plants. When Hitler ordered a raid against the major oil fields in Baku a month later, it was just not feasible. By October 1942 the forces available to Luftflotte 4 had become too weak to enable it, even on the Stalingrad front, simultaneously to carry out its central tasks of isolating the battlefield and directly supporting the Army in combat.

Moreover, while the Germans were at the limits of their supply chain, the Soviet railway system carried men and matériel to the eastern bank of the Volga where they were ferried across on barges, steamers and rickety bridges. Luftwaffe aircraft circled the Volga looking for targets of opportunity, but sinking relatively small vessels from the air was very difficult and once most ferries began crossing at night, the Fliegerkorps lost the ability to inflict serious damage upon them. Furthermore, all German bombing attacks against Soviet supply routes east of the Volga produced only temporary restrictions. In each instance, rail traffic was resumed within a few hours, enabling trains to continue carrying forward matériel and personnel replacements.

VVS numbers and effectiveness were also increasing steadily. Fifty new airfields were completed on the east side of the Volga, while eight airfield maintenance battalions were rushed to the region. In early September, the two VVS air armies up against Luftflotte 4 were flying an average of 354 sorties per day. By November 1942, of the 4,544 aircraft in the VVS, around 1,400 were committed to Stalingrad.[174] And these airmen and women were becoming more experienced and flexible. Based on

experience gained in the battle for Moscow, the 102nd Fighter Air Div of the PVO assigned to protect Stalingrad started to use its fighters in the ground-attack role. At the suggestion of 16th Air Army aviators, their engineering crews installed rear cockpits for machine gunners in their Il-2 ground-attack aircraft. As no machine gunners were on the unit strength, technical and other support crews flew two or three sorties a day in this capacity after completing their technical duties. Adapting fast, the aviation industry began to send two-seater Il-2s to the front in early November.

The RAF won the Battle of Britain because it invested in a radio communications network that enabled radar early-warning information to be passed expeditiously to fighter aircrew. Similarly, the German Blitzkrieg strategy was made possible by a sophisticated system of accurate and timely air-land radio communications. The austerely equipped Soviet air units enjoyed no such luxury in 1941, and one of Gen Novikov's first tasks was to organise a radio network for target control within 16th Air Army. Gen V. N. Zbdanov, deputy commander of the Leningrad Front's 13th Air Army, and Gen G. K. Gvozdkov, VVS HQ Signal Directorate Chief, were tasked to set it up. This air-ground communications network consisted of a central radio station, located near the 16th Air Army headquarters, radio stations in the divisions and regiments located on airfields, and target controlling stations 2-3km from the front line at intervals of 8-10km with direct communications links to fighter pilots in the air. Twenty-five commanders of air regiments from reserve air brigades were recruited as controllers to gain battle experience, and the VVS introduced the first manual for radio direction of fighter aircraft in September 1942. This communications system tightened the control of VVS operations, and such was the timeliness of information that flowed back and forth that the radio stations soon expanded their operation to include ground-attack operations as well.

Initially, Soviet AAA defences were very weak, but they grew increasingly stronger, particularly in light and medium guns, and an increasing number of AAA gun crews were made up of women. New modern types of aircraft, their increasing operational availability, improvements in air tactics and acquisition of experience by both command and flight personnel, all combined to greatly improve VVS effectiveness. During a 27-day period 'our aircraft flew about 16,000 sorties on the near approaches to Stalingrad, destroyed 655 enemy aircraft and caused great losses to enemy troops and equipment. During that period our aircraft doubled their night activities. Air power increased its total efforts.'[175]

German heavy bomber attacks on the Barrikady gun factory in Stalingrad reminded Richthofen of the ruthless Sevastopol bombardment and, despite the parlous supply state, many of his strike units continued to fly up to four missions per day. Dive-bomber crews oriented themselves over the city by using the roof of the railway station, adorned with an enormous red sledgehammer, as a landmark. But German airmen found it impossible to neutralise all Soviet artillery and other heavy weaponry, which was appearing in ever greater numbers. Luftwaffe effectiveness was also being limited because early in the battle for Stalingrad, the fighting general Chuikov realised that he would succeed only if he neutralised German superiority in air power and artillery.

Above:
Twin-seat Il-2 Shturmoviki en route to do battle. *IWM*

Consequently, he directed his troops to 'hug' the Germans, which meant remaining so closely engaged that Luftflotte 4 often could not use air strikes for fear of endangering its own men. For weeks on end, small combat groups of Red Army infantrymen and combat engineers were separated from their opponents by only a single wall. By November, fighting was at such close quarters that Richthofen's dive-bombers had to drop their bombs 'less than a hand grenade's throw from the German infantry'.

As it was hard enough for aircrews to differentiate between friend and foe in daylight, the Luftwaffe carried out very few tactical air attacks at night. 'At night we have no fear of the Luftwaffe,' noted Gen Chuikov, which allowed his hard-pressed forces to resupply and regroup under cover of darkness and along lesser-known routes.[176] Once again, the Stavka policy of maintaining large operational and strategic reserves allowed the Soviets to accept incredible casualties and absorb the German offensive capability.

Soviet forces holding strongpoints inside Stalingrad were regularly rotated and continuously reinforced at night — almost 60,000 fresh Soviet troops crossed the Volga in the last two weeks of September alone — whereas German forces committed to the meat grinder of urban fighting had been in constant action since the start of the summer offensive. In contrast to the Red Army's

apparently inexhaustible supplies of ammunition, it became a standard Stalingrad joke that 'hundreds of German batteries are in position before the city, but each of them had only one round of ammunition.'[177] The German Army had to fight with what it had, and what it had was growing ever more tired and weary.

Richthofen put the failure to take Stalingrad expeditiously down to 'weaknesses in nerve and leadership' among senior army commanders like Paulus. C-in-C Sixth Army may well have been a far better staff officer than he was a dashing field commander, but in truth German combat power had passed its peak before the battle within Stalingrad had even begun. After a massed raid by all Fliegerkorps VIII's Stukas on 1 November, the army was capable of striking with a force of only 37 men, who not surprisingly promptly stopped after initial losses. Richthofen was unwilling to concede that the close air support capability he had perfected with Fliegerkorps VIII had reached the end of its usefulness in the battle for Stalingrad.

*   *   *   *

Air Commander Novikov and a small group of senior commanders briefed Stalin on a regular basis. The Stavka was subordinated to Stalin's will and, as Supreme Commander, he could be exacting in his demands as well as petty and vindictive. But Stalin was a quick learner of military realities and he kept himself abreast of VVS air operations though daily briefings. Two high-ranking air force officers systematically studied the detailed reports on the previous day's major operations whereupon Gen N. A. Zhuravlev, 'who possessed the ability to say a great deal in a little space', wrote a briefing note for Stalin. These daily briefs provided a snapshot of missions flown, targets hit, number of air engagements, summary of VVS and Luftwaffe losses and an evaluation of VVS effectiveness. Stalin also learned about Luftwaffe deployment, air actions and aircraft development.[178] By the climax of the Stalingrad crisis, Stalin and the Stavka had the understanding and capacity to plan complex defensive and offensive air-land operations.

Both Stalin and Hitler refused to be impressed by the complexity of issues, and they would have agreed that any problem could be solved if the will was there. Hitler's faith seemed vindicated in December 1941 when he gave the order to stand fast after the Red Army attacked in force. The retreat was halted and the front stabilised deep inside Russian territory, in defiance of the professional advice of his generals. The fact that his Blitzkrieg had been insufficient given the sheer size and scale of the USSR, and that German casualties in the East had reached 918,000 men by the end of January 1942, did not dent Hitler's confidence in his own sense of mission or military expertise.

After the winter of 1941-2, the German Supreme Commander was even less prepared to listen to advice, or even information, which invalidated his perceptions. Throughout 1942 Hitler remained convinced that Soviet resistance was in its dying throes, and that the Wehrmacht could simultaneously capture Stalingrad and march on the Caucasus, which had originally been sequential. There was no recognition that the disasters in the Crimea and at Kharkov were occasioned by Soviet blunders, or that the scales were turning against Germany as Soviet production got into full stride and Western aid reached the USSR in increasing quantities.[179]

Visitors to the Stavka would comment on how Zhukov, now deputy to Stalin as Defence Commissar, 'spoke brusquely, in a very authoritative way. The effect suggested that the senior officer here was Zhukov. And Stalin took it all for granted. At no time did any trace of annoyance cross his face.'[180] The atmosphere in Hitler's war HQ was very different. After an all-out air and ground assault on Stalingrad in September, when Gen Chuikov won back at night the ground lost during the day, Gen Halder recommended that the attack be broken off. Hitler responded by sacking his Army Chief of Staff, declaring: 'We need National Socialist ardour now, not professional ability.'[181] Shortly afterwards the Soviet Government would get rid of the military commissar system whereby every military unit was assigned a party official who shared responsibility with the commanding officers. Henceforward, the political officer was a subordinate to the commander and responsible only for political education. With Germans on the Volga, the military situation had become too parlous for political meddling. The gulf between the two Supreme Commanders would grow wider as Stalin became more appreciative of sound military advice, and Hitler increasingly cut himself off from reality.

A good commander tries to throw his opponent off balance, and Soviet counter-attacks on the Stalingrad front were initially launched to relieve Chuikov's men. However, from mid-September Vasilevsky and Zhukov began planning a much more ambitious move intended not just to relieve Stalingrad but also to encircle Paulus's Sixth Army. They eventually envisaged two arms making a wide sweep covering a 320km front from north and south of Stalingrad. Learning from the hurried mistakes of the past, the Stavka insisted that the attack would not be launched until a force of over a million men had been assembled and briefed.

In the German drive southeastward, neither Army Group A nor B had adequate forces to hold their extended front lines, which meant an increasing dependence on Romanian, Italian and Hungarian troops. Early in November, as deteriorating weather further degraded Luftflotte 4's operational capability, German air reconnaissance photos showed the Soviets constantly increasing the number of bridges being thrown up over the Don in front of the Romanian Third Army. A Ju88 was on a strategic reconnaissance mission over railways north of the Don River bend, returning southward from Tambov. Flying at low level, the aircraft broke through the almost unbroken cloud cover. At an altitude of 50m, the crew suddenly noticed widely spaced dark groupings, in between which were massive shapes — tanks! The same picture was repeated everywhere: there was no room for doubt. Secretly, and cleverly, under cover of bad weather, the Russians were concentrating forces north of the Don River bend. Hitler ordered the Luftwaffe to make additional heavy air strikes upon all bridge sites and Russian troop assembly areas in the wooded tracts along the northern banks of the Don. But in most cases these very urgent missions could not be carried out because all available Fliegerkorps VIII units were supporting Sixth Army's efforts to take Stalingrad.

In the past, German ground forces, with Luftwaffe support, had always been able to deal with this sort of situation. But just as Luftflotte 4 could now not stop all the reinforcements crossing the Volga into Stalingrad, so it proved unable to stop the build-up around the Don. According to Oberst von Heinemann of Fliegerkorps VIII, 'the Soviets cleverly exploited periods of bad weather and the dark of night. That the movements were discovered at all was down largely to chance.'

Unlike Stalin, Hitler had to provide for other theatres of war besides the Eastern Front. But his preoccupation with Russia reflected his fundamental inability to grasp the unity of the war he was fighting. He neglected the Atlantic and the Mediterranean until it was too late, and nothing typified Hitler's failure to grasp the big picture than his decision, just when Luftflotte 4 needed every combat aircraft it could lay its hands on, to send the Ju88s of KG76 to Field Marshal Rommel in distant North Africa to take part in a struggle that was already lost. Worse than that, the 81,000 German troops sent to Tunisia between November 1942 and January 1943, plus the 250 Ju52s used to ferry them, would have been far better employed in helping save Sixth Army and supporting Luftflotte 4.

When Stalin told Zhukov on 12 November that 'the experience of war . . . indicates that we can achieve victory over the Germans only if we gain air supremacy', he showed he had taken on board the first principle of air power. To support the 1,005,000 men, 13,540 artillery pieces and mortars, and 894 tanks gathering in the staging areas, the VVS amassed 1,414 aircraft in the Stalingrad sector.[182] By comparison, the day after the offensive began, Luftflotte 4 had only 732 combat aircraft, of which 402 were operational.

Gen S. A. Krasovskiy's 17th Air Army supported the 5th Tank Army and 21st Army, Rudenko's 16th Air Army flew in support of the 65th Army, and Khryukin's 8th Air Army deployed 75% of its operational aircraft in support of the 50th Army.[183] Support also came from the 2nd Air Army of the Voronezh Front. No fewer than 426 of these combat aircraft, such as U-2s and R-5s, were there to operate at night and keep the pressure on around the clock. Besides numerical superiority, the VVS would benefit from Novikov's insistence that units assigned to the offensive would have the most modern aircraft. By mid-November, 75% of all aircraft and 97% of all fighters in the Stalingrad sector were the newer models. Among the 125 fighters of the 16th Air Army, only nine were older vintage and almost all its 103 *Shturmoviki* were the new twin-seat Il-2s.[184] To confuse the enemy, alongside 25 new VVS airfields, 19 decoys were built with mock night exercises conducted on 14 of them.

Novikov would run the air campaign alongside Zhukov, and the air-land campaign plan for what the Soviets codenamed 'Uranus' was pure Blitzkrieg. The VVS would first gain superiority by hitting German airfields for three days prior to the attack. Soviet airmen would then concentrate on the breakthrough areas, clearing the opposition from the skies while providing the Red Army with effective close air support. Fighters and Il-2s were to continue attacking airfields and any German aircraft that managed to get airborne, while bombers and other ground-attack aircraft would bomb and strafe in front of advancing Red Army formations. ADD squadrons would hit more distant Luftwaffe airfields and transport nodes, and interdict reserves moving toward the front. Once the Axis line broke, the VVS would pursue retreating forces relentlessly to prevent them re-establishing a stable defensive line.

As it happened, bad weather thwarted much of this air plan when the Soviet onslaught began at dawn on 19 November. The Romanian Third Army defended at first but was then overwhelmed. Realising the scale of the threat, von Richthofen ordered his last strike assets in the Caucasus to fly north as soon as the weather allowed, but throughout 19 and 20 November 'very dreadful weather' hampered Fliegerkorps VIII's efforts to halt the Soviet advance. In the face of barely 120 German sorties a day, the Soviets pressed on unhindered, threatening Fiebig's command post at Oblivskaya and his airfields in the immediate vicinity. Meanwhile, the second great Soviet thrust was setting out south of Stalingrad and, shortly before dusk on 23 November, the two Soviet pincers met 20km south of Kalach. Zhukov's armoured trap had succeeded beyond all expectations. Inside a pocket measuring only 50km from west to east and 40km north to south, the Soviets were amazed to discover that they had trapped well over 250,000 men, 100 tanks and nearly 2,000 guns.

It was not until 23 November that 'tolerable weather' allowed Fliegerkorps VIII and the Romanian squadrons to increase their tempo of operations, by which time it was far too late for air power to stem the Soviet tide. That same day, the Luftwaffe airlifted supplies into the Stalingrad pocket for the first time. Thereafter, Fliegerkorps VIII would do little other than fly food and matériel into a shrinking space in an ever more hopeless effort to save Paulus and his trapped army.

If the Sixth Army was to establish itself within perimeter defences to hold the Stalingrad area until relieved at some future date, airlift was its only hope for survival. Among over 12,000 Luftwaffe personnel trapped in the Stalingrad pocket were most of Gen Wolfgang Pickert's 9th Flak Div, their supply trains and signal units, the groundcrews of two airfields, and elements of JG3 and the 12th, 14th and 16th short-range reconnaissance Gruppen. As Pickert was the ranking Luftwaffe officer, von Richthofen put him in charge of all Stalingrad Luftwaffe units. It fell to Pickert, plus his bosses at Luftflotte 4 and Fiebig at Fliegerkorps VIII, to advise on the best way forward.

Two days after the Soviet encirclement began, Gen Fiebig told Paulus and Gen Schmidt, his Chief of Staff: 'Supply an entire army by air? Impossible! Our aircraft are heavily engaged in Africa and on other fronts. I must warn against exaggerated expectations.'[185] He repeated this emphatic advice the following day, a view endorsed by Pickert who had fought on the Eastern Front in World War 1. Pickert's view, that the Sixth Army should break out immediately and pull back to the southwest while it could, had much to commend it. But Arthur Schmidt was adamant that the airlift 'simply has to be done', and that his men could help ease the supply problem by first eating their horses.

Richthofen's views are clear from his diary entry for 21 November. 'The Sixth Army believes that it will be supplied by the Luftflotte in its hedgehog [perimeter defence] positions. Every effort is being made to convince that army that this cannot be done because the required amount of transport space is not available. In the same way I have tried to convince the Commander in Chief of the Luftwaffe, the Army High Command and the Army Group.' Gen Fiebig's diary indicates that neither Richthofen nor Jeschonnek believed it possible to carry out the immense operation of supplying the Sixth Army by air.

On the evening of 22 November, Hitler was travelling with Keitel and Jodl on his special train from Berchtesgaden to Leipzig, from where he would fly to Rastenburg. The train was halted every few hours to allow Hitler to talk to Halder's successor as Army Chief of Staff, Gen Kurt Zeitzler. During one of these conversations the Führer told Zeitzler: 'We've found another way out.' Zeitzler did not know it but Hitler had been talking to Hans Jeschonnek who, despite all advice to the contrary from Richthofen, had indicated that an air bridge to supply Sixth Army might be possible on a temporary basis.

On hearing this, Göring immediately summoned a meeting of his transport staffs. To support 100,000 men in the Demyansk pocket had required an airlift of 300 tons a day, so the Sixth Army's request for 700 tons per day to support around 250,000 men was not unreasonable. But the Reichsmarschall told his planners that 500 tons a day was needed. They replied that 350 tons was the top limit, and then only for a short period. Göring translated this into an assurance to Hitler that the Luftwaffe could maintain the Sixth Army in its present position by air. He did not mention that the staff estimate did not allow for bad weather, unserviceable aircraft or enemy action.

There has been much debate over whether Hitler pressured his advisers to come up with the airlift answer, or whether they were derelict in giving him flawed advice. On the Army side, Paulus reported to Field Marshal von Weichs at Army Group B, who suggested immediately to Hitler that the Sixth Army should fight its way out of encirclement.

The best option would have been to destroy all communications from the Caucasus and Stalingrad while withdrawing Army Groups A and B behind the Don River, leaving the Soviets to cope with the manifold difficulties of supply and the approaching winter. Instead, Field Marshal von Manstein was told on 21 November to abandon the planned attack in the far north and take over the Sixth Army, the Fourth Panzer Army and the Romanian Third Army in a new command, Army Group Don. Manstein supported the breakout option but Weichs' eminently sensible recommendation received no emphatic endorsement from the Sixth Army leadership.

The ultimate decision rested with Hitler, who was in a difficult position having assured the Nazi Party faithful only two weeks earlier that Stalingrad was all but taken. He may also have thought that Manstein would break the encirclement and restore the southern front. Certainly, Hitler's Luftwaffe adjutant, von Below, recounts that on their arrival at Rastenburg his Führer was worried about whether the Sixth Army could be supplied from the air. 'He had long conversations with Göring and Jeschonnek about this,' which implied that Hitler had doubts over what he was hearing. 'Göring assured him that the Luftwaffe could supply the Sixth Army for a certain time, Jeschonnek did not contradict him.'[186]

If von Weichs had found firm and articulate support for his line, Hitler might have been spared the disaster that was to befall him and the Sixth Army. However, those at the top of the Luftwaffe committed their service to the air supply of Stalingrad rather than pointing out firmly that such operations could not be carried out in any sustained fashion. The Luftwaffe, which after all was most affected by the decision, should have derived sufficient warning from its earlier Kholm and Demyansk experiences. It ought to have been able to point to losses incurred in those two air supply actions, together with a study of all the pros and cons. If such data had been available, Göring and the OKL would have been in a position to give an unqualified and well documented 'no' when asked if air supply of Sixth Army was possible. Otherwise there was no point in the C-in-C Luftwaffe maintaining an air historical branch!

The origin of the Stalingrad disaster lay with Luftwaffe personalities. Göring, who was going through a hard patch after blunt criticisms over the Luftwaffe's failure to stop the increasingly successful British night bomber raids, was probably ready to promise anything in order to restore his Luftwaffe's reputation. Jeschonnek, who should have known the facts, was an idealist who 'always considered it to be his sole duty to execute to the letter, without criticism, the desires of his Führer'.[187] It can be assumed that Jeschonnek made no positive stand against the airlift, because this would have created a serious disagreement with Göring and some record of this would have been found in the documents.

Gen Zeitzler witnessed the fateful decision on 23 November.

'Göring said: "My Führer, I report to you that the Luftwaffe will supply the Sixth Army by air."

'I interjected: "That the Luftwaffe cannot do."

'Göring replied: "You are not qualified to judge that matter."

'I then asked: "Reichsmarschall, do you know what quantities of supplies have to be daily flown in to the army?"

'Göring replied uneasily: "Not I, but my staff."

'I immediately summarised. "Allowing for all stocks at present with the Sixth Army, allowing for absolute minimum needs and the taking of all possible emergency measures, the Sixth Army will require delivery of 300 tons per day. But since every day is not suitable for flying, as I myself learned at the front last winter, this means that 500 tons will have to be carried on each and every flying day if the irreducible minimum average is to be maintained."

'Göring shot back: "I can do that."

'"My Führer, that is a lie."

'Needless to say, this led to a very heated debate, which was cut short by Hitler with the words: "The Reichsmarschall has reported to me that the air supply movement will work. I must believe his reports. My decision [to hold Stalingrad and supply it by air] remains unchanged."'[188]

Richthofen, one of the most realistic men in the Luftwaffe, when told of the decision to attempt what he considered to be an impossible airlift operation, could only resign himself to writing: 'We have only one chance to cling to; so far the Führer has always been right, even when none of us could understand his actions and most of us had strongly advised against them.'

Richthofen's Luftflotte now had two major missions in the battle for Stalingrad — airlifting supplies to the encircled Sixth Army, and providing air support for German ground forces fighting against vastly superior Soviet units advancing along both banks of the Don. There was a synergy between these two because ground forces had to establish a defensive line along the Chirnaya River if the main supply airfields at Morozovskaya and Tatsinskaya were to be kept operational for the airlift. The closer the supply bases were to Stalingrad, the greater the number of sorties that could be flown into the *Kessel*, or encircled area. But while Fliegerkorps VIII managed to help slow down the Soviet advance all along the Chir River line, on 30 November it was relieved of its combat role and ordered to concentrate on flying supplies in to Sixth Army.

Working on a load of two tons per Ju52, and a 40% serviceability rate that was on the high side for the Eastern Front, at least 375 Ju52s would be required to carry a minimal 300 tons a day into the *Kessel*. The *Transportverbände* (Air Transport Service) was already overstretched by the German bridgehead in North Africa and although the French aircraft industry had been pressed into supplementing German factory output, the total production of the most advanced Ju52/3m for 1942 was only 504, barely *half* the year's attrition.

The Stalingrad airlift started on 24 November: out of the 47 Ju52s available to Richthofen, just nine aircraft flew in 75 tons. Richthofen reported this shortfall to Göring, just as the Sixth Army's quartermaster was reporting that he needed the Luftwaffe to bring in 500 tons a day (300 tons of fuel, plus 200 tons of food and ammunition). Göring stated on 25 November that the Luftwaffe could deliver an average of 500 tons of supplies a day, by assembling every possible aircraft including Lufthansa's precious four-engined Ju90s. Shortly afterwards he left for Paris.

While the Reich was being scoured for Ju52s, the 300-ton-per-day goal could be met only by temporarily misemploying He111

Above:
Loading a Ju52 during the Stalingrad airlift.
Author's collection

Below:
The Ju290A-5 long-range transport and reconnaissance bomber, earlier versions of which assisted in the Stalingrad airlift. There is an unconfirmed story that in the early spring of 1944, three Ju290A-5s, each capable of a maximum take-off weight of 44,970kg (99,141lb) and fitted with two additional 550gal (120-litre) internal fuel tanks, flew nonstop from Odessa and Mielec to Manchuria with special cargoes, before returning to Mielec with strategic materials. *IWM*

Above:
Ju52s assembled in the snow during the Stalingrad airlift.
Smithsonian Institution

Left:
The Luftwaffe air supply corridor into Stalingrad.

Map legend:

— German front 18 Nov 1942
--- First line of defence
➡ Soviet attacks
▲ Airfields
Strong Soviet artillery
···· Encircled German forces

Don River
Krivaya River
Bokovskaya
Kletskaya
Shishikin
Sixth Army
Volga River
Perelazovskiy
Third Rom Army
Dubovka
Chernyshevskaya
Yerzovka
Golubinskaya
Gumrak
Berezovaya River
Chernaya River
Pitomnik
Bassargino
Stalingrad
Kalach
Armoured Attack
Skasyrskaya
Obliyskaya
Krasnolobodsk
Morozovskiy
Nizhne-Chernovskiy
Luftwaffe Air Supply Corridor
Soviet counter attacks
Tatsinskaya
Fourth Panzer and Fourth Rom Army
German Counter Thrust
Donets River
Don River
Aksay River
Aksay
Sadovoye
Tsimlyanskiy
Fourth Panzer Army
Kurroyarskiy River
Don River
Kotelnikovo

front-line bombers for transport purposes. By 5 December, Luftflotte 4 had assembled 11 Ju52 Gruppen (some 200 aircraft) which, along with two Gruppen of obsolete Ju86 bombers pulled out of the training schools, were placed under the very experienced Oberst Fritz Morzik's air transport wing HQ at Tatsinskaya. Elements from four He111 Gruppen (KG4, KG27, KG100 and KG55) were in place under the command of Oberst Dr Ernst Kühl — 'Cool' by name and reputed to be cool by nature — at his KG55 headquarters at Morozovskaya. By mid-January the Stalingrad resupply force had grown to elements from no fewer than 14 He111 Gruppen, including the entire effective strength of KG55 and KG27. To these were added at intermittent intervals long-range maritime patrol Fw200 Condors, Ju90s and the prototype of the giant Ju290V1.[189] The last, capable of carrying eight tons, crashed with heavy loss of life during the airlift. It was a measure of Luftwaffe desperation that when 20 of the long-awaited He177 strategic bombers were sent to Zaporozhye in south Russia in early December for winter trials, they were promptly redirected to the Stalingrad air transport role even though only seven aircraft were serviceable. On the first operation the Gruppe commander, Maj Scheede, was lost. Not surprisingly, the He177 was found to be totally unsuited to the airlift role. I./KG50 eventually reverted to bombing missions in support of the Army, but not before five more aircraft had been destroyed by engine fires in mid-air.

Given limited serviceability rates, a new term, *Kesselklar* (cleared for flight into the pocket), was coined to maximise the number of functioning airlifters. Previously, the standard had been *einsatzbereit* ('operational'), which meant that standby flight instruments were functioning. Now, if the primary systems worked, you went. To give some idea of what the transports crews were up against, on 5 December 36 Ju52s flew into the *Kessel*, some having to make completely blind take-offs. At Pitomnik airfield in the pocket, the ceiling was only 130m and lowering, with visibility ranging up to 700m. Yet Luftwaffe transports continued to land, some aircrews having made seven attempts in the process. By 8 December temperatures had dropped and there were dense fog patches throughout the Stalingrad area. None the less, about 70 He111s delivered 140 tons of supplies. The slower Ju52s could manage only 60-70 tons because VVS fighters were able to scatter the lumbering transports. On 9 December Soviet aircraft twice attacked Tatsinskaya, destroying four Ju52s, 75 tons of fuel for the army and 6,000 rounds of ammunition.

The Soviet 17th, 16th and 8th Air Armies, plus the ADD, were used to blockade *Kessel* airspace. Whenever weather permitted, Bf109s of Maj Wolf-Dietrich Wilcke's JG3 provided fighter escort for the transports into the Stalingrad area. For all that its narrow fuselage and lack of a loading hatch made the He111 an indifferent air transport, it stood a chance of getting through at night when fighter escorts were not practicable. The He111s were generally feared by VVS airmen because of their well-disciplined flying formations and mutually interlocking fields of fire. It was far easier to go for the unmanoeuvrable, weakly armed and slow Ju52s and Ju86s. But the main factor that adversely affected the airlift was bad weather, not Soviet air attacks.

In the beginning, a flight into the *Kessel* normally took around 50 minutes, homing into the radio beacon at Pitomnik airfield. On landing, the transports were quickly unloaded and wounded men were taken out on the return leg. The Soviets soon learned to position powerful AAA batteries along the main air corridors to the Sixth Army. Luftwaffe aircrew tried to counter AAA by constantly varying flight routes, but this usually increased flight duration and, consequently, consumption of precious fuel. Within a short time, Soviet commanders became aware of the most suitable transport aircraft routes, and they laid their anti-aircraft batteries accordingly.

The Soviets knew that Luftwaffe transports could fly several missions on a good day. If the Red Army could capture the nearest replenishment airfields and drive the fighter escorts back out of range, Sixth Army would be left high and dry. Manstein knew that time was not on his side, and on 12 December he launched his relief operation to try and free Sixth Army.

Gen Fiebig rather tersely noted that the proper role for his bombers was to support Fourth Panzer's drive, which he felt was 'of far greater worth than a few tons of supplies more or less flown into the fortress'.[190] But by 19 December, which was the highlight of the airlift campaign with 73 He111s, 50 Ju52s and 13 Ju86s delivering 270 tons into the Stalingrad pocket, von Manstein's leading panzers had penetrated to within 50km of the southern front of the *Kessel*. Now was the time for Sixth Army to break out, not least because Fiebig lodged an appeal to the Führer via Luftflotte 4 HQ at Novocherkassk stressing his force's inability to transport large amounts of fuel and food.

But as the Luftwaffe was destroying more than 60 Soviet tanks along the lower Chir, Gen Schmidt at Sixth Army was rejecting the breakout option as a 'catastrophic solution'. Then on the morning of 20 December, the Soviet Fifth Armoured Army pushed forward towards the Luftwaffe airfield at Millerovo, whereupon KG27 immediately began to transfer out to bases further away.

The important rail and supply depot at Tatsinskaya, and the airfield nearby, were crucial to continuation of the airlift. Soviet tanks reached Tatsinskaya airfield on Christmas Eve, and because Hitler had refused to allow the transports to pull out in measured fashion, Soviet tank and artillery were able to set fire to a number of Ju52s on the airfield. The remainder succeeded in taking-off at the last possible moment, including one carrying the Fliegerkorps VIII command staff that lifted off under heavy fire in clouds of snow. Some 108 Ju52s and 16 Ju86s were saved out of a total of 180 aircraft, which was a magnificent achievement under the conditions but which would never have been necessary but for Hitler's obduracy. The surviving airlifters were finally assembled with great difficulty at Salsk airfield, but two valuable airlift days had been lost.

Soviet reinforcements eventually forced the entire Fourth Panzer Army to fall back, and with it went the last hope of freeing Paulus's trapped army. On 2 January 1943, the He111s of KG55 had to take-off at Morozovskaya in a dense fog to avoid being overrun in a surprise Soviet attack as the Ju52s had been at Tatsinskaya. From their new base at Novocherkassk, on the lower reaches of the Don, the He111s could fly only a single daily supply because the distance to the pocket was about 330km. Ju86s, because of their inadequate range, could no longer be used at all.

With Ju52s now at the limits of their range, and distances to the pocket too great for fighter cover, Ju52 operations became restricted to night-time. As Fourth Panzer Army was pushed further back, Salsk airfield had to be evacuated. The one relatively suitable site left within range of Stalingrad was a cornfield at Cherekovo, where all loading and servicing had to be done outside in sub-zero temperatures.

Of the seven airfields originally in the pocket, initially only Pitomnik and Bassargino were suitable as logistical airheads. An alternative should have been constructed at an old Soviet airfield at Gumrak but Sixth Army originally rejected this option because of its close proximity to its HQ, even though it would have allowed a greater air traffic flow. Incredibly, neither Paulus nor his Chief of Staff ever visited the logistical airheads within the *Kessel* or made any real effort to secure a personal impression of the conditions under which the men at those crucial places were working.

In the last two weeks of December, 80% of VVS combat time was flown in support of its ground troops slowly strangling the Stalingrad pocket. There was no doubting the level of Soviet effort, persistence and bravery to match that of the Ju52 crews. On one occasion, VVS Sgt Nurken Adbirov of the 808th Ground Attack Sqn, having run out of ammunition, flew his *Shturmovik* into a group of German tanks. By 1 January 1943 the German

fighter detachment stationed in the Stalingrad pocket claimed its 130th Soviet aircraft, while four days later the 9th Flak Div notched up 63. Yet on clear nights in January, airfields in the pocket were under constant surveillance by Soviet airmen in harassing aircraft (generally U-2s), and if a landing or taxiing aircraft was hit on the ground, the wreckage stopped all operations for several hours, compelling others to airdrop their supplies.

By January VVS tails were up around Stalingrad. The number of German night airlift flights increased dramatically but the VVS held the advantage in terms of geography, choice of attack time and overwhelming numbers. A real long-range fighter was something the Luftwaffe General Staff had long demanded and on 27 January, nine Bf109s and five Bf110s fitted with reserve fuel tanks pitched up to serve as long-range escorts. Despite serving under the experienced Maj Wilcke, they did not enjoy much success because the Bf110s were the old, slow 110-Cs and the 109s were restricted by low cloud ceilings. The fighters soon were withdrawn to defend rear airfields that were coming under frequent Soviet attack.

The airlift averaged 145 tons per day during the first 16 days of 1943, but that was all to change. On 16 January, Pitomnik, the

Below:
A German fighter down in the ruins of Stalingrad. *Author's collection*

only airfield with a night capability, fell to the Soviets. Shortly beforehand, von Richthofen had ordered his men to prepare Gumrak. Gumrak was small and its runway in a poor state but, undaunted, 10 of Kühl's He111s landed there on the day Pitomnik fell. However, they only brought a miserable 13 tons of supplies and carried out 62 wounded. The He111s brought in almost 32 tons three days later but even when added to 30 tons air-dropped, this was still only 20% of the minimum for survival. The fate of the Stalingrad garrison was sealed.

Because of the constant complaints emanating from Sixth Army HQ over inadequate supply deliveries, and the steady

bickering over suitable landing fields, Hitler did not know whom to believe so he sent Field Marshal Milch to the area in mid-January to assume command over all airlift operations into Stalingrad. From Luftflotte 4's special command train, Milch set about remedying the air transport serviceability rate that had sunk to a lamentable 20%. He also had an impact by pushing the use of cargo gliders but otherwise Milch had to concede that Luftflotte 4 had done everything humanly possible to support Sixth Army and that the failure of the airlift operation was beyond its control. Basically, even Milch could not stop the Soviet ground advances that forced a continuous rearward

Right:
Field Marshal Paulus and his staff surrender in Stalingrad. *Author's collection*

Opposite:
A Ju52 after coming to grief in the ruins of Stalingrad. *SCRSS*

displacement of base airfields and consequent reduction in already limited airlift effectiveness.

Gumrak, plus a crude airstrip in the immediate vicinity of the city, fell to the Soviets on 23 January. The last German aircraft flew out of the pocket that day — on board the He111 were 19 wounded and seven bags of mail. Paulus's army was now cut off from all help other than that which could be air-dropped by parachute, much of which fell into Soviet hands. Forward elements of the Soviet 21st Army made contact with Chuikov's 62nd, which had been tying down German forces in Stalingrad itself. The German Sixth Army was now split into two small pockets in the north and south of the city.

In the southern pocket, Paulus moved his HQ into the basement of the Univermag department store. Such was the shortage of food that none could be given to the wounded and sick, of whom there were now some 30,000. On the night of 29/30 January, out of 151 Luftwaffe transports that took off, 132 succeeded in dropping 130 tons of supplies on the pockets. The following day, Paulus surrendered; 14 German generals, two Romanian generals and over 90,000 Axis troops accompanied him into captivity.

During the night of 31 January/1 February, 110 transports took off for the still fighting northern pocket, followed by 108 the next evening. The drop zone, marked with a red-lighted swastika, was clearly defined on the night of 2 February until 24.00hrs, after which it was seen no more.

The VVS flew 35,929 sorties between 19 November 1942 and 2 February 1943, as against 18,500 by the Luftwaffe. Over that time, Soviet aircraft dropped 141,000 bombs and incendiary containers, and fired 30,000 rockets.[191] After Stalingrad, 10 Soviet air divisions were given the designation of 'guards' units for 'daring, persistence and effectiveness'. Seventeen 8th Air Army pilots were awarded the highest decoration for bravery, Hero of the Soviet Union. The air commanders and aircrew who won their spurs over the Stalingrad pocket were now ready to support Novikov in bolder endeavours.

Officially, the Soviets claimed 1,200 German aircraft shot down, of which about 80% were transports.[192] As it happened, between 24 November 1942 and 2 February 1943 the Luftwaffe lost 488 aircraft, made up of 266 Ju52s, 42 Ju86s, 165 He111s, nine Fw200s, five He177s and one Ju290.[193] It was more than a whole Fliegerkorps and around 1,000 aircrew also perished. In trying to satisfy Hitler and the Sixth Army, the Luftwaffe air transport service was bled white.

By 13 January 1943 there were 317 Ju52s, 181 He111s, 20 Fw200s, one Ju290 and 10 He177s on hand for the airlift, augmented by 87 Ju52s and 219 He111s en route from other fronts and the Reich.[194] Even assuming a 25% serviceability rate, this lot should have been able to fly 456 tons a day into the pocket. But cold winter weather, Soviet air-land pressure and the loss of landing strips ensured that an average of only around 100 tons per day could be flown in between 22 November 1942 to 16 January 1943. This figure became even lower after the loss of Pitomnik and Gumrak airfields. Although it had been possible to fly out about 30,000 wounded, in the absence of any breakout attempt the sacrifice of hundreds of aircraft and highly trained aircrews was in vain. Worse still, large numbers of aircraft and personnel were drawn from German training establishments that

were vital to the life of the entire Luftwaffe. For example, II./ and III./KG55, which had been pulled out of the Stalingrad battle in autumn to re-equip and convert onto a new precision bombsight, were hauled back in late December to join the air transport force. Many of the Ju52 formations came from the multi-engined training schools and were crewed by skilled pilot and navigation instructors. The long-term consequences for the already overstretched Luftwaffe bomber arm were considerable.

After the débâcle, a 'disappointed' Göring announced his intention of court-martialling Jeschonnek and his Chief of Luftwaffe Supply and Administration as those 'responsible for the Stalingrad catastrophe'. But the blame lay full square with Hitler. In von Manstein's view, as Supreme Commander, 'it was Hitler's duty to examine the reliability of the declaration made by Göring. In the first place, he knew Göring, and secondly, he was very well informed on the strength etc of the Luftwaffe.'[195]

In accepting the Reichsmarschall's unconditional promise, Hitler was doubtless influenced by the Luftwaffe's successful supply of 100,000 German troops in the Demyansk pocket in early 1942. But in lauding that successful outcome, little importance was apparently attached to the fact that the Luftwaffe was then much stronger and had suffered no serious losses in matériel and irreplaceable personnel. Furthermore, over Kholm and Demyansk the Luftwaffe enjoyed air supremacy. Given that by November 1942 the Luftwaffe in the East was weaker in operational strength than it had ever been, while the VVS had steadily increased in strength and capability, it should have been obvious to all concerned that the Luftwaffe could not supply around 250,000 men of the Sixth Army for any length of time. Experience in Russia should have indicated that it was equally impossible for Hitler to promise to relieve the Sixth Army by prompt ground action. Much of the fault for these planning errors can be laid at the disjointed and dictatorial methods of command at the highest military headquarters. The Chief of the Luftwaffe Operations Staff, for instance, had no role in the deliberations concerning the airlift operations, while Hitler's orders were passed directly to Sixth Army. In Moscow, there was no way in which Stalin would have felt the need to bypass Zhukov and Novikov in any equivalent air-land operation.

The Führer appears to have been motivated to hold ground at all costs, and by the prestige attached to the name 'Stalingrad'. As Supreme Commander of the Wehrmacht, it was Hitler who ordered Luftflotte 4 to supply the beleaguered army, as he himself accepted at a conference with von Manstein on 5 February 1943. 'I alone am responsible for Stalingrad. I could perhaps aver that Göring gave me inaccurate information on the supply-carrying capabilities of the Luftwaffe, and could thereby unload part of the responsibility on him. But he is the man I myself have appointed as my successor. I therefore cannot burden him with the responsibility for Stalingrad.'[196]

While it was commendable that Hitler did not try to find a scapegoat, it was regrettable from the German point of view that he failed to listen to his air advisors at the outset. The first priority in any campaign is to give friendly forces at least local air superiority, if not supremacy. That point was ignored around Stalingrad and the Luftwaffe was worn down in consequence. To ask air power to retrieve a seriously flawed strategy is to rely on a wing and a prayer.

MARITIME AIR

'No airman can do his job properly if he is engaged one day in combined operations with the Army over land; the next day in operational flying kilometres behind the enemy line; and the third day over the sea with both his own and enemy naval units below him.'
Grossadmiral Erich Raeder

The best strategic thinkers understand that air power is all-pervasive. In March 1942, British and American leaders spent a great deal of time debating the best means of easing the burden on their Soviet ally. Most vociferous were those who argued for an immediate opening of a Western Front, but as Gen Sir Alan Brooke noted in his diary: 'What can we do with some 10 divisions against the German masses?'[197] However, while it was impossible with the British and US land forces then available 'to force the Germans to withdraw land forces from Russia, we might induce them to withdraw air forces.'[198] This was an aspect that those who criticise the RAF strategic bomber offensive often overlook. Increasingly powerful Bomber Command and Eighth Air Force raids on the Reich forced the OKL to withdraw fighter units from the USSR, which relieved the pressure on the Soviet military. AVM Don Bennett, the great RAF Pathfinder leader, was awarded a Soviet medal in recognition of the impact his bomber raids made on the outcome at Stalingrad.

In like fashion, air activity over the waters around the Soviet Union was bound up with the war on land. Prewar German naval co-operation theory envisaged the use of dive-bombers in co-operation with surface vessels to destroy enemy shipping. The aircraft carrier *Graf Zeppelin*, launched at Kiel in 1938, was intended to carry Ju87s, but the Stukas' limited range was a major drawback. However, Göring's antipathy to the very idea of a separate fleet air arm ensured that all German airborne maritime units, be they coastal or shipborne, remained Luftwaffe controlled and manned, apart from seconded Kriegsmarine observers. In these circumstances, it was not really surprising that the Luftwaffe failed to give any priority to producing a maritime dive-bomber of the required range. In the end, the overwhelming bulk of bombing attacks against shipping were made using normal twin-engined Luftwaffe bombers in horizontal low- or high-level attacks.

The Luftwaffe units most closely integrated with the German Navy were the six Staffeln employed on battleships and cruisers. Back one step were units tasked with anti-shipping attacks, coastal and sea reconnaissance, air-sea rescue, coastal patrol, and minesweeping operations. Torpedo-carrying aircraft were part of the Luftwaffe prewar air plans, but notwithstanding the obvious appeal of launching a stand-off attack rather than flying directly over a capital ship with all AAA guns blazing, the OKL was very

backward in developing a torpedo bombing capability. It was only when the full implications of the Battle of the Atlantic became clear in 1941 that energetic measures were undertaken and intensive anti-shipping training carried out. Crack Luftwaffe land-based bomber squadrons were set aside for almost full-time attacks on shipping, and operational anti-shipping commands established to rectify the omissions of the prewar period.

One such was Luftwaffe Commander Baltic, activated at Swinemünde on 1 April 1941. This post was given to Oberst Wolfgang von Wild, who had been a naval cadet in World War 1 and commanded coastal attack group (*Küstenfliegergruppe*) 806 from 1939-40. Luftwaffe Commander Baltic was organised (i) to provide continuous armed reconnaissance in the eastern Baltic and Gulf of Finland to prevent 'surprise attacks by enemy surface and submarine forces'; (ii) to mine Kronstadt and Leningrad harbours, the Neva River between Leningrad and Petrokrepost, and the White Sea-Baltic Canal; (iii) to attack the canal lock installations in the Lake Onega area; (iv) to provide submarine defence and escort convoys, together with anti-submarine warfare, in the Baltic Sea east of longitude 13° and (v) to attack enemy merchant shipping wherever necessary.[199] To meet this varied remit, Wild was given the short-range AufKlGr125 (See) with its Ar95, He60 and He114 floatplanes, KuFlGr806 with its coastal attack Ju88As, and the 9th Air-Sea Rescue unit.[200] Later, Wild would be assigned the Bf109s of IV./JG54, the Ju88As of KuFlGr506, the He115 three-seat general-purpose and torpedo bomber floatplanes of 1./KuFlGr406, and the Ar196 twin-seat reconnaissance and coastal patrol floatplanes of 1./1BFGr (*Bordfliegergruppe* or ship-based reconnaissance group) 196.

Between 22 June and 31 August 1941, Luftwaffe Commander Baltic's aircraft flew 1,775 sorties and sunk 66,000 tons of merchant shipping, five destroyers and one torpedo boat. An additional 17,000 tons of merchant shipping were deemed to have been so badly damaged that sinking was probable, while ships definitely damaged or considered to be damaged by near misses included a heavy cruiser, one flotilla (destroyer) leader, one auxiliary cruiser of 6,000-7,000 tons, 17 destroyers, five motor torpedo boats, two minesweepers, two picket boats, one cutter and 132,000 tons of merchant shipping. Wild's aircrew claimed 46 enemy aircraft destroyed in the air plus 11 on the ground, for the loss of 11 Ju88s, three Ar95s, one Ar196 and five Bf109s.[201] And it was all done in close co-operation with naval authorities committed in the Baltic.

On 27 October 1941 Luftwaffe Commander Baltic was disbanded, the Ju88As of KuFlGr806 were assigned to Fliegerkorps I and AufKlGr125 (See) was transferred, because of ice conditions, to Pillau. The staff together with a Luftwaffe signals company were transferred in early November to Berlin before being moved early in 1942 to Saki in the Crimea.

At the beginning of 1942, Luftflotte 4 established *Sonderstab Krim* (Special Staff Crimea) to support Eleventh Army operations. Special Staff Crimea, reporting to von Greim at Fliegerkorps V, had at its disposal AufKlGr125 (See), Bf109s from JG74, Ju87s from StG77 and twin-engined bombers from KG27, KG51 and KG100 that came and went. It was indicative of the rudimentary nature of Luftwaffe maritime air operations so long after the outbreak of war that I./KG100, designated as a mine-laying unit for Special Staff Crimea, had been given no training in anti-shipping operations, while III./KG27 often had no bombs or detonators suitable for air-sea attacks. Furthermore, Ju88 operations by the crews of III./KG51, who had been specially trained for anti-shipping attacks, were often curtailed for lack of the right types of bombs. Night interdiction missions carried out against Soviet supply shipping were often frustrated by bad weather and the condition of Saki airfield, which was poorly equipped for night operations.

Despite the fear of Soviet amphibious landings at any time, such were the demands from other sectors of the Eastern Front that on 11 February 1942 Göring closed down Special Staff Crimea. Aircraft were withdrawn and at midnight on 18 February Oberst von Wild's Air Command South (*Fliegerführer Süd*) assumed command of remaining Luftwaffe units in the Crimea. Wild's reconnaissance units would fly regular surveillance over the Crimean and Sea of Azov coastlines and, when feasible, over the outer Black Sea reaches. Their other mission was to interdict Soviet supply vessels in the Kerch Strait and en route to Soviet forces on the other end of the Crimea. These tasks were undertaken in close co-operation with the small but steadily expanding German Black Sea Fleet.

On 24 February — a typical day — Wild's HQ launched 47 Bf109s, 26 Ju87s, 23 Ju88s/He111s and one reconnaissance aircraft. Throughout daylight from 06.00 to 17.10hrs, the Bf109s worked to maintain local air superiority over Saki airfield, carry out reconnaissance and surveillance over Sevastopol and enemy lines and escort various bomber raids including that by 24 Stukas against Red Army artillery batteries near Semisotka and Ak Monai. The Bf109s also rode shotgun for eight Ju88s in a fruitless raid on the Soviet battleship *Pariskaya Kommuna*, but such was the threat posed by Wild's bombers that the commander of the Soviet Black Sea Fleet, Vice-Admiral Oktyabrsky, directed that the battleship and two new cruisers were not to leave the safety of port without his direct permission.

Once von Manstein's spring offensive got going, supporting Eleventh Army became the highest priority. The odd He111 torpedo bomber was spared for anti-shipping work but by 6 March the German Black Sea Fleet commander had to be told that no aircraft could be spared for sea mine laying off the south Crimean coast. Manstein was also informed that if Eleventh Army wanted mining operations to go ahead to protect his rear, in addition to the 'also-requested long-range reconnaissance and defensive missions, [then] Luftflotte 4's operations against ground targets at the front must be cut back.'[202] Suffice to say that no Luftwaffe units were withdrawn from direct support of German ground troops to drop mines offshore.

When von Richthofen committed virtually all his aircraft at Kerch or Sevastopol, he was only adhering to the sound military practice of concentrating his forces on the main centre of gravity, believing that success or failure in the Crimea depended on the army's efforts. Only when success looked imminent did Luftflotte 4 HQ divert flying units back to support Air Command South in its more peripheral anti-shipping mission.

When additional Ju88s, He111s and Ju87s could be spared, Wild would immediately concentrate his units against Soviet naval bases. They damaged ports and sank several warships but Wild could deploy those reinforcements for only a few days before they were sent back north again to help the army. After the fall of Sevastopol, Wild was left with two credible anti-shipping Gruppen — I./KG100 and the torpedo bombers of II./KG26 — from which he was lucky to have 30 aircraft serviceable on any given day.

Air Command South's last mission of any consequence was a strong attack on Novorossiysk harbour on 2 July, which sank the flotilla leader *Taskent* and badly damaged the cruiser *Komintern*. Wild's Stukas and bombers were then reassigned to the battle for Rostov. Richthofen disbanded Air Command South on 9 August, deeming it no longer necessary to have a separate maritime air command in the Crimea once Fliegerkorps IV moved into Kerch. Fliegerkorps IV absorbed Wild's specialist anti-shipping and long-range reconnaissance forces for the drive towards the Caucasian oil fields.

The growing prowess of Soviet air forces would cost Wild six bombers destroyed and three damaged in July 1942 alone. When he launched a force of 24 bombers against Soviet warships in distant Poti harbour on 16 July, the defences prevented destruction of a single vessel. By the end, Air Command South's two dozen operational fighters and two flak regiments were far too few to deter or destroy the opposition.

In the six months of its existence, Air Command South had never been allocated more than 20% of Luftflotte 4's aircraft and often had to make do with 5-10%. None the less, Wild's units conducted 3,481 air operations and flew 16,626 individual sorties, of which 462 were long-range missions to continuously and systematically reconnoitre the Crimea, Caucasus and Black Sea. Daily armed reconnaissance sorties along the Caucasus coast placed particular emphasis on Soviet ports and naval bases, with any warships or merchant vessels found being bombed, strafed or torpedoed on an opportunity basis. Air Command South claimed the destruction of 68 freighters (totalling 131,500 tons), a flotilla leader, two destroyers, a submarine chaser, three submarines and a variety of smaller warships and merchantmen. They claimed to have damaged even more. When diverted to army support missions they claimed to have destroyed 510 trucks, 280 motor vehicles, 65 tanks, 30 artillery pieces, 11 artillery batteries, 11 fortified gun emplacements, eight trains, four locomotives and a variety of bunkers, installations and railway lines.

Neither Special Staff Crimea nor Air Command South was ever strong enough to sink a significant number of vessels or heavily damage Soviet naval bases. Their greatest leverage lay in their very presence, which persuaded the overcautious Vice Adm Oktyabrsky to keep his large warships penned up in the ports of Poti and Batumi, where strong flak defences could protect them.

In threatening Oktyabrsky with the loss of his capital ships, the Luftwaffe protected German land forces from any Soviet amphibious landings in the Crimea.

After Richthofen transferred all combat aircraft from the Caucasus to the Stalingrad sector, Luftwaffe maritime activity over the Black Sea was confined to limited reconnaissance missions, and anti-shipping operations ceased for good. In consequence, Oktyabrsky's fleet became increasingly active. By the time Paulus surrendered at Stalingrad, Soviet warships were again pounding Crimean, Ukrainian and, on occasion, Romanian coastlines and attacking Axis supply convoys.

*   *   *   *

Murmansk is the only ice-free port in northern Russia, and the only serious link south in 1941 was the railway to Leningrad. The Karelian sector from Lake Ladoga, northeast of Leningrad, to the south shore of the Barents Sea stretched over 950km, and on 22 June 1941 just two Soviet armies — the 7th and the 14th — opposed the Germans and Finns in the far north. The main VVS and naval air bases were around Murmansk, and most of the 200 aircraft they housed were pretty clapped out. There seemed to be no co-ordination between VVS and naval air operations and it was symptomatic of the state of Soviet aviation that on the rare occasion when their aircraft penetrated German airspace, it never amounted to much. Only Soviet formation leaders were entrusted with an attack objective, so German pilots concentrated on shooting down the lead aircraft in the knowledge that the remainder of the formation would disperse and flee back to base.

Generaloberst Hans-Jurgen Stumpff's Luftflotte 5, with its HQ in Oslo, had 240 aircraft in Norway and a small detachment in Finland. The Chief of Staff controlled the Luftflotte's flying operations, most of which consisted of reconnaissance and fighter activities in the Skagerrak and along the west coast of Norway. A separate tactical staff, based at Kirkenes close to the Russian border, had operational control of all air units committed against the USSR in the far north. Air Command Kirkenes (*Luftwaffenkommando Kirkenes*) was given to Oberst Andreas Nielsen, a participant in Hitler's Munich 'Putsch', who underwent flying training in the USSR in 1928 and had been Condor Legion bomber force commander in Spain. Nielsen's principal mission was to support all army and naval operations in the Finnish area. This was broken down into (i) the establishment of German air superiority over all combat areas and coastal portions of northern Norway, (ii) operations against hostile land and sea forces, (iii) operations against Soviet supply routes (especially the Arctic Canal, Murmansk, Arkhangelsk and Kandalaksha), and (iv) protection of German shipping against attacks by the Western Allies. Air Command Kirkenes was given a good fist of

Below:
The arrival of Generaloberst Stumpff at Kirkenes. *Goss/Rauchbach Archive*

Above:
A pretty scene. A Ju88 of KG30 'Adler' in northern Norway, winter 1941-2. *Goss/Rauchbach Archive*

reconnaissance aircraft plus 10 Ju88s of 5./KG30 at Banak and 36 Stukas of IV./StG1 at Kirkenes, 10 air defence Bf109s of 13./JG77 and a *Schwarm* of five to six Bf110s from ZG76.

The West had used Murmansk, and Arkhangelsk on the White Sea, to supply Russia in World War 1 and a study by the Luftwaffe's 8th (Military Science) Branch recognised that more than half of the Soviet Union's overseas imports came in through these northern ports. It needed no great strategic genius to recognise the importance of cutting off at least the crucial all-year-round Murmansk lifeline. But once again the Germans split their combat focus rather than concentrate on the single specific strategic objective of closing the Salla-Kandalaksha gap and then mopping up Murmansk. Hitler was largely to blame by insisting in the 'Barbarossa' Directive that 'the most important task remains the protection of Norway'. Any forces available thereafter were to be employed 'at first to protect the Petsano area and its iron ore mines and the Arctic highway, then to advance with Finnish forces against the Murmansk railway and thus prevent the passage of supplies to Murmansk by land.' In effect,

the Directive recognised the importance of the Murmansk-Leningrad railway only in so far as it enabled traffic to pass from south to north. Hitler worked on the assumption that the USSR would fall before overseas imports could make any difference.

So instead of one concerted effort to sever the Soviet Union's northern supply line, German troops were wasted securing the long Norwegian coast against an invasion that was way beyond British capabilities. Of those forces that were available, Mountain Corps Norway was to drive from Kirkenes through the Petsano nickel area towards Murmansk, while to the south, XXXVI Corps and the Finns were expected to envelop Salla before pushing on to Kandalaksha on the White Sea. But this two-pronged operation did not make good progress. The northern thrust was halted in the Petsano sector and, soon after, XXXVI Corps with the Finnish 6th Div were halted over 60km from the railway at Alakurtti. Andreas Nielsen's air strength was dissipated over the extensive Finnish-Norwegian theatre as aircraft were shifted quickly to extinguish 'fires' at crucial points. And then the winter came.

The initial phase of operations in the far north must therefore rank as another example of Hitler's failure to think strategically, both in not realising that the British were incapable of providing adequate air cover for an amphibious operation against Norway and in his narrowly confined continental appreciation of sea trade. Murmansk was there for the taking in June 1941, and the German failure to secure it must rank as one of the significant lost opportunities of the war.

In response to an appeal by Stalin to Churchill for munitions and supplies, the British agreed to ship 200 aircraft a month to the USSR up to June 1942. In July 1941 the first 40 Hurricane IIBs arrived in Russia, followed by 200 Curtis Tomahawk[203] low-level ground-attack fighters. They came in crates via Murmansk, together with more mundane but equally crucial supplies like rubber. In 1941, the OKL and Hitler did not seem to realise that it would make more sense to prevent hundreds of Hurricanes and Tomahawks from getting to the front line in the first place than to shoot them down individually once they got in the air.

Once the penny dropped, Luftwaffe bombers were condemned to the thankless, and ultimately impossible, task of permanently interdicting the Murmansk railway line. In mid-December 1941, Air Command North (East) (*Fliegerführer Nord [Ost]*) was established at Rovaniemi in Finland to conduct air operations in the Finnish-Karelian area. Combat aircraft were moved to airfields along the Kemi-Salla road but although the force was endowed with a *Freya* early warning radar station, no extra combat aircraft were forthcoming.

Air operations in the first months of 1942 were restricted by the brief daylight hours, snowfalls and fog. Whenever the weather permitted, the relatively weak German bomber and dive-bomber forces carried out interdiction missions against the Belomorsk-Murmansk section of the rail route, and branch lines leading from it to various sectors of the front. The rail depots at Kandalaksha, Loukhi, Kovda, Kem, Ambarnyy and Apatity were also attacked frequently, and the line from Murmansk to Kandalaksha must have been one of the most heavily bombed railways in Russia. Luftwaffe units succeeded in cutting the rail line repeatedly, as well as in destroying large quantities of rolling stock and rail installations, yet they were unable to halt the traffic on the route for any considerable period. Soviet leaders were well aware of the importance of maintaining traffic on this line, especially once the ice had formed in the navigable channel of the White Sea leading to the railhead at Arkhangelsk.[205] Repair materials were stockpiled at various trackside points to ensure quick repairs by the gangs of thousands whose job it was to keep the trains running. Many had come from villages around Leningrad where German bombs had already killed their families.[206]

The Soviet fighter presence was strengthened along the Murmansk railway and Soviet bombers were dispatched with increasing frequency to bomb German airfields that were launching the offending Ju87s and Ju88s in the first place. German dive-bomber and slower reconnaissance aircraft were therefore compelled to operate with fighter escorts, while a pair of Bf109s was required to remain alert-ready at each airfield in case of unexpected enemy attacks. This reduced the operational status and availability of German fighters for offensive missions.

The upshot was that there were too few Luftwaffe attack aircraft in the far north to close down the Murmansk railway for any meaningful length of time. It was a matter of both limited numbers and delivery accuracy — in the second half of May 1942, four missions flown by 54 of Air Command North (East)'s aircraft managed to drop 25 tons of bombs on a rail bridge south of Olenegorsk, but the bridge was only damaged.

As supplies started to pour across the Atlantic — Moscow asked Britain for three million gas masks in May 1942 alone — Führer Directive No 44 was issued on 21 July 1942:

'We must now cut the northern supply route which links Soviet Russia with the Anglo-Saxon powers. This is principally the Murmansk railway, along which by far the largest proportion of supplies from America and England were delivered during the winter months. The importance of this supply route will increase further when the season and weather conditions prevent successful operations against northern convoys . . . 20th Mountain Army therefore proposes, in co-operation with Luftflotte 5, to prepare an offensive this autumn to seize the Murmansk railway near Kandalaksha.'

However, the Stavka was equally determined not to let the railway be cut, and it backed up this resolve with more and much improved ground and air reinforcements.

On 3 November Air Command North (East) was ordered to release the greater part of its aircraft to reinforce Combat Zone South. After their withdrawal and the beginning of winter weather, Luftwaffe operations against the Murmansk railway gradually tapered off. This was not unexpected because, since 25 March 1942, the major emphasis for Air Command North (East) had been the Allied convoys passing through the Norwegian and Barents Seas.

According to one German estimate, out of a total of 2.3 million tons shipped into the USSR in 1942, 1.2 million came into Murmansk and Arkhangelsk.[207] Among the crucial war materials coming through northern ports were 1,880 aircraft, 2,350 tanks, 8,300 trucks, 6,400 other vehicles and 2,250 field guns. By March

Above:
Run in and break. Stukas returning from an attack on Murmansk. *Goss/Rauchbach Archive*

1942 there were a number of heavy ships in the Norwegian area including the battleship *Tirpitz*, the 'pocket battleship' *Admiral Scheer*, and the heavy cruiser *Prinz Eugen*. Given the ever-increasing logistic boost to the Soviet war effort, it is not surprising that Hitler decided that he might as well use the naval and air units gathered for defence of Norway against Anglo-US convoys.

Luftflotte 5 was therefore ordered, in co-operation with the local naval command, to use its air assets primarily for reconnaissance and attack operations against convoys approaching from the west, with the assurance that additional bomber and torpedo-bomber units would be assigned to it when needed. On 25 March 1942, Air Command North (East), now under former Stuka pilot Oberst Alexander Holle, was told to transfer its command post back to Kirkenes and to organise for attacks against approaching Allied convoys and the ports of Murmansk and Arkhangelsk. Working in concert were Air Command Lofoten Islands, with its HQ at Bardufoss under the former commander of KüFlGr106 and KG28, Oberst Ernst-August Roth, and Air Command North (West) (*Fliegerführer Nord [West]*) at Trondheim under another He111 pilot, Obstlt Hermann Busch.

The British gave the designation 'PQ' to convoys travelling west-east, and 'QP' when returning to the UK. According to German intelligence, a PQ convoy departed every four weeks. When Luftflotte 5 HQ heard that a convoy was assembling, Air Command North (West) would initiate systematic reconnaissance cover of the ports of northern Scotland and Iceland. For this, Air Command North (West) had BV138 long-range maritime reconnaissance flying boats (three-engined aircraft known as 'flying clogs'), Ju88s and, most impressive of all, Fw200 Condors. Designed by Kurt Tank as a long-distance airliner, the four-engined Fw200C, with its ability to carry 4,400lb (2,000kg) of bombs over a range of 4,650km, operated as a potent maritime reconnaissance-bomber out of Trondheim-Vaernes with I./KG40.

The aim was to keep each convoy under constant surveillance, weather conditions permitting, from the moment it was detected. Thereafter, all Luftwaffe units suitable for an attack, especially those of Air Command North (East), were withheld from other missions and deployed for action against the convoy. In theory, Luftflotte 5 was allocated attack units from other sectors as soon as a convoy was discovered, but because of bad weather, generals

Below:
The Arctic convoy route and Luftwaffe maritime aircraft ranges

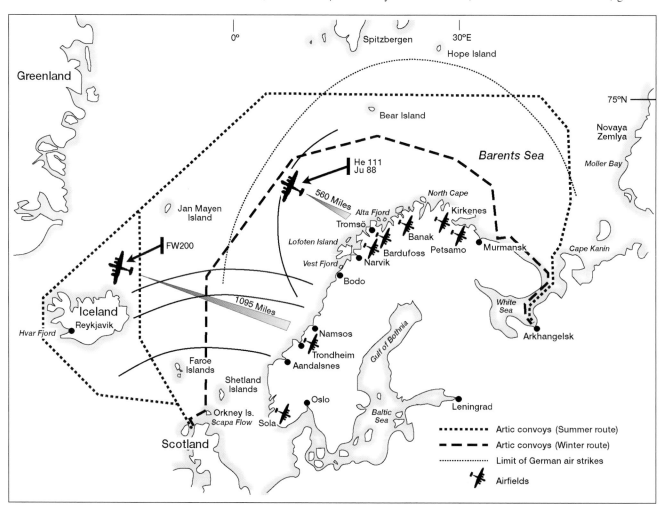

arguing and the pull of equally pressing concurrent commitments, redeployed aircraft almost always arrived late. Unless aircrews were proficient in naval attack, their value was also often doubtful.

Newly arrived units were stationed on a space-available basis at Bodø, Bardufoss or Banak airfields. Air Command Lofoten Islands directed any attack until the convoy reached a line extending from the North Cape to Spitzbergen. From then on, combat and reconnaissance responsibility passed to Air Command North (East), whose mission was to keep the convoy under continuous attack for the remainder of the voyage, up to and including its arrival in the terminal ports. From the point at which a convoy came within range of Air Command North (East)'s bombers, not a single aircraft was to be used in support of ground forces along the Finno-Russian front without Gen Stumpff's personal approval.

In the beginning, reconnaissance missions flown by Luftflotte 5 over northern waters as far as the ice line were rendered fruitless by storms and poor visibility. Between the third week of March and the end of May 1942, German naval and air forces managed to sink only 21 out of a total of 166 merchantmen that sailed from the UK to Russia, of which the Luftwaffe accounted for a dozen.[208] Gen Stumpff did not have a great deal to show for Luftflotte 5 being brought up from 152 combat aircraft in January to 221 by late March. But things were about to change. The Luftwaffe had started to take torpedo-bombing seriously only in December 1941, and as its Italian allies were far more adept at this technique, Staffeln from KG26 were rotated through Grosseto in central Italy for conversion training, beginning with 3./KG26. The first torpedo-adapted He111Hs and 12 crews arrived at Bardufoss on 1 May, together with 60 extra Ju88 bombers.

The British newspaper correspondent Alexander Werth set sail from Iceland on 20 May in a 10,000-ton cargo vessel *Empire Baffin* that helped make up convoy PQ16. Luftflotte 5 learned that PQ16 might be at sea that same day, and the convoy was soon under constant Condor observation. On 27 May, a force of 101 Ju88s, operating as both horizontal and dive-bombers, and seven He111 torpedo-bombers struck the convoy southeast of Barents Island. It was a classic all-axis attack, with the bombers coming in from all directions to swamp the escort destroyers' air defences. 'For 40 long minutes they attacked,' wrote Werth, 'usually in twos and threes, usually coming straight out of the sun, some diving low, others dropping their bombs from two hundred feet (60m). From the yellow shark-like bellies one could see the obscene yellow eggs dropping . . . Then there was another attack. This time they weren't merely dive-bombers, but torpedo carriers as well . . . Then the Focke-Wulf tried to provoke the destroyers by coming almost within range, and while the destroyers were firing at him, one of the planes which had been quietly hiding in the clouds suddenly came diving down.'[209] Four merchantmen were sunk and two others received heavy damage, while three German aircraft were lost. PQ16 was heavily attacked again on 28 May and during the following night. As a result, only 25 out of the more than 50 ships in the convoy reached Kola Bay by the evening of 30 May, and that night these 25 ships fell under another heavy German air attack. Another seven ships (31,000 tons) were sent to the bottom.

On his fraught trip to Murmansk, Werth heard much from a Russian passenger about 'our fighter ace Safonov'. Boris Safonov, who flew with 72 Comp Air Regt of the Air Force of the Soviet Northern Fleet based in Murmansk, was the best known Soviet fighter ace during the first months of the war. His first 14 'kills' were achieved during the first three months of the war while flying the I-16 fighter.

Following the arrival of the first 40 Hurricane IIBs in Russia, aircrew and ground personnel belonging to Wg Cdr H. N. G. Ramsbottom-Isherwood's 151 Wing (81 and 143 Squadrons) set up for business on Vaenga airfield near Murmansk in September 1941. Although they flew in combat, their main role was to convert Soviet pilots and groundcrews to the new aircraft. On 26 October a Bf110 was claimed as the first Soviet Hurricane kill, by which time over 100 Hurricanes had been delivered. Once the Soviets had established 72, 78, 152 and 760 Hurricane Fighter Air Regts, 151 Wing personnel returned home by sea. Lt-Col Boris Safonov, now in command of 78 Regt, claimed one Bf109 on 17 December and one He111 on 31 December in his Hurricane fighter.

For those on convoy PQ16, there was little to do but wait as the ships edged ever closer towards the protective cover of Kola-based Soviet fighters. Then, at about 10.30hrs on Saturday 30 May, just after the last of Air Command North East's bombers had gone, 'three pairs of aircraft began to fly in a large circle above the convoy — Hurricanes.' By this time 78 Fighter Regt had converted to US-delivered P-40s, and Safonov was leading three Kittyhawks when he spotted a group of Ju88s from 3./KG30 near the convoy. During the ensuing battle, Safonov was credited with downing three Ju88s, but soon afterwards the engine on his Kittyhawk stopped and at 10.35hrs his aircraft hit the water. On 14 June 1942, with 20 personal 'kills', Boris Safonov posthumously became the first person to be twice appointed Hero of the Soviet Union in the war against Germany.

At 16.00hrs on 27 June 1942, the ships of convoy PQ17 left the Hvalfjord in Iceland and headed northwards. The 35 merchant ships were heavily laden with 297 crated aircraft, plus enough tanks, vehicles, raw materials and victuals to equip an army of 50,000 men. Two tankers were there to replenish the numerous close escort force of six destroyers, four corvettes, three submarines and two AAA ships. Medium-range cover for PQ17 was to be provided by four cruisers and three destroyers.

The Germans knew from agents in Iceland that PQ17 was forming up. Under their new *Gruppenkommandeur*, Maj Ernst Henkelmann, the crews of I./KG40's Fw200s set out to find it but their initial efforts were thwarted by fog. Just after PQ17 set sail, a Condor had flown across so low that it nearly hit the cruiser HMS *London*. As the convoy edged forward in poor visibility, one ship was rammed and another ran aground. This left 33 ships en route through the Denmark Strait.

On the fourth day of the voyage, the protective fog lifted. PQ17 was spotted at 01.04hrs on 2 July whereupon two U-boats trailed the convoy and sent a fix to the Luftflotte 5 command post at Kemi, which had overall control of the operation. Air Command North (West)'s Fw200s and BV138s were off the convoy in the afternoon. From then on, until 10 July, PQ17 was kept under constant observation by the Luftwaffe from just outside shipboard flak range, apart from a few brief interruptions for weather.

Left:
Hurricanes taxying into Vaenga airfield in northern Russia in difficult snow conditions. Note the addition of Russian numbers and letters to identify individual aircraft to each squadron. *Via Air Historical Branch (RAF). Crown Copyright 1941-2/ MOD. Reproduced with permission of the Controller of Her Majesty's Stationery Office*

Below:
Inter-allied co-operation — RAF and Soviet Navy pilots at Vaenga aerodrome. *Via Air Historical Branch (RAF). Crown Copyright 1941-2/ MOD. Reproduced with permission of the Controller of Her Majesty's Stationery Office*

PQ17 was passing Jan Mayen Island, still outside the range of the bombers based at Bardufoss, Banak and Kirkenes. But north of Bear Island, the convoy had to turn east to avoid the ice cap. That was the moment the attack crews of Luftflotte 5 had been waiting for. On 2 July four U-boats went for PQ17, only to be driven off by the strong naval escort. Towards 18.00hrs eight He115 seaplanes from 1./KüFlGr406 out of Tromsø-Søreisa pitched up. The lumbering floatplanes each launched one torpedo as they flew in flat out at 180mph, but their crews were put off their aim by savage escort fire. One He115 was brought down.

Luftflotte 5 HQ decided to launch an all-out attack against the convoy on 4 July. Air Commander Lofoten Islands put together the air plan, which aimed to get the best synergy out of the Ju88s of III./KG30 and the He111 torpedo-bombers of 1./KG26. Two hours after the flying boats of I./KüFlGr906 had taken off from Billefjord, Roth ordered the Ju88s airborne, led by Hptm Hajo Hermann who had been decorated with the Knight's Cross at Dunkirk. They were to be followed into the air 30min later by 23 He111s led by Hptm Bernd Eicke. The 27 Ju88s were to dive-bomb the convoy and while the anti-aircraft defences concentrated on them, the 23 He111s were to hit in two groups, one a low-level beam attack and the other from the stern.

But it did not work out that way because the Ju88s were grounded by bad weather. As the first He111 broke through the grey clouds at around 08.20hrs, the guns of the merchant ships and escorts threw up a barrage of steel. The cruisers *London* and *Norfolk* were blazing away as Hptm Eicke corrected his position a little and ordered Lt Rentz to fire the two tin fish. On the Liberty ship *William Hopper*, Lt Brian G. Welch of the US maritime gunners watched as the He111 came directly at him. 'One of our 7.5cm shells exploded near his starboard side and I saw smoke coming from that side of the aircraft. Then I saw the torpedo. It came from the starboard side and hit the ballast tank with such an explosion that the boiler was sent through the skylight. The ship shuddered and began to sink stern first.' The He111s struck three ships and lost three of their own, including Lt Hennemann, who received a posthumous Knight's Cross for sinking a US destroyer.

Just as the Germans knew of PQ17's departure from the Kriegsmarine's communications monitoring service, so the British code breakers at Bletchley Park had an Enigma decrypt by 3 July confirming that the battleship *Tirpitz* had left Trondheim. The First Sea Lord, Admiral Sir Dudley Pound, visited the Admiralty Operational Intelligence Centre on the evening of 4 July, where Cdr Ned Denning advised from *Tirpitz's* previous behaviour and earlier Kriegsmarine policy decrypts that the battleship was unlikely to leave Altenfjord while the Germans incorrectly believed that a battleship, and probably an aircraft carrier, was shadowing PQ17. But the 64-year-old Pound, then a very sick man with a brain tumour, was convinced that the *Tirpitz* was fast bearing down on the convoy. The First Sea Lord could not be persuaded to wait and at 21.30hrs PQ17 was ordered to scatter. The situation was made worse because the officer in charge of the escorts misunderstood the message and headed his six destroyers south to join the now redundant cruiser force, leaving the merchant vessels to make for whatever ports they could reach. To the seamen left to fend for themselves, it had all been brought about by the He111 torpedo attacks.

On 5 July, Luftflotte 5 found the convoy scattered with the bulk of PQ17 still within a 60-290km area. The aircrew could not believe their luck, and torpedo-bombing He115s fell on the ships with combined gusto. When the fog lifted over northern Norway, no fewer than 69 Ju88s from KG30 managed to get airborne. At 17.30hrs a Fw200 guided them to a cluster of vessels making for the refuge of Novaya Zemlya. As the bombs rained down, Capt Owen Charles Morris, commander of the good ship *Zamalek* and the first Merchant Navy seaman to be awarded the DSO, had one of his crew lie on the deck centreline watching through binoculars and shouting avoidance instructions to 'steer port' or 'steer starboard'. Twelve Allied ships were sunk that day.

Because fog covered the area north of 72° North, no action could be taken against the last ships of PQ17 from the evening of 7 July, when they were near the northwest coast of Novaya Zemlya, until 9 July. Four merchant ships, escorted by a couple of AAA ships, three minesweepers and three trawlers, had found their way into the Kara Sea barred by ice. Their only hope was to head south for Iokanga on the Kola peninsula, but this meant running towards the German airfields. Two BV138s picked them up and brought in the bombers and U-boats. Thirty-eight Ju88s from KG30 were launched from Banak. Although it was just before midnight, conditions were perfect. Attacking out of the sun that was still above the horizon, and with 30km visibility, the Ju88s sank a 7,000-ton US freighter and seriously damaged another.

On 10 July another attack was launched, this time by 16 Ju88s against two merchant ships and four patrol boat escorts north of Iokanga. An 8,000-ton freighter was badly crippled, another of 5,000 tons was sunk and the other ships were damaged. This close in, the Soviets were able to fight the attackers off with Pe-3 twin-engined fighters and Hurricanes, but not before Gen Stumpff signalled Göring to claim that not one ship of PQ17 had reached Iokanga.[210]

Stumpff was over-egging it because several merchant vessels did stay briefly in Iokanga before moving on to the White Sea. But in destroying two-thirds of the convoy, the combined German air-submarine effort had exceeded all expectations. A total of 130 Ju88s, 43 He111s and 29 He115s were committed against PQ17, dropping a total of 210,000kg (206.7 tons) of explosives and 61 aerial torpedoes in 202 sorties. Aircraft sank eight of the 24 merchant ships lost, and damaged another eight that had to be finished off by U-boats. Various naval vessels were also sunk or damaged by the Luftwaffe. German air losses consisted of a single Fw200 with its crew, a BV138 flying boat and crew, two He111s with crews, two He111s from which only two men were lost, and one He115, the crew of which was rescued.

The Germans did not expect their opponents to take the PQ17 disaster lying down, especially as the Arctic convoy shipments were considered vital to the Soviet war effort. Soviet air attacks on Luftflotte 5 airfields were also expected to increase during the passage of convoys, and immediate steps were taken to prepare Glockensund airfield on Spitzbergen for more effective maritime missions.

PQ18 consisted of 41 merchant ships (totalling 167,000 tons), which were to be accompanied by the Fighting Destroyer Escort

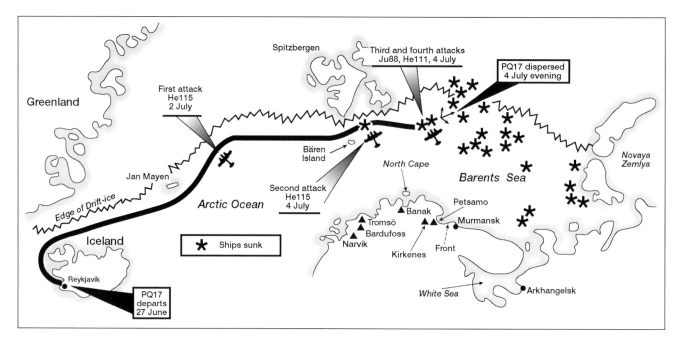

made up of 10 destroyers, numerous corvettes, minesweepers, submarines and AAA ships, plus the escort carrier HMS *Avenger* with 12 Sea Hurricane fighters, three Swordfish anti-submarine aircraft and two dedicated destroyers. The transfer of some of RAF Coastal Command's seek-and-strike aircraft to North Cape bases supplemented the air umbrella. PQ18 left Loch Ewe in Scotland on 2 September. It was sighted at sea for the first time at 03.15hrs on 13 September about 40km southwest of Spitzbergen, and was kept under surveillance until 18.00hrs by aircraft that included one Ju88 equipped with an ASV (Air/Surface Vessel) variant of the FuG200 Lichtenstein radar. Four Luftwaffe raids were mounted that day, which sank eight ships between 15.00 and 20.35hrs. But five German aircraft were lost and during further attacks on 14, 15 and 18 September, continual British combat air patrols over the convoy plus determined escort anti-aircraft fire took their toll. Göring ordered on 17 September that 'PQ18 is to be attacked with all available means until it enters port. Destruction of the ships in this convoy is of decisive importance,' but by the following day KG26 could put only a dozen out of its original 92 He111 torpedo-bombers into the air.

Plans were made for another attack in the Gorlo Straits and in the White Sea by the rather weak torpedo forces still in operation, but worsening weather made this impossible. PQ18 reached Arkhangelsk with 27 ships. The shallow water in Dvina Bay made it impossible to launch torpedoes against the ships once they reached the vicinity of Arkhangelsk.

In over 330 sorties against PQ18, Luftflotte 5 aircraft sunk 10 ships and contributed to the loss of three more. However, it lost 44 aircraft in the process, of which 38 were He115 and He111 torpedo-bombers. The Luftwaffe 8th (Military Science) Branch calculated that while only one vessel was sunk for every 19 high- or dive-bombing sorties, air-launched torpedo bombing sunk an Allied vessel every eight sorties. This proportion would have been even better if many of the torpedoes dropped had not turned out to be duds.

Although the relatively meagre results achieved against PQ18 were due in part to bad weather, Luftwaffe forces available for anti-convoy operations were now too weak to accomplish anything decisive. The British and US navies were now using powerful escort forces, together with specialist long-range aircraft. Just as important were the growing numbers of North Cape-based Soviet aircraft that regularly attacked the Luftflotte's airfields at Petsamo, Kirkenes and Banak, often timed to prevent aircraft from getting off the ground to hit the convoys. While these hit-and-run sorties were not very destructive, parallel jamming of Luftflotte 5's radio frequencies showed the extent to which Soviet air power was developing.

Luftflotte 5's war diary reported no convoys of any size from October to December 1942, and the assumption that the British would try to move supplies to Russia on single ships, travelling alone, proved to be correct. Air reconnaissance was increased to try and find these individual merchantmen but when a heavily protected convoy left Loch Ewe on 15 December, it was not discovered by the Luftwaffe or by German naval units, and it arrived safely in Murmansk on Christmas Day 1942.

What finally did for the anti-convoy effort was the land campaign. The battle in the Far Northern theatre was waged on two very separate levels — the tactical battle to close the Murmansk railway, and the strategic interdiction of Allied shipping across wide expanses of sea. Success in these missions demanded very different aircrew skills and experience, and as the air wars over the UK, the Mediterranean and Russia made increasing demands on German bombers and haemorrhaged the cream of bomber crews, Luftwaffe hopes of building up a serious anti-shipping capability, as in so much else, had to recede.

Gen Stumpff relied on the temporary assignment of bombers whenever an Arctic convoy was sighted, but such reinforcements were just not available once the Red Army started to fight back with a vengeance. After Stalingrad was encircled, there were far too few air assets that could be spared from the Russian front for the Far North. The degree to which Luftflotte 5 became weakened and incapable of making a major difference over land or sea showed the extent to which the Luftwaffe had become badly overstretched. From now on, even priority air operations to sever Soviet supply lines could only be performed 'as far as possible' under the circumstances.

In January 1943, anyone standing on the docks at Basra in Iraq would have seen crate after crate being unloaded from British and US merchant ships. Inside these crates were components which made up bombers that were operating in support of Soviet troops around Stalingrad within eight days of a ship docking in Iraq. From now on the Persian Gulf route would supply three times as much to the USSR as the weather-dependent Arctic lifeline. None the less, between December 1942 and May 1945, Arctic convoys delivered a massive 4,964,231 tons of equipment and materials, including 5,218 tanks, 7,411 aircraft and 4,932 anti-tank guns. Some have argued that the Germans lost the maritime war because Göring sabotaged all efforts to create a specialist naval air arm. But that was a red herring. Given the state of German aircraft production even as late as 1942, there were never going to be enough German air assets for prolonged land and sea campaigns against two of the largest nations on earth.

Opposite top:
Map showing the fateful path of PQ17.

Opposite bottom:
A merchantman of convoy PQ18 being bombed by the Luftwaffe, September 1942. *IWM*

KUBAN HEEL

'The art of air combat is clearly a German privilege. Slavs would never be able to master it.'
Adolf Hitler

During 1942 the Eastern Front had solidified over half its length. From Murmansk, round the siege of Leningrad, due south to Lake Ilmen and across the pine forests of the Rzhev salient and down to Orel, ground positions stayed pretty much the same for 12 months. Then, taking advantage of the German fixation with Stalingrad, the Stavka went over to the offensive at the beginning of 1943. On the Moscow front an offensive was launched which brought the Red Army to Rzhev and Vyasma before the winter was over, and the Soviets recaptured Voronezh on the Upper Don before the end of January.

But it was down south, where the three great rivers of the Ukraine flowed into the Black Sea, that Soviet progress was most marked. Bypassing German forces outside Stalingrad, they swept forward to the Donets while covering their northern flank by an advance to Kursk. Such was the speed and scale of Soviet action

Below: Situation on the Russian front, December 1942–January 1943.

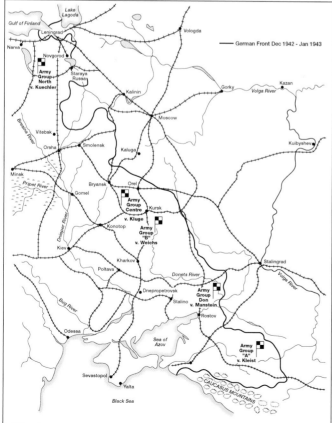

that the Germans were forced to make a precipitate retreat from the Caucasus. After the loss of the Sixth Army, German commanders would have preferred to fall back on their railheads to await better weather. But while trying to stabilise his line, von Manstein had to extricate Army Group A from the Caucasus, which meant holding Rostov at the mouth of the Don as the key to rail lines and supplies.

Early in February, Army Group Don was redesignated Army Group South. What saved the Germans in early 1943 was von Manstein's brilliance in mobile warfare and von Richthofen's airmanship. Hitler liked von Richthofen, a committed National Socialist who was aggressive, inspiring, honest but completely loyal. And there was no disputing the skill with which von Richthofen handled the air forces under his command.

Aware that Manstein would need effective air support to stop Soviet advances and rebuild the Southern Front, von Richthofen began reorganising Luftflotte 4 even before Stalingrad fell. From his command train at Taganrog-South airfield, on 20 January von Richthofen ordered Oberst Kühl to transfer all He111s not used for transport duties from the makeshift Novocherkassk airfield, east of Rostov, to a much better base at Stalino, 180km to the northwest. He also ordered Obstlt Hans-Henning von Beust, commander of KG27 at Voroshilovgrad, to withdraw his He111s to Konstantinovka, 80km due west. These redeployments moved precious bombers away from Soviet air and ground attack. The He111s were now able to operate out of established airfields with excellent runways, hangars and all the facilities needed to improve serviceability rates, and which were connected by road and rail to German supply centres in the Ukraine. As German armies retreated northwest these airfields came back into combat range.

On 23 January, Hitler approved the temporary 'borrowing' of 30 He111s from the Stalingrad airlift for combat operations against attacking Soviet troops. These bombers never returned to 'trucking' and von Richthofen quietly 'borrowed' more and more He111s after 24 January, further enhancing operational attack rates.

Leaving Martin Fiebig's Fliegerkorps VIII to provide air supply and combat support to Stalingrad and the Caucasus, von Richthofen tasked Kurt Pflugbeil's Fliegerkorps IV to operate southeast of Rostov in support of delaying battles of the Fourth Panzer Army and the remnants of the Fourth Romanian Army withdrawing across the Manych River towards the Lower Don. Richthofen briefed on 25 January that he would strengthen Fliegerkorps IV with a Zerstörer Geschwader and the return of most of KG51. Back on 2 January, von Richthofen had created an ad hoc close air support *Fliegerdivision Donets* under Gen Alfred

Mahnke, an 'old eagle' who had learned to fly before 1914. Mahnke's fighters, dive-bombers and ground-attack aircraft had operated pretty autonomously in support of hard-pressed German troops in the Don-Donets region, and von Richthofen now subordinated Air Division Donets to Fliegerkorps IV to optimise the employment of these crucial assets. What was left of the Royal Romanian Air Corps, which had been working alongside *Fliegerdivision Donets*, was pulled out of the line for a time after the loss of 79 aircraft since 16 October 1942.

To support von Manstein along his extended front, the OKL put *Luftwaffen Kommando Don* under Luftflotte 4. Commanded by Gen Günther Korten, Air Command Don had been formed on 26 August 1942 from Fliegerkorps I to support the army northeast of Kharkov. It became Fliegerkorps I again on 17 February 1943, and from his Poltava HQ Korten looked after operations in Luftflotte 4's northern sector. Fliegerkorps IV, with its HQ at Dnepropetrovsk, covered the central sector, while its subordinate command, *Fliegerdivision Donets*, controlled powerful close-support forces in the southeastern sector. Richthofen retained control of the bulk of his long-range bombers through his own HQ.

As Soviet advances became more worrying, a number of second-line Luftwaffe units launched harassing bomber attacks on Soviet forward concentrations and lines of communication. These units, of which there were eight, were known as *Störkampfstaffeln* (harassment bomber Staffel) and were equipped with obsolescent or training aircraft such as the He46, He51, Ar66 and Hs126, fitted with underwing or under-fuselage bomb racks and at least a single fixed 7.92mm machine gun. These auxiliary units, which could carry 50kg (110lb) bombs or 70kg (154lb) cluster-bomb dispensers, were thrown together as a crisis response to reinforce first-line strength. Similar to the Soviet biplane night harassment units, they were reorganised on a permanent footing from March 1943 from which the later *Nachtschlachtgruppen* (Night ground-attack Gruppen) were formed. Nevertheless, initially they were few in number — probably only 85-100 aircraft in the whole of Russia — and their offensive capacity was small. Not surprisingly, such Luftwaffe expedients failed to halt or even slow down the Soviet drive, which crossed the Donets River on 5 February.

By mid-February, the Red Army appeared to be advancing in strength towards Pavlograd and Dnepropetrovsk. As the Soviets occupied Kharkov, von Richthofen flew himself to within sound of Soviet artillery to be co-located with von Manstein at Zaporozhye. Soviet forces were perilously close when the Luftflotte 4 command train subsequently trundled into Zaporozhye, and Gen Otto Dessloch's 200 flak guns positioned in front of the town could only have done so much.[211] But von Manstein was sure that the Soviet advance had become over-extended, and von Richthofen backed his colleague by moving the considerable air power of *Fliegerdivision Donets* to the increasingly vulnerable Stalino area on 20 February to succour the hard-pressed troops.

Spearheading six Soviet armies was Mobile Group Popov, a modern tank army led by Lt-Gen Markian Popov, which pressed forward into the German rear. The Luftwaffe was the only mobile instrument available to stop such a threat, and Luftflotte 4's radio intercept service picked up transmissions revealing the locations and intentions of Popov's Group, plus its critical shortage of fuel.

It was the right time for a concentrated air attack. Mustering all available bomber and tactical support aircraft, Fliegerkorps IV carried out very effective attacks in the Pavlograd-Kramatorsk area against Popov's armour, halting its advance and eliminating all the tanks which had advanced upon Zaporozhye. Gen Popov admitted later that his Group was halted by the Luftwaffe's ceaseless assault.

The destruction of what remained of Group Popov five days after the Soviet occupation of Kharkov showed how the Red Army in the southwest was operating well beyond its logistic reach. The canny von Manstein then closed the trap, sending First and Fourth Panzer Armies and Army Force Kempf to regain the Donets River line, with the main effort of Luftflotte 4 in support. The Soviets recognised an entrapment when they saw one and started withdrawing from Kharkov on 10 March. The following day saw Fliegerkorps IV supporting the army and Fliegerkorps I harassing retreating forces.

When von Manstein's counter-offensive began, Luftflotte 4 had 928 aircraft or a third more than it possessed at the end of January. A total of 493 (53%) were operational, a 16% increase in three weeks despite von Richthofen having withdrawn eight weak or depleted units (some 250 aircraft) for resting and refit during February. Korten's Fliegerkorps I added a further 198 serviceable aircraft (out of a complement of 314) to the order of battle. Luftflotte 4's improved strength and serviceability dramatically increased sorties flown from an average of around 350 per day in January to 1,145 and 1,486 on 22 and 23 February respectively. 'The Russians were stopped everywhere and suffered heavy losses,' wrote von Richthofen enthusiastically.

Having secured unified control of all Luftwaffe assets in the south, von Richthofen threw his Air Fleet into the battle for Kharkov as an integrated whole. He concentrated units from one or more Fliegerkorps against crucial single targets as the tactical situation demanded, and Fliegerkorps commanders were instructed to ensure that their units could immediately bring their firepower to bear in other operational sectors.

Richthofen's successes owed everything to the flexibility, co-ordination and concentration with which he deployed his assets. The last two were exemplified by the creation of ad hoc air battle groups to support spearhead forces such as SS Division *Das Reich*, which led the assault on Kharkov. Thereafter, the concentrated effort was sustained until Belgorod was taken, strengthening the German hold on the Donets line. The phrases 'massive concentration', 'drastic concentration' and 'concentration of all forces to the highest degree', appeared repeatedly in Luftflotte 4 battle orders, just as they did in the joint campaign planning for 'Desert Storm' in 1991 and 'Allied Force' over Kosovo in 1999.

By mid-March, the Combat Zone South front was again firmly integrated and all Axis divisions were contiguous along a line (albeit thinly manned in places) extending from Taganrog to Belgorod. Richthofen's ability to pick his Luftflotte off the floor and win clear air superiority for a major German counter-thrust so soon after the Stalingrad hammering explained why Hitler promoted him to Field Marshal on 15 February 1943.

However, an early thaw prevented the Germans from carrying the offensive northwards from Belgorod to Kursk, where the

Above:
Everyone knows about Russian winters but few appreciate the impact
on operations of the awful Russian rasputiza. Ju88D in the spring thaw.
Price

Soviets remained in possession of a consolidated salient
outflanking the new positions that von Manstein had established
on the Donets. In addition, concentration of Axis forces in the
battle for Kharkov allowed the Soviets to consolidate their
bridgeheads over the Donets further to the south around Chuguev
and Izyum. German armoured groups, with air support, were
thrown against these bridgeheads but without success. These
Soviet vantage points would prove their worth when the summer
campaign began three months later.

*   *   *   *

Manstein would have preferred to pull all German troops out of
the Caucasus but on 23 January 1943, Hitler ordered that a
bridgehead 'kept as small as possible' be maintained on the
Taman peninsula, which divided the Black Sea from the Sea of
Azov. Through this peninsula flowed the Kuban River, and the
Seventeenth Army, along with some Romanian troops, were to be
maintained in a series of defensive positions on both banks to
secure what Hitler envisaged as a jumping-off point to threaten
the Caucasian oil fields later in 1943. Given the limited German
naval presence in the Black Sea, it fell to the Luftwaffe to sustain
all the troops on the Kuban bridgehead, or what the Germans
called the *Gotenkopf Stellung* (Goth's Head Position).

Three days before Stalingrad fell, Fliegerkorps VIII set up Air
Transport Mission Crimea (*Lufttransporteinsatz Krim*). Gen
Fiebig's men had two tasks: to transport troops and wounded from
the region east of the Kerch Strait to the Crimea, and on the return
leg to ship supplies (especially vehicle fuel) from the Crimea, as
well as from airfields north of the Sea of Azov, to the region east
of the Kerch Strait.[212] Fiebig's He111s, Fw200s, Ju90s and Ar232s
operated from the well-founded airfields of Saki and Sarabus in
the Crimea, while the Ju52s flew out of equally good bases at
Taganrog and Mariupol. The Me321 *Gigant* heavy transport
gliders that Field Marshal Milch had ordered for the Stalingrad
airlift, but never used, operated from Bagerovo on the Kerch
peninsula.

Operating from airfields with good supply and maintenance
facilities, and with the weather generally favourable, Fiebig's air
transports unloaded a daily average of 500 tons of fuel,
ammunition and rations into the Kuban bridgehead, which was
much more than they had ever managed to ferry into the
Stalingrad *Kessel*. Flying out of Krasnodar, Timashevskaya and
Slavyanskaya while the Germans still held these airfields, the air
transport crews completed a major evacuation. On 28 February,
Field Marshal von Kleist, C-in-C Army Group A, thanked
Fliegerkorps VIII for having airlifted 50,000 men from the
southeast Caucasus to the Crimea and Ukraine.

The last airlift mission into the Kuban bridgehead was flown on
30 March. The following day, Fliegerkorps VIII was withdrawn
and transferred to Luftflotte 4's northern flank. In its place,
Fliegerkorps I assumed command of German air forces supporting
the Kuban bridgehead through Gen Korten's HQ at Simferopol in
the Crimea, and an advanced command post at Kerch.

Korten's personnel faced increasingly serious Soviet
opposition. During the Seventeenth Army's slow withdrawal from
the Caucasus and establishment of positions on the Kuban,
growing numbers of Soviet aircraft attacked German airfields and

ports, especially around Kerch. A beefed-up 9th Flak Div under Gen Wolfgang Pickert, who commanded all AAA in the Seventeenth Army area in collaboration with two weak fighter and one dive-bomber Gruppen, became vital to the defence of Axis ground forces as well as rear installations. None the less, during February and March, and mostly in support of von Manstein's counter-offensive, the Luftwaffe in the East lost 56 dive-bombers, 217 bombers and 163 fighters.[213]

On 10 March 1943, Luftwaffe combat forces in the USSR stood at 15 fighter or fighter-bomber Gruppen, one twin-engined Bf110 Gruppe, 15 bomber and eight dive-bomber Gruppen, and 27 short-range and 18 long-range reconnaissance Staffeln. Heading up the other side was Alexander Novikov, who was promoted to Marshal of Aviation on 17 March 1943, the first appointment of its kind in the Soviet Union. The 42-year-old Novikov now mustered 13 air armies supported by 19 aviation corps of the Supreme Commander's Reserve, with special fighter regiments of the PVO air defence forces assigned to cover front-line airfields, and Golovanov's eight bomber corps for independent operations. Where the Luftwaffe in the East had around 1,800 combat aircraft, Soviet front-line strength stood at 5,892 aircraft, most of which were modern, very capable and tangible tributes to the skill, expertise and exertions of the Soviet designers, engineers and workers.

In the UK and USA, there was no way in which the respective senior airman, Sir Charles Portal or 'Hap' Arnold, would have been expected to run their air services *and* direct a major air campaign. The Soviets did it differently. Not content with being VVS commander, Air Marshal Novikov represented the Stavka where the action was, and in this case he controlled and

Below:
Me323 Gigant near Riga. Operated by I. and II./TG (Transportgeschwader) 5 from main bases at Warsaw (Poland), Lecskemet (Hungary) and Focsani (Romania), these giant transports flew several thousand sorties over an area stretching from Riga to Kirovgrad, from Galatz to Sevastopol for the Crimean airlift, and from Bucharest to Zilistov between 5 November 1943 and 2 May 1944.
R. Bauer via Goss/Rauchbach Archive

co-ordinated the air forces of the North Caucasus, Southern and Southwestern Fronts. Under him, Gen K. A. Vershinin was North Caucasus Front Air Force commander with a brief to centralise control of the 4th and 5th Air Armies. At the beginning of April, the North Caucasus Front Air Force consisted of 4th Air Army's 250 aircraft under Gen N. F. Naumenko, 200 from the 5th under Gen S. K. Goryunov, 70 from the Black Sea Fleet and 50 from the ADD. And these air units were systematically reinforced during the Kuban air operation, especially as the Lend-Lease flow of UK and US aircraft such as P-39s, A-20s and Spitfires started to kick in.[214] When, on 20 April, the Stavka raided its reserves to add the 2nd Bomber Air Corps and the 3rd Fighter Air Corps to the 4th Air Army, and the 2nd Composite Air Corps and 282nd Fighter Air Div to the 5th, this brought Vershinin's air component up to 900 military aircraft of which 370 were fighters, 170 ground-attack aircraft, 165 day bombers and 195 night bombers. New types made up 65% of the bomber force, compared with 25-30% six months earlier, while almost all the interceptors were the latest Yak-1, Yak-7B or La-5.[215] Opposing them in Luftflotte 4 were 24 combat Gruppen and 17 reconnaissance Staffeln. Although the Soviets would hold the advantage in fighter numbers, Luftflotte 4 had more bombers, better bases and space for manoeuvre.

Back in February, a surprise attack by Soviet marines on the coast at Mount Myskhako, south of Novorossiysk, threatened German control of the Kuban. By mid-April, Luftflotte 4 had concentrated some 820 aircraft in the Taman region and the Crimea, and von Richthofen could draw on at least 200 additional bombers from airfields in the southern Ukraine as required. However, this build-up had not gone unnoticed by VVS reconnaissance, and when he ordered attacks on German supply traffic in the Black Sea and across the Strait of Kerch, Novikov forced Korten to maintain defensive forces in the Crimea.

The German Seventeenth Army had 15 divisions around the Kuban and on 17 April, three of them were launched in Operation 'Neptune' against the Soviet occupation at Myskhako. Fliegerkorps I put up 450 bombers from two dive-bomber and two bomber Gruppen, and 200 fighters from two Gruppen reinforced by Romanian and Slovak squadrons. Against this, Vershinin had

500 aircraft of which 100 were bombers, but most of his airfields were some 150-200km from Myskhako and the approach route for the 4th Air Army's aircraft was over the often cloud-shrouded Caucasus Mountains. From Luftwaffe airfields 50-100km back on the Taman peninsula, groups of 30-40 German bombers began to

Above:
G. A. Rechkalov. *Author's collection*

bomb Soviet troop positions. On 17, 18 and 19 April, Luftflotte 4 flew 494, 511 and 294 Ju87 dive-bomber sorties respectively. Operating in groups of 16, the first Stuka wave on 18 April took off at 04.45hrs and the last landed at 18.30.

The air battle over Myskhako reached a climax on 20 April. A German push in the morning made almost negligible progress, despite being supported by all available combat aircraft, whereupon I./KG2 and II./StG77 attacked a high-level Soviet HQ

in the afternoon. At dusk all available bombers attacked jetties and other landing sites reinforcing the Soviet beachhead, and during the night 165 Ju87s re-attacked from 10,000ft. That same day, Novikov committed the three air corps of the Stavka reserve, making it possible to carry out two powerful strikes against German infantry and artillery directly in front of the Red Army line of troops. As Gen K. N. Leselidze, Commander of the Soviet 18th Army wrote succinctly: 'Massed raids made by our aircraft against the enemy trying to annihilate our troops in the Myskhako region disrupted his battle plans. The men on the bridgehead were greatly encouraged.'

The arrival of the Stavka air reserve swung the battle in the Soviets' favour. In the skies above the VVS tactical command post near the village of Abinskaya, Gen Vershinin saw an aircraft fall every 10 minutes. On certain days, up to a hundred air battles took place over the Kuban and the Germans were forced to retrench after Luftflotte 4 had lost 182 aircraft and the Soviets half that number. The number of German missions was halved on 21 and 22 April, and VVS aircrew were now able to bomb and strafe enemy troops more actively.[216] Vershinin reported delightedly that 'control of the air passed to our hands'.[217]

In the thick of it was often the elite 16th Guards Fighter Air Regt flying US-supplied P-39 Bell Airacobras. Grigori Rechkalov was born on 9 February 1920 near Yekaterinburg. He was taught to fly in the Sverdlovsk aero club and in 1939 he graduated from Military Air College. By the end of 1942 he had claimed four kills plus two shared victories in 20 combats. 16th Regt's Yak-1s were then replaced by P-39s that had been ferried across the Caucasus from Tehran. After converting at Baku, the Regt moved to Krasnodar in the spring of 1943 from where it operated over the North Caucasus Front alongside the 9th Guards Fighter Regt.

Rechkalov led a four-aircraft *zveno* in the *eskadrilya* commanded by Capt Alexander Pokryshkin and on the regiment's first mission with the P-39 on 9 April, he and Pokryshkin both claimed a Bf109. During April 1943, Rechkalov claimed seven Bf109s and one Ju88. On 24 May he was awarded the Gold Star of a Hero of the Soviet Union, and he was credited with 11 kills during the Kuban operations. Only in the spring of 1944, when Rechkalov was deputy commander of the 16th Guards Regt, was he removed from his post for the air power sins of 'losing control, indecisiveness and lack of initiative'. As for 'Sasha' Pokryshkin, who criticised Rechkalov for putting the pursuit of further personal victories ahead of proper leadership, he was credited with 20 kills over the Kuban. Pokryshkin's kill total rose to 48 (including several through ramming) while flying the Airacobra, and he was shot down four times. And his 'score' did not include aircraft downed during free hunts over German territory during the Kuban campaign because, at that time, the Soviet Command only confirmed aircraft destroyed over their own area.

Above:
A. I. Pokryshkin gets down from his P-39 Airacobra to receive the acclaim of his fellow pilots. *Author's collection*

Having seized the initiative, the Soviets launched their 56th Army at Krymskaya on 29 April, aiming to split the German Seventeenth Army groupings and drive to the Black Sea. Five radio stations had been set up near the front lines, three being in the 56th Army offensive zone, for guiding fighter aircraft and directing them during air battles. On the night before the offensive, 4th Air Army and ADD units flew 379 missions to drop 210 tons of bombs to soften up German positions. Saturation averaged 21 tons per sq km, and post-action reports noted that 'the daring women pilots of the 46th Guards Night Bomber Regt were especially active'.

Soviet women pilots were first organised into three combat regiments in October 1941 by the famous prewar long-distance flier, Marina Roskova. Of these, the 586th Fighter Air Regiment went into action flying Yak-7Bs during the battle for Stalingrad. Its squadron commander, Olga Yamshchikova, flew 93 sorties, had three confirmed kills and became the first Soviet women to fly a jet aircraft after the war. Valeriia Khomiakova was the first woman to shoot down an enemy aircraft at night when she destroyed a Ju88 over Saratov on 24 September 1942.[218]

The two female bomber regiments were designated guards units and the 46th arrived on the Southern Front in May 1942. Commanded by Maj Yevdokia Bershanskaya, the women flew their U-2s from the Kuban to Berlin, during which time they totted up 24,000 combat missions and dropped 23,000 tons of bombs from their hardy biplanes. The Ju87 crews of StG2's operational training Gruppe at Kerch-Bagerovo received nightly visits from the U-2s, which chiefly bombed the railway station, harbour and airfield. 'Our adversaries are not very skilled at night fighting; they evidently need much practice. They have an occasional stroke of luck every now and again. A bomb drops on an ammunition train standing in a siding and for hours explosives light up the night sky, the earth trembles from the detonations. Very soon these raids become part of our daily routine, and we generally stay in bed and sleep. Otherwise we feel the effect of lack of sleep on our own raids the following day.'[219]

Other women flew with men's units, including Lt Lydia Litvak who scored 12 kills in her year with the 73rd Fighter Air Regt before being shot down on 1 August 1943. But the fact that 23 U-2 pilots and navigators became Heroes of the Soviet Union explains why their opponents called these doughty Soviet women pilots the 'night witches'.

At 07.00hrs on 29 April, 4th Air Army launched a massive raid to coincide with the opening of 56th Army's ground offensive. For three hours, 144 bombers, 82 ground-attack aircraft and 265 fighters pounded Axis positions. By the end of the day, Soviet aircrews had flown 1,308 sorties and claimed 81 enemy aircraft. On 4 May the 56th Army 'liberated' the village of Krymskaya and advanced 10km over the following few days. It was dogged stuff. Three or four pairs of VVS fighters would arrive over the battlefield to check on the air situation. They would report back to the central radio controller and, around a quarter of an hour later, larger groups of bombers or ground-attackers with fighter escorts would pitch up over the target. If German AAA was not in evidence, they would make several attack runs.

Tank warfare was one area in which the Soviets excelled and during the winter of 1942-3, a number of tests were carried out

with Ju87 'Gustav' anti-tank aircraft at the Rechlin test and evaluation establishment in Mecklenburg. These Stukas had a 37mm anti-tank gun mounted under each wing which fired tungsten-hardened shells, and together with Ju88Ps fitted with a single 75mm gun under the pilot's cockpit, they formed an Anti-tank Air Command (*Panzerjagdkommando*) working to Obstlt Otto Wiess.

Ju87 Gustavs were deployed under Oberst Hans-Ulrich Rudel on their first combat assignment over the Kuban bridgehead. But the Ju87G and Ju88P were never to be great successes. Soviet philosophy was such that, in the event of a breakthrough, their tanks never advanced beyond the protection of their permanently installed, and therefore very strong, AAA defences. Which meant that when Rudel took on Soviet tanks that had penetrated German defences south of Krymskaya, Soviet AAA hit his Stuka while he was still over his own lines, and other aircraft in his unit fared no better. Rudel noted that the VVS were using an early model of the British Spitfire over the Kuban and it was indicative of the way in which German aircraft technology was falling behind that he felt the Spitfire performed well in combat against Luftwaffe aircraft.

From 29 April to 10 May the VVS 4th Air Army, Black Sea Fleet air units and ADD flew 12,000 sorties, over half of them against Axis troops and equipment on the battlefield. During this time, the Soviets fought 285 air battles, but the Germans managed to stop any further inroads. From 10-26 May, the ADD flew 152 sorties against Luftwaffe airfields in the Crimea.

The Kuban air battles marked a new phase for the Soviet air forces. The arrival of new high-speed interceptors at the front stimulated the development of new battle tactics. Ivan Kozhedub, the only Soviet fighter pilot beside Alexander Pokryshkin to be awarded the Gold Star of a Hero of the Soviet Union three times during World War 2, recalled that 'the famous formula of air-to-air combat was, *altitude-speed-manoeuvre-fire*. The fighter pilot gained altitude, converted it into speed by diving, and then used that speed to manoeuvre into a good firing position. A pair of fighters — a *para* — became the permanent combat tactical unit in fighter aviation, and two *para* made up a *zveno*. Squadron formations came to include several groups, each of which had its own tactical mission (assault, protection, AAA suppression or air defence). The massive use of aviation, its increasing influence on the course of combat and operations, required its concentration in those major specialties.'[220]

Altitude-speed-manoeuvre-fire sounds pretty straightforward but the main VVS task was to protect Soviet ground troops from enemy air attacks. The accepted tactic was to fly a combat circle over the area being protected, in part to give a psychological boost to the poor bloody infantry down below. But the Germans sent their Bf109s in first to clear the airspace for the following bombers and ground-attackers, which meant German fighter pilots coming down to shoot into the circling Soviet fighters.

Alexander Pokryshkin argued that Soviet air defenders should fly pendulum profiles over the battle area, converting between altitude and speed all the time. Ground-pounders would see their fighters only when they reached the lowest point, but the manoeuvre would be much more effective in other combat respects. Pokryshkin's squadron used the combat pendulum for the first time during the air battle over Krymskaya, and it met

Above:
Lieutenant of the Guards Akhmet Kankoshev, a Kabardinian from the Caucasus, at a camouflaged aircraft dispersal. Kankoshev was credited with bringing down five German aircraft during nine days of fighting over the Kuban. He was killed in action on 28 December 1943. *Author's collection*

by air commanders at forward posts at the front. Kuban air operations showed that control of the air depended on successful interaction between several air armies on a broad front, to deprive the Luftwaffe of the opportunity to manoeuvre air power freely.

Soviet air defenders did not get everything right over the Kuban. In their enthusiasm, they often concentrated on the fighters escorting the German bombers, which left those bombers free to strike their targets with little interference. But growing co-ordination between aircraft and ground command posts enabled Soviet fighters to respond to urgent requests for air support more effectively, and kept VVS aircraft clear of their own AAA batteries. Once enemy bombers entered an anti-aircraft zone, VVS fighters withdrew and flew parallel flight paths.

The 'Kuban escalator' or 'Kuban bookshelf' was another development designed to improve the effectiveness of the Soviet air umbrella. Following on from Pokryshkin's emphasis on altitude and mutual support, the 'escalator' had VVS fighters staggered in pairs, with each patrol separated vertically by some 1,000m, to allow larger formations to fly attack and escort roles. This staggered arrangement, with the lower patrols extended forward, conferred greater all-round coverage, defensive firepower and operational flexibility. 'Each shelf of the bookcase fulfilled its own distinct role,' recalled Gen Vershinin. 'Where enemy aircraft were successful in escaping the attack of one shelf of the bookcase, they immediately came under another's fire.' When set alongside growing VVS numbers, which would soon provide one escort fighter per ground-attack aircraft, and an expanding technological capability, tactical innovations such as the 'Kuban escalator' marked an important shift in the war. Although impossible to confirm, Ivan Kozhedub was convinced that the air support lessons learned over the Kuban would eventually ensure that 'out of all the aircraft lost by Germany on the Soviet-German front, 90% were downed by fighters.'

The Soviet 4th Air Army had an operational strength of 924 aircraft at the start of the final Kuban air phase on 26 May, compared to Luftflotte 4's 700. But this was now more than just a matter of raw numbers. Part of the Stavka's purpose in putting pressure on the Kuban was to force the Luftwaffe to sacrifice its air assets fighting for a strategically peripheral piece of real estate. Soviet action throughout May compelled the Luftwaffe to average some 400 sorties every 24 hours at a time when the Luftwaffe should have been resting and recuperating for Hitler's summer offensive.

Besides supporting the Kuban sector, Luftflotte 4 reverted to its 'proper' mission of interdicting Soviet military forces and logistics, including communications routes and feeder lines. A number of successful strikes were carried out against industrial targets in Saratov and Kamyshin, and shipping (including mine laying) on the Volga as far as Astrakhan and the Caspian, while continuous and increasingly heavy bomber attacks were made against Soviet trains, rail installations, bridges and depots to hinder the forward movements of Soviet supplies and troops. Once the early thaw turned all main and secondary roads into quagmires, particular emphasis was placed in interdicting Soviet railways, which were often the only reliable means of bringing up reserves and supplies. For these attacks, the Ju88s of 9./KG3, and the He111s of 14./KG27 and 9./KG55 were converted into specialist rail interdiction *Eisenbahn* (Railway) Staffeln.

with great success. Gen Vershinin acknowledged that Pokryshkin's practical, hard-nosed approach prevailed. The new tactics were disseminated widely, partly through the army newspaper *Red Star* and by experienced fighters pilots, including Pokryshkin and Rechkalov, briefing at numerous tactical seminars. 'This was not done without heated quarrels,' recalled Vershinin. 'Sometimes one or other tactical method was tested in the air, but finally a single idea was worked out. We accepted many useful recommendations which were later codified and accepted by all air organisations.'[221]

As the scale of air battles increased, Soviet fighter pilots became adept at complicated vertical manoeuvres and multi-layered formations. This was vital in supporting Novikov's concept of the 'air offensive'. His ground-attack aircraft learned to operate in close co-operation with ground forces, and strikes by groups of 50-60 aircraft were found to have a formidable piercing and crushing effect on enemy defences and troop concentrations. In the subsequent command conference analysing the results of the Kuban fighting, Novikov stressed the vital importance of operational air supremacy, the 'air offensive' and the effectiveness of radio control

Formed on 1 June 1943 at Dnepropetrovsk from parts of 9.(Eis)/KG55, which had been trainbusting with Ju88C-6s fitted with cannon since February 1943, 14.(Eis)/KG55 was an autonomous outfit flying with both Ju88C-6s and He111H-16s. The latter were fitted with six forward-firing 20mm cannon, and an electronic altimeter that allowed the crew to fly down to 20m above the tracks. In over 5,000 hairy missions, the Staffel lost nine crews. And while these units were committed regularly against Soviet rail traffic, powerful concentrations of their bomber colleagues went for the larger rail installations and junctions. Luftflotte 4 operations against rail and air installations continued until the end of June but although these attacks achieved considerable local success, the forces available to the Luftwaffe in Combat Zone South were too weak to completely destroy or interrupt for any considerable period enemy rail, road or air activity.

Although fighting was concentrated in southern Russia, combat was taking place elsewhere on the Eastern Front. The battle around the town of Velikiye Luki on the road to Moscow from 25 November 1942 to 15 January 1943 was a case in point. Soviet forces had isolated 7,000 Axis troops in Velikiye Luki, and by the time 15 officers and 87 men were brought out on 16 January, supporting Luftwaffe units had lost 55 aircraft destroyed (including three Ju87s, eight Bf109s and 20 He111s) and 26 aircraft damaged on sacrificial air supply and attack missions.

On the opening day of 'Barbarossa', the Luftwaffe had 2,815 operationally ready (*einsatzbereit*) aircraft in the East. Just before Stalingrad fell, that figure stood at 989, of which 479 were Ju52 transports. It was a measure of the recuperative powers of the Luftwaffe and its personnel that the German air presence in the East had built back up to 3,415 *einsatzbereit* aircraft by 31 May 1943, which was just over half of the entire air force.[222]

However, although the Luftwaffe in the East was still a force to be reckoned with, from November 1942 it had been continuously employed in a vain attempt to avert disaster at Stalingrad and then one Luftflotte after another had to give up aircraft to boost Luftflotte 4. The effects on Luftwaffe dispositions in Russia were clear.[223]

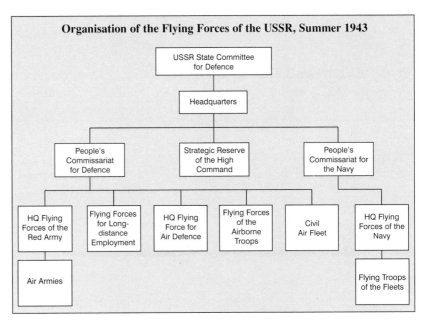

Organisation of the Flying Forces of the USSR, Summer 1943

	Mid-October 1942	Early December 1942	Mid-January 1943
Leningrad Front	485	270	195
Moscow Front	425	480	380
Don Front	545	700	900
Caucasus and Crimea	495	330	240

In February 1943, approximately 950 out of some 1,800 German first-line operational aircraft based in Russia from Murmansk downwards were concentrated in the Don-Donets sector. More disturbingly, the majority of aircraft left around Leningrad, Moscow and in the Caucasus were army co-operation and reconnaissance types, of little use for serious strike work. In certain sectors, German air cover was virtually suspended — when the Red Army advanced across the Elista Steppes south of the Lower Volga, only a few Luftwaffe long-range reconnaissance aircraft were available on a front stretching over 300km. The lack of a meaningful German close-support capability on the exposed northern flank of the Stalingrad salient allowed the Soviets to advance rapidly to Voronezh and beyond.

This imbalance also seriously disrupted the organisation of the German Air Force. There were now seven HQ Staffs from Velikiye Luki southwards, of which the majority were short-term creations that had sprung up in response to immediate and tactical requirements. Notwithstanding the vision of a Luftwaffe bomber command, there was now even less time for strategic air power thinking. After Stalingrad, all air planning efforts were concentrated, under local control, on the day-to-day task of hampering and stemming any Soviet advances so far as local air resources permitted. This resulted in the nonsense of von Richthofen's beloved Fliegerkorps VIII, hitherto the spearhead of every major German offensive, being pulled out of operations and placed in tactical control of *air supply*, first of the Sixth Army, and then of the Kuban bridgehead.

And much of this steady and wearing attritional pressure on Luftwaffe organisation and capabilities was so pointless. After an air campaign during which the Soviets flew around 35,000 sorties and claimed the destruction of 1,100 German aircraft, 900 of them in air-to-air combat, in early September 1943 the OKW decided to abandon what remained of the 'Goth's Head' and withdraw Seventeenth Army across the Strait of Kerch into the Crimea. The covering fire deployed by 9th Flak Div on both sides of the Strait to protect the evacuation from greatly superior Soviet air power paralleled the superb German evacuation from Sicily across the Strait of Messina a few weeks earlier. From now on there would be more such 'Dunkirk' victories as the VVS got stronger and wiser, and the lack of Luftwaffe forward planning and numbers started to tell.

FROM KURSK TO KIEV

'The future battle on the ground will be preceded by battle in the air. This will determine which of the contestants has to suffer operational and tactical disadvantages, and be forced throughout the battle into adopting compromise solutions.'
Gen Erwin Rommel

On 1 March 1943, over 250 four-engined RAF bombers dropped 600 tons of bombs on Berlin. Five hundred big fires ranged out of control, 20,000 homes were damaged, 35,000 people were rendered homeless and 700 civilians were killed. The following day, a photo-reconnaissance Mosquito circled high over Hitler's capital taking damage assessment photographs in broad daylight. Neither German fighters nor flak could touch it.

Field Marshal Erhard Milch knew that the Luftwaffe was saddled with a disparate assortment of aircraft designs, many of which had been overtaken by the changing nature of modern air warfare. And the good ideas that were around were often negated by poor application. For example, at Rechlin in the summer of 1939 Hitler had seen the Hs129 tank-killer easily pierce 80mm of armour plate with its 30mm cannon shells. But such was the unfocused and inept nature of Luftwaffe procurement that, notwithstanding the awesome nature of Soviet tank production, the Hs129's 30mm cannon would not enter production until mid-1943.

On 5 March 1943 as RAF Bomber Command launched the Battle of the Ruhr, Milch dined alone with Hitler. Milch's argument to his Führer was straightforward. Germany must now go on the defensive, conserving strength for a resumption of the offensive in 1944 if need be but at all costs overhauling defence procurement and leadership to keep the home base secure. The subtext was that Hitler should make peace but failing that, Göring should hand over the Luftwaffe to a professional airman, not least

because Milch could not fault Soviet wartime leadership.[224]

After Stalingrad, Hitler should have realised that the Soviets had learned enough from their opponents now to plan, organise and conceal an operation involving over a million men, to handle mobile armoured units, co-ordinate air-land operations, mass artillery and run a sophisticated, real-time communications network. And with Stalin effectively handing over the operational running of the war to Marshal Zhukov and Air Marshal Novikov, Hitler should at least have made von Manstein C-in-C in the East.

But Hitler probably felt that only he could stiffen the will of his generals to achieve another great victory, both to avenge Stalingrad and to crush the Red Army before it completely surpassed the Wehrmacht in size and quality. The obvious objective was the Soviet-held Kursk salient, some 200km wide and 150km deep, which ran from just south of Orel in the north, bulged westward into the German line around the city of Kursk before curving back east to end up around Belgorod. This bulge not only severed Army Group Centre's rail link with Kharkov but also forced the Wehrmacht to deploy considerable forces to seal it off in the north, west and south.

Codenamed Operation 'Zitadelle' ('Citadel'), the plan envisaged forces from south of Orel and north of Kharkov converging on Kursk to pinch off the salient. The attack was scheduled for the end of the mud season, while the Soviets were still off balance after Kharkov, to encircle another mass of Soviet troops as per the heady days of 1941. But space and numbers had greatly altered German perspectives over two years. In 1941, German armies had attacked over a 1,600km front with the aim of toppling the Soviet Union. In 1942, the drive on Stalingrad and the Caucasus had been along a 570km front aiming for a far-flung objective. In 1943, with Luftwaffe power in the East down to two-thirds of that employed in 'Blue', the 'Citadel' frontage was just under 200km against an objective less than 150km away.

Gen Hoth's Fourth Panzer Army, supported by Luftflotte 4, was tasked with breaking through to Kursk from the south to meet up with Gen Walter Model's Ninth Army coming down from the north with the help of Luftflotte 6. Back on 1 April 1942, Fliegerkorps V had become *Luftwaffenkommando Ost* at Smolensk with responsibility for Fliegerkorps VIII's area when it moved south. Some believed that Luftwaffe Command East had been set up only to confer an organisation of appropriate status on Gen Robert Ritter von Greim, but it was renamed Luftflotte 6 on 11 May 1943 and given responsibility for the sector between Smolensk and Orel.

For 'Citadel', the Germans brought together 900,000 men, about 10,000 guns and mortars, and 2,700 tanks and self-propelled guns. To strengthen Luftflotten 4 and 6, 13 Gruppen were brought in from Germany, France and Norway after 15 March. Eventually, 17 Geschwadern were based near Kursk, which when supplemented by over 200 bombers based at Smolensk, Stalino, Zaporozhe and Kirovograd, meant that the two Air Fleets could call on 1,200 bombers, 600 fighters, 100 ground-attack and 150 reconnaissance aircraft. This left Luftflotte 1 in the north with just one Gruppe each of bombers, fighter-bombers and light night bombers. In the Arctic, Luftflotte 5 could still draw on KG30, JG5 and I./StG5, but the Black Sea area had to rely on Romanian air force units and a much-reduced Fliegerkorps I.

Early in April, two Ju88s photographed some 12,000sq km of the Soviet bulge at Kursk from 17,000ft, the largest tract ever taken in a single sweep by the Staffel. On 22 April Soviet bombers attacked the strategic reconnaissance bases at Orsha and Orsha-South, destroying the Ju88s of the 4.(F)/121 and 1.(F)/100. This left 4.(F)/14 as the only strategic recce unit available to Army Group Centre.

Attacking the Kursk salient was as obvious to the Soviets as it was appealing to the Germans. Based on intelligence including British *Ultra* intercepts passed on to Moscow, Marshal Zhukov briefed the Stavka on the exact nature of the two-prong German movement to envelop Kursk as early as 8 April. Stalin and his more punchy front commanders argued for pre-emptive action against massing German formations, but Zhukov prevailed in his belief that they should wait until the Germans exhausted themselves against stubborn and active Red Army defences before launching a massive counter-offensive to crush the panzer groups.

The Stavka tasked the military and 300,000 local civilians with laying a massive array of dug-in tanks and guns, anti-tank strongpoints, ditches and traps and other defensive positions on both shoulders of the salient. Huge minefields were laid specifically to channel the panzers towards the anti-tank defences where it was hoped German armour would burn itself out trying to break through. And behind no fewer than eight defensive lines, Marshal Zhukov created a new Steppe Front 100km back, wherein he placed the full weight of Gen Pavel Rotmistrov's 5th Guards Tank Army, supported by the 5th Air Army.

Looking to the two threat axes, Marshal Novikov tasked Gen Rudenko's 16th Air Army with countering advancing Germans from Orel to Kursk (the Central Front), and the Voronezh Front's 2nd Air Army plus part of the neighbouring Southwestern Front's 17th Air Army to cope with the thrust from Belgorod-Kursk. ADD bomber forces were expected to operate along both axes at night, and two PVO fighter divisions were responsible for air defence of airfields. The Germans had lost any element of surprise — a report sent to Stalin in the second week of May proclaimed that 'the 16th Air Army has intensified aerial reconnaissance and is keeping the enemy under vigilant observation. Air formations and army units are alerted to repulse enemy air attacks and frustrate possible enemy offensive action.'

Hitler's 'Citadel' Directive of 15 April promised that 'the best units, the best weapons, the best commanders, and large quantities of ammunition shall be committed to the area of main effort.' The offensive was to have started on 4 May but Hitler postponed it to 12 June and then to 5 July because he wanted to reinforce his panzer forces with the latest 40-ton 'Panther' and 60-ton 'Tiger' tanks. His army commanders argued that such delays only

favoured the Soviets, and Hans Jeschonnek confirmed during a conference in Munich on 4 May that postponement offered the Luftwaffe no advantages whatsoever. It was at this stage that Hitler should have halted 'Citadel' and gone over to the defensive for the rest of the year. Heinz Guderian, now Inspector-General for Armoured Troops, spoke for all thinking German military men when he asked Hitler: 'was it really necessary to attack Kursk, and indeed in the East that year at all? Do you think anyone even knows where Kursk is?'

In the breathing space given to them, the engineering battalions of 2nd and 16th Air Armies built or renovated 154 airfields, many of them camouflaged, 'with the help of the local population'. The VVS also built 50 dummy airfields, which were so realistic that of 35 Luftwaffe raids against VVS airfields in June, 29 were made against the dummies and some were attacked several times. In 2nd Air Army's area, 18 ground-attack aircraft and 18 fighters were kept at 30min dawn-to-dusk readiness for operations against Axis personnel and equipment. These 36 aircraft could be launched only on the direct orders of the Air Army commander.

On 12 June, Hitler sent von Richthofen to command Luftflotte 2 in the Mediterranean following the Axis surrender in North Africa. Manstein protested about the breaking up of his double act so close to 'Citadel', but in vain. 'My efforts to secure the return of von Richthofen to command the Fourth Air Fleet failed, and led only to a sharp controversy with Göring, who was unwilling to admit how decisively important the influence of a personality such as von Richthofen was for the combat forces.'[225] Gen Otto Dessloch took over the Luftflotte 4 command post at Dnepropetrovsk but Oberst Schulz, Richthofen's Chief of Staff, stayed on to provide continuity in the conduct of air operations.

German intentions became even more obvious when Fliegerkorps VIII, with its long experience in close-support operations, was moved from the Crimea to assume operational command in the Kharkov-Belgorod sector. Gen Hans Seidemann, who had been too young to see World War 1 service but had held a succession of operational chief of staff posts since the Condor Legion in 1939, now commanded Fliegerkorps VIII. From his HQ at Mikoyanovka, some 27km south of Belgorod, Seidemann had the following complement of around 1,100 aircraft:

- strategic reconnaissance Ju88s of 4.(F)/14
- eight Bf109 and Fw189 tactical reconnaissance Staffeln
- six Bf109G fighter Gruppen of JG3 and JG52
- two Ju88A and six He111H bomber Gruppen of KG3, KG27 and KG55
- six Ju87D dive-bomber Gruppen of StG2 and StG77
- two Hs123A and Fw190A fighter-bomber Gruppen of SchG1
- four Hs129B and one Ju87G anti-tank Staffeln
- one night harassing bomber Gruppe with old biplanes
- one Ju88 strat recce sqn, one Fw189 tac recce sqn, one Bf109 fighter sqn, one Ju87 dive-bomber sqn and one Ju88 bomber sqn of the Hungarian Air Division

In the north, Gen Paul Deichmann's *1.Flieger-Division* (1st Air Div), with its command post near Orel airfield, was responsible for Luftflotte 6 combat air operations. At the end of June, 1st Air Div had 730 aircraft, consisting of three tactical recce units (one each for Second and Ninth Armies, and Second Panzer Army), plus the following units based at airfields in the Orel-Bryansk-Shatalovka area:

- six Fw190A fighter Gruppen with JG51 and JG54
- I/ZG1 Bf110F fighter-bomber Gruppe, incl 12./ZG1 night fighters
- three Ju88A and four He111H bomber Gruppen with KG1, KG4, KG51 and KG53
- three Ju87D dive-bomber Gruppen with StG1
- one Staffel each of anti-tank Hs129B, Ju87G and Bf110G
- one night harassing bomber Gruppe with old biplanes

On the credit side, German bomber numbers had appreciably increased, and newly formed ground-attack (*Schlacht*) units equipped with Fw190 fighter-bombers and Hs129s were now in the field. On the debit side, total Luftwaffe single-engined fighter strength stood at 1,800, of which some 800 were defending the Reich and the European coast from Norway to the Bay of Biscay. Another 400 were employed in the Mediterranean, which left no more than 600 over the Russian front. This was little more than had been in the East a year earlier, but the Germans had been

Below:
The battle of Kursk and its aftermath.

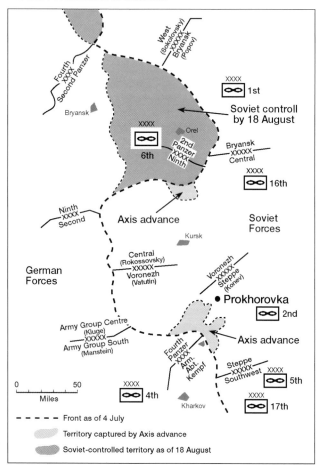

forced on the defensive since July 1942, and Soviet air strength had grown both in quantity and quality.

Up to the summer of 1942, the German pilot training programme had been run on peacetime lines, with dancing classes on the syllabus. Fuel shortages and front-line demands reduced training hours but after a revamp in 1943, the Luftwaffe doubled the number of new fighter pilots passing out of the training system. However, as the British, Russians and Americans were doing much better, German output barely kept up with losses.[226] One solution was to equip Romanian and Hungarian air forces with modern German aircraft. While the operational value and efficiency of some satellite units was doubtful, they were adequate for defensive operations on static sectors of the front. Their employment certainly released Luftwaffe flying units to escort and spearhead German land attacks.

In the run-up to 'Citadel', Luftflotte 6 frequently took control of bomber forces from Luftflotten 1 and 4 to launch big wing attacks on the tank works at Gorky, 400km east of Moscow. State Motor Vehicle Plant No 1 Molotov, known as the 'Soviet Detroit' after being built with US assistance between 1927-32, turned out around 60% of total Soviet light tank output. This largest automotive plant in the USSR was the aiming point for 420 bombers that dropped 636 tons of bombs on successive nights during 5-8 June.[227] Gorky was attacked again, along with the synthetic rubber factory and asbestos works at Yaroslavl (240km northeast of Moscow), the petroleum refinery and ball bearing industry at Saratov (640km east of Orel) and oil depots at Astrakhan at the mouth of the Volga, almost nightly during the second and third weeks of June. Intended as major blows to the Soviet war machine immediately prior to 'Citadel', these raids were reinforced by sustained smaller-scale attacks on Soviet airfields and rail communications immediately behind the front line between Orel and Kursk.

As German bombers struck industrial targets, the Soviets countered with night attacks against German airfields, communications centres and depots crowded with supplies for the upcoming offensive. Strong Soviet groups flew repeatedly into the Orel and Kharkov areas, and since Luftflotte 6's night fighter *Schwarm* was down to just three operational aircraft, it was able to down only a few from the many Soviet aircraft that penetrated German airspace. On 26 June the Chief of the Luftwaffe Night Fighter Arm, Gen Josef Kammhuber, was ordered to transfer a regular night fighter Gruppe east. The only available formation was Hptm Prince zu Sayn-Wittgenstein's IV./NJG5, which had already gained experience in fighting Soviet bombers, and it moved to airfields at Bryansk and Orel at the end of June. Divided into several *Schwärme*, IV./NJG5's operations were controlled by one *Freya* early warning and two *Würzburg* ground control radars mounted on a railway train.

From 25 June, Luftwaffe missions flown over the Central and Voronezh Fronts were reduced by 75%. Maintenance of surprise and deception prior to 'Citadel' were paramount, with no fewer than 300 Luftwaffe aircraft only deploying forward into Luftflotte 4's sector between 17.00 and 18.30hrs on 4 July. But the Luftwaffe was becoming seriously short of aviation fuel. Luftflotte 6 received only 5,722 tons of 91-octane B-4 bomber and general-purpose aviation fuel in June 1943, as against a total consumption of 8,634 tons, and only 441 tons of higher performance C-3 fuel, so necessary for its Fw190s, against a total consumption of 1,079 tons.[228]

Enough ammunition was stored at each Fliegerkorps VIII airfield for 10 missions, and bombs for 15 days of major battle at each 1st Air Div base. But an already serious rail transport situation was worsened by steadily increasing partisan sabotage attacks against the few available Axis supply routes. Encouraged by the Stavka, partisan action peaked in June 1943 with 841 separate acts of sabotage, destroying or damaging 298 locomotives, 1,222 railway wagons, and 44 bridges in Combat Zone Centre alone. The partisans stopped rail movements at an average of 24 points daily, which rendered any parallel VVS interdiction effort superfluous. In 1943, the Stavka estimated that half a million Axis auxiliary troops and 25 active divisions were tied down on anti-partisan activities.[229] Given that German supply lines ran through areas with no great love for the communist regime back in 1941, to have alienated the local population to the extent the Germans did by their cruelty and arrogance was the height of strategic irresponsibility. No air war can be won without secure bases or logistic lifelines.

As Stalin was willing to stake everything on the outcome of the battle, the Soviet force outnumbered the attackers by about 2.5 to 1 in men and exceeded the Germans in tanks and guns.[230] Relative air dispositions were as follows:[231]

	16th, 2nd, 17th Air Armies operational (unserviceable)	Luftflotten 4 and 6
Fighters	1,007 (199)	600
Ground attack	756 (78)	100
Bombers	676 (52)	1,000
Recce	14 (10)	150
Totals	2,453 (339)	1,850

While the Luftwaffe had a preponderance of bombers, the VVS had a marked superiority in ground-attack aircraft and nearly twice the number of fighters. In the first 24 hours of the operation, the Luftwaffe flew 4,239 combat sorties as against 3,157 by the VVS.[232] Most 'Citadel' air activity took place over the two lines of advance, and on 5 July over 4,300 German and Soviet aircraft operated in these narrow front sectors covering no more than 100km.

1st Air Div bombers took off on their first 'Citadel' attack missions at 03.30hrs on 5 July. While Fliegerkorps VIII bombers were getting airborne further south, reports came in from the aircraft warning listening service and *Freya* radar units that very powerful Soviet air formations comprising 417 aircraft were approaching German airfields, especially around Kharkov. All German fighters at Kharkov and southwest of Belgorod took off immediately, not to escort the bombers as planned but to go for the incoming Soviet formations. The Bf109s came out of the greyish haze of the early dawn and enjoyed a turkey shoot. Too many Soviet aircrews were still inflexible in their tactics, sticking rigidly to their set course long after it was suicidal.

Marshal Zhukov was unimpressed by the initial Soviet counter-air operation. 'Air force participation [the night before] was negligible and, putting it bluntly, ineffective, while dawn strikes at enemy airfields failed to accomplish their purpose, as by that time the enemy already had his aircraft up to support ground troops.'[233] While 16th Air Army had over 1,000 serviceable aircraft, only 520 sorties were flown before noon on 5 July. That evening, Stalin asked Marshal Konstantin Rokossovsky: 'Have we gained command of the air?' The Central Front commander's response was a gem: 'Fierce air battles are going on with alternating success.' Stalin directed that no effort be spared to gain control of the air.[234]

The Luftwaffe gave almost full support to the ground assault on the first day, with dive-bombers flying five to six missions in the fine summer weather. As Ninth Army advanced from the north, 1st Air Div close support aircraft repeatedly hit opposing Soviet artillery concentrations while its bombers attacked crowded VVS airfields around Kursk. From 04.25 to 11.00hrs over the Orel-Kursk axis, the Soviets recorded as many as 1,000 German sorties of which around 800 were flown by bombers.

Just ahead of Fourth Panzer Army driving from the south towards Oboyan, Fliegerkorps VIII's ground-attackers and dive-bombers hit Soviet batteries, pockets of resistance and reserves while its bombers attacked targets immediately behind the Soviet front. At 14.45hrs on 5 July, five Stuka Gruppen spent a concentrated 10 minutes 'shaping' an area 3km long and 500m deep. For all their superiority in fighter numbers, the Soviets admitted that 'our aviation… did not have air superiority over the enemy's main attack axis — the Belgorod-Oboyan Highway — until 10 July.'[235]

The VVS learned during the first days of Kursk that air superiority meant more than having the largest number of fighters. Waiting passively for the enemy to appear was not good enough — as the Soviet post-action report concluded: 'Aviation must shift its operations to enemy territory and, while there, extensively employ the method of free search, destruction and blockading of aircraft at airfields.'[236] If large numbers of fighters cleared the battle space, bombers and assault aircraft would only need a small number of fighter escorts. On 6 July, 16th Air Army laid on a massive fighter sweep to disperse and tie up German fighter forces so that Soviet ground-attack and bomber aircraft could have a relatively clear run at the German Ninth Army. As Gen Rudenko noted with some relief, these operations were 'more orderly . . . with more purpose'.[237]

The Soviets had developed their own mobile early warning radar, and a derivative for tactical air control. Once these were co-ordinated with the burgeoning radio control net, the VVS quartet of aircraft that would epitomise Soviet tactical air power started to play on song over Kursk. The Yakovlev and Lavochkin family of fighters provided air defence cover. The clean, low-wing Yak family of fighters were lightweight, fast and highly manoeuvrable machines capable of holding their own with later Bf109s and Fw190s, but they also mutated into bomber and anti-tank variants. Both the Yak-9 and the LaGG-5 and LaGG-7 were true swing-role aircraft.

Yakovlev and Lavochkin fighters flew escort missions for the two most important Soviet ground-attack aircraft — the Il-2

Above:
Pe-2s on their way to do battle in 1943. *Author's collection*

Shturmovik and the Pe-2 dive-bomber. Six eight-ship *gruppa* of Il-2s running in at up to 292mph between 10m and 50m were known to German soldiery as *der Schwarzer Tod* — the Black Death. The two-seat Il-2m3, which appeared just in time for Kursk, could dispense 37mm cannon for tank-busting plus 132mm rockets, a 600kg (1,323lb) bomb load and up to 200 PTAB hollow-charge anti-armour bombs, while the aircrew sat in an armour-plated forward fuselage that was invulnerable to anything less than a 20mm shell. The twin-engined Pe-2 was the Soviet equivalent of the Mosquito. It served as a long-range escort fighter but with a rugged 11'g' limit, it could dive-bomb and attack at low level with more agility than the heavily armoured Il-2.

These four types were every bit as good as their German counterparts, and they made up a significant proportion of the 8,300 aircraft in the VVS inventory in mid-1943.

Hitler continued to believe that the Soviets were on their last legs, whereas the German fighting man's impression was that the Russians were always able to make up their losses by committing reserves and flying in new aircraft and replacement personnel. On 5 July, 1,958 German aircraft operated over the 20-60km Belgorod-Kursk area but within 24 hours the daily combat sortie total had dropped to 899. Notwithstanding the need to interdict Soviet rear rail links to isolate the battlefield as had been done around Kiev in 1941, there were insufficient Luftwaffe aircraft available for such missions. The Luftwaffe supply system could not keep pace with the required aircraft rate.

As the Luftwaffe became overstretched, Soviet combat rates increased steadily and VVS formations penetrated up to 25km behind German lines to attack supply routes and airfields. German fighter crews could still assert local air superiority and even air supremacy over their VVS counterparts, but they were often redeployed for air defence in the rear. This left German ground troops increasingly exposed to VVS attack especially, as one German commander noted: 'powerful Russian flying formations were in the air at all times'.[238] The Luftflotte 4 war diary subsequently admitted that Soviet airmen had learned a lot in the past years of warfare, and had come a long way from their primitive condition of 1941. 'The performances of some hostile air units, especially among the ground-attack forces, were commendable.'[239]

Soviet engineers had transformed the heavily forested terrain, dissected in many places by numerous gorges, into one gigantic field of fortifications. As a result, German forces attacking from north and south made slow progress in spite of strong air support. On the afternoon of 8 July, the Red Army launched an attack deep into the right flank of the Fourth Panzer Army from the vast forests. Fliegerkorps VIII had been expecting this. It had ordered constant air surveillance of the area and had put all available dive-bomber and anti-tank air units on readiness to go into action at short notice. Even before Fourth Panzer Army HQ knew what was happening, Fliegerkorps VIII units were on their way to counter the oncoming Soviets.

StabIV./SG9 was the *Führer der Panzerjäger's* anti-tank Gruppe, and its Hs129Bs were launched from Mikoyanovka to attack a Soviet tank brigade with mounted infantry, which had crossed the Donets River and the Belgorod-Kursk railway line on a broad front. The armoured brigade was sighted west of Belgorod and under the overall command of Hptm Bruno Meyer the four Hs129B Staffeln, each with 16 aircraft, attacked from astern and abeam in relays. As one Staffel attacked, another was en route to the target, a third was refuelling and the fourth was returning to base after attacking to replenish for the next wave. The Soviet brigade scattered, the bulk of its tanks destroyed while accompanying infantry were laid low by anti-personnel bombs dropped from Fw190s.

But this success could not mask the fact that Luftwaffe units were now being shuttled from point to point along the front, denying ground troops the continuous and potent air support they had been used to. Obstlt Paul-Werner Hozzel, former Kommodore of StG2, recalled that from Kursk onwards 'we could not break the Russian front, it was too heavy, too massive, too deeply entrenched.' A whole Geschwader could no longer be brought to bear as an entity because its Gruppen were forever being sent to firefight hither and yon.

As early as the afternoon of 7 July, Fliegerkorps VIII was directed to surrender KG3, JG3 and SG3 — 30% of its bomber force, 40% of its fighters and half its ground-attack strength — into the Orel sector to help Ninth Army which was getting bogged down. In responding to panicky army pleas for air support, the OKL negated Fliegerkorps VIII's careful preparations for 'massive concentration' which, then as now, is a fundamental tenet of the successful employment of air power.

With the balance now weighted on their side, Il-2s and Pe-2s began to achieve successes that were way beyond a handful of Panzerjäger Staffeln. The Soviets made great use of joint air-ground command posts from division up to 'front'. Air and ground liaison officers working side by side would receive information, filter requests, check availability and pass requests for air support. To save time, all radio communications were done in 'clear' so that everyone knew what was afoot. This 'open' system allowed the Germans to intercept launch orders for attack missions, vector Luftwaffe fighters in and forewarn their ground troops, but it was very successful in focusing mass quickly.

No later than 10 minutes before an attack, Soviet artillery would be told to deconflict their fire with approaching *Shturmovik* and Pe-2 formation strikes. If German AAA was light, the aircraft would fly on the deck; otherwise, they would fly in between 800m and 1,100m. The Il-2s would move into a circle, 500m between each aircraft. With the formation leader starting off, the circle

Above:
'Chocks away' on an Il-2
in camouflaged dispersal.
IWM

Left:
Oblt Diekwisch's view
from his Orel-based
Stuka of 9./StG1 hitting
Soviet tanks at Kursk,
July 1943.
Goss/Rauchbach Archive

would continue as one aircraft pulled off target, one aircraft attacked and another rolled in to attack, until they were all fired out. Some *Shturmovik* attacks would involve 36 aircraft, with one portion of the team suppressing German anti-aircraft batteries. It was not uncommon to have multiple circles in place, some just formed, some in progress and some peeling off to return to base. In among the bombs and cannon shells, VVS aircraft could fire some pretty mean air-to-ground rockets. *Shturmovik* and Pe-2 attacks brought daylight movement of German troops to a standstill and in the words of one German officer, the cluster bombs they dropped 'would fall within a radius of 100m to such a dense pattern that no living object within the effective beaten zone could escape the splinters. The bombs fell into even the narrowest trenches and, because of their great fragmentation, were very dangerous and greatly feared.'[240] One *Shturmovik* attack on 7 July accounted for 70 tanks out of one German tank division, while four hours of another Il-2 strike destroyed around 240 tanks out of 300.

By 11 July, 16th Air Army had flown over 7,600 sorties against the German advance from Orel, supported by some 800 long-range ADD bomber missions. The official history recorded that during this defensive phase: 'Soviet fliers destroyed 517 fascist aircraft, captured control of the air, and gave great help to our ground forces in their efforts to break the enemy offensive.'[241] Both sides over-exaggerated their kill rates, but the Germans suffered most from close air support losses, declining unit serviceability and increasingly alarming fuel shortages. The Luftwaffe had to exercise very tight control over all of its forces to ensure meaningful concentrations in the decisive sectors.

The leading German assault units — Fourth Panzer Army in the south and the Ninth Army in the north — were still 100km apart when the Soviets opened their decisive offensive on 11 July against the projecting Orel bulge. The VVS recorded 477 missions that day as against 691 by Luftflotte 6, but the Soviets had vastly superior ground forces and by the Germans' own accounts, VVS aircrews operated over the front at will. Soviet armies cracked through the thinly manned defences of the Second Panzer Army east of Zhizdra, and, heavily supported by tanks and ground-attack aircraft, rapidly gained ground. A rerun of Stalingrad loomed ominously large and within a matter of hours, the main emphasis had shifted from Ninth Army's offensive to the defensive positions of Second Panzer Army.

Luftflotte 6, reinforced by Fliegerkorps VIII fighter, dive-bomber and anti-tank units, committed all available forces in the hope of halting or at least slowing down the Soviet advance, pending arrival of German ground reserves. This shift of air emphasis northwards weakened the counter to 2nd Air Army around Belgorod, but every aircraft was needed continuously to bomb and strafe all visible Soviet forces and the forested areas where they were suspected of hiding. 1st Air Div repeatedly struck Soviet railheads around Sukhinichi and attacked rail installations and trains along the Kozelsk and Kaluga areas to interrupt the forward flow of supplies and reinforcements. However, they had little impact owing to limited aircraft numbers and adverse weather that temporarily halted all flying operations.

For two whole days, the Luftwaffe alone denied Soviet armoured units access to the Bryansk-Orel railway, keeping the route open until the first Wehrmacht ground reinforcements arrived. By its dashing and annihilating anti-tank attacks, the Luftwaffe destroyed most of the enemy tanks that had broken through and were directly threatening the Orel-Karachev rail and road routes. A Soviet armoured brigade reached the railway line but it was eliminated before consolidating its position, an achievement Gen Model acknowledged by signal: 'For the first time in military history the Luftwaffe has succeeded, without support by ground forces, in annihilating a tank brigade which had broken through.'

In the southern sector, having failed to reach Kursk by the direct Oboyan route, the Germans regrouped before trying to punch northeast through the Soviet lines at Prokhorovka. Prokhorovka is a small land bridge between the Psel and the Don, leading to open country beyond, but the Stavka had moved up the 5th Guards Tank Army and 5th Air Army to meet the panzers. The Battle of Kursk has come to be represented by the head-to-head battle at Prokhorovka, where in excess of 1,200 German and Soviet tanks clashed in the largest armoured battle of all time. Over half the armour was destroyed in barely 24 hours.

German air liaison officers were unable to participate to any great degree because their command vehicles could not keep up, but that did not stop a furious air battle raging overhead. 'Although enemy air resistance was still quite strong,' recorded the Soviet General Staff study, 'from this time on our aviation had superiority.'[242] By 14 July, Soviet aviation was mounting 1,491 day and night sorties as against 1,238 by the Luftwaffe.

At this stage the Germans had lost some 20,720 men, including 3,330 dead, in 'Citadel'. Soviet losses were heavier — 17,000 dead and 34,000 taken prisoner — but having absorbed everything German air and land forces could throw at them, the Soviets launched their counterstroke against the Axis positions above and below Kursk, at Orel and Kharkov.[243] The embattled German Ninth Army had to shift forces north to Orel, while the OKW was distracted by Anglo-US amphibious landings in Sicily. Given the serious threat to Italy, Hitler abandoned 'Citadel' with the irritable exclamation: 'The Russians manage everything, and we manage nothing at all.' The Germans would never again advance in the East.

*   *   *   *

There has never been a concentration of aircraft operating with such combat intensity over such a small area as during the battle of Kursk. Although the Germans had the air edge at the beginning, by the end of 12 July the 2nd, 16th and 17th Air Armies, plus the ADD, had flown 20,668 missions as against 16,038 by Luftflotten 4 and 6.[244] The qualitative differential would only get wider during the Soviet thrusts towards Orel and Kharkov.

The now formidable VVS had three main roles: to establish air control over the battle zones to protect advancing Soviet troops and armour; to provide sustained air support along breakthrough corridors; and to follow this by graduated air strikes into Axis rear areas. The Luftwaffe lost 487 combat aircraft in July and 785 in August because up to 35% of Soviet sorties were dedicated to achieving and maintaining control of the air. Among those who distinguished themselves in the battle for air superiority were Free French fighter pilots of the Normandy Squadron. After that, the

Above:
'There I was . . .' Snr Lt Mikhail Forofontev, destroyer of 15 German aircraft during the battle for Orel, passes on his experiences to Jnr Lt Valentin Fedorov, whose smile betrays that he is being shot a line. *SCRSS*

weight of VVS air power focused on narrow breakthrough corridors that had been opened by tremendous amounts of artillery. The VVS and tanks were sent to enlarge and expand these gaps to force the enemy back along a broad front. Soviet tactical air power put down German anti-tank forces, isolated the battle area from any reserves that the Germans might bring up, and protected tank and motorised units from Luftwaffe attacks. As Axis forces withdrew, the VVS played an active part in their pursuit.

For their Orel counter-offensive, three Soviet air armies — Gen M. M. Gromov's 1st, Gen N. F. Naumenko's 15th and Sergei Rudenko's 16th — attacked on three sides of the German-occupied bulge. The maximum strength of Luftflotte 6 in 1943 was three fighter, three dive-bomber and five bomber Gruppen, which if they had been at full strength — which they never were — would have given a force of over 300 aircraft. When ADD and 15th Air Army bombers hit German defences near Novosil, east of

Orel, the OKL was compelled to move Fliegerkorps VIII units north to try to check the Soviet advance. Then followed a secondary Soviet offensive down south on the Lower Donets, a sector which by this stage had been left largely to Romanian and Hungarian air forces, so Fliegerkorps VIII was forced to move units south from the Belgorod battle zone. The shuffling back and forth was exemplified by I./StG77, the only permanent component of Fliegerkorps VIII, which was transferred to Fliegerkorps IV at Kramatorsk on 16 July, to Stalino on 22 July, back to Kramatorsk three days later and to Makeyevka on 27 July, before being returned to Fliegerkorps VIII at Tolokonoye because air support was urgently needed east of Kharkov and at Belgorod. The upshot was that Luftflotten 4 and 6 had to spread their combined total of around 1,200 aircraft into three distinct forces. Far from the Luftwaffe securing air superiority over the VVS, the tactics of the Soviets completely wrested the initiative from their opponents.

While the Germans mixed and matched, 15th Air Army — 120 ground-attack aircraft, 112 bombers and 200 fighters — was dedicated to support and protect just the 3rd Guards Tank Army. And Soviet air forces were more adept at hitting German supply routes, storage areas and airfields around the clock. By 18 July, 1st, 15th and 16th Soviet Air Armies had flown 7,272 night missions as against just 469 by the Germans. On some nights as many as 500 sorties were flown, around half of which were by the ADD's Il-4s which dropped more than 400 tons of bombs per night. Much of the disruptive night activity was still carried out by the elderly U-2 biplanes, but spreading Soviet air superiority placed an added strain on hard-pressed German flak batteries, which were now much less free to act as supplementary field artillery.

Once the Soviets broke through German lines, the devastating combination of infantry and tanks moving forward with powerful air support proved irresistible. In five days, 15th Air Army flew around 4,800 sorties and 16th Air Army more than 5,000, of which over 50% were by *Shturmoviki* and Pe-2s against retreating troops. The 60,995 sorties flown by the VVS and ADD, and the 15,000 tons of bombs they dropped, helped the Soviets destroy 21 German divisions and occupy the Orel bulge.[245]

The Soviets employed 14 combined armies, a tank army and several mechanised corps for the Stalingrad battle whereas 'the counter-offensive at Kursk was carried throughout by 22 strong combined armies, five tank and six air armies, and large long-range air formations.'[246] It was a measure of the Soviets' strength that even before the fall of Orel they launched an attack towards Kharkov via Belgorod. On the night before the offensive began on 3 August, 370 ADD sorties bombed German defensive positions. More anti-artillery and counter air missions followed after dawn, while 2nd and 5th Air Armies flew repeatedly in support of the Red Army's land assault. As gaps opened in the German line, VVS fighters (now enjoying a 3:1 advantage) flew in force to maintain visible air superiority. Below them, Il-2s and Pe-2s provided the cutting edge for Soviet armour by hitting strongpoints, suppressing artillery and isolating forward troops from their reserves. It was aggressive and brutal stuff, costly in VVS aircrew and aircraft but no more than Marshal Zhukov expected from all his people. Gen V. Z. Ryazanov, Commander of the 1st Ground-Attack Air Corps, received the following signal from the commander of 48th Infantry Corps: 'The ground troops were able to advance thanks only to the attack aircraft.' The 2nd Hungarian Air Div and a few German units could not stem the tide, and Belgorod was liberated on the same day as Orel.

By 11 August, the VVS had developed a powerful momentum in the south. Large numbers of front and ADD aircraft were directed against the German rear, hitting railway stations, roads and reserves trying to move forward together with Axis airfields where the most vulnerable aircraft concentrations and fuel stores were identified by air reconnaissance. To stop German tanks moving forward to defend Kharkov, ADD bombers flew 2,300 missions against trains and stations from 6 to 17 August. At the height of the Kharkov offensive, the VVS committed 50-80% of its daily sorties to close air support. When Soviet air reconnaissance detected the Germans trying to withdraw in good order from Kharkov for Poltava, 1,300 sorties were dispatched against the columns.

After the evacuation of Kharkov airfields on 23 August, the bulk of Luftwaffe forces withdrew to air bases around Dnepropetrovsk, Kremenchug and Mirogorod to defend the Dnieper line. This concentration in the south was dictated by the German desire to hold on to the Crimea, but it exposed the northern flank of the Ukrainian salient which soon became clear to VVS air reconnaissance.

Three VVS air armies — the 16th, 2nd and 5th — supported the Central, Voronezh and Steppe Fronts in a co-ordinated Soviet offensive to cross the Dnieper River and capture Kiev.[247] These air armies had 1,450 aircraft as against the Germans' 900, but more importantly it was now a case of makeshift versus methodical air power. Within Luftflotte 4's area, Fliegerkorps I HQ at Nikolayev had responsibility for the southern sector including the Crimea. Fliegerkorps IV looked after the central sector from its HQ at Kirovgrad, and later Novo Ukrainka, while in the northern part Fliegerkorps VIII's command post at Belaya Tserkov covered the Poltava-Kharkov sector. The loss of German airfields when the Soviets overran Stalino and Taganrog led to the strengthening of Fliegerkorps IV at the expense of Fliegerkorps VIII.

But then the Stavka launched another offensive from Orel southeast towards Konotop, forcing the Germans to raise Luftflotte 6's strength in the area to 400 aircraft, which left the adjacent sector from Kiev to Chernikov virtually devoid of air cover. The gradual southward concentration of German close-support forces drained air support for the central front, leaving only some 500 aircraft, a high proportion of which were reconnaissance and army co-operation types, to cover a line of around 600km. Not surprisingly, the Soviets came through here.

Although satisfied with the outcome at Kursk, Stalin had been furious at the failure of Gen Sokolovsky's offensive operations aimed at Smolensk. Luftflotte 6 was giving a good account of itself in supporting the defensive action east and north of Smolensk, and in late August Stalin ordered Air Marshal Novikov to help get a grip of the offensive. Working with Sokolovsky and other army colleagues, Novikov came up with an extensive deception plan. Golovanov's long-range bombers were sent to pound an apparent line of advance and having diverted German reinforcements, Sokolovsky's main thrust was able to recapture Bryansk and Smolensk, the city where Novikov had learned to fly and where his wife and young son were buried, by 25 September.

The Soviets established bridgeheads across the Dnieper at the beginning of October. On 10 October Luftflotte 4 committed 867 aircraft against Soviet troops, railways and southern bridgeheads while that same day, Luftflotte 6 concentrated 960 aircraft in support of the Third Panzer Army west of Smolensk. It was all hands to the pumps, with He111 bombers being seriously misused on close air support missions just ahead of German lines. But in the short term Army Group Centre held the wide arc from north of Velikiye Luki to just north of Vitebsk because Luftflotte 6 was able to summon the air support to master many a seemingly hopeless situation.

For about a week from 20 October, the Luftwaffe operated intensively against Soviets advancing from Kremenchug on the Dnieper towards Krivoi Rog. At the beginning of November, 2nd Air Army had increased its aircraft strength to 603 whereas Luftflotte 4's had dropped to 610. However, the Soviet air army was optimised for ground-support missions whereas 70% of the opposition were long-range bombers. All of those on the whole southern front were committed to stopping the Soviet advance, with many units flying two such sorties a day plus a third in the

Kiev sector, 280km to the north. This intensive air effort — some 1,200 missions per 24 hours over 4-5 days — played an appreciable part in halting the Soviet advance short of Krivoi Rog. On the down side, such a concentrated and sustained air effort was possible only by weakening the Luftwaffe between Kiev and the Pripet Marshes which, in parallel with a ground force shift southwards, left the way open for the Red Army to capture Kiev on 6 November.

By December 1943 the Red Army had advanced up to 1,300km and liberated almost two-thirds of the territory seized by its enemy. The fall of Kiev and consolidation of substantial bridgeheads over the Dnieper further south, less than five months after the Germans threw everything at Kursk, showed what combined air-land power could achieve over vast distances, provided it was given the right resources and directed with single-minded purpose.

Right:
Oblt Diekwisch of III./StG1 receives the Knight's Cross from Generaloberst Alfred Keller, commander of Luftflotte 1, at Gorodjets on 15 October 1943. *Goss/Rauchbach Archive*

Below:
Air-land co-operation at its most formidable. Soviet tanks and Il-2 Shturmoviki go into action together at the start of the Soviet counter-offensive at Kursk. *SCRSS*

REAPING THE WHIRLWIND

'What a giant machine a Corps with a number of divisions is on the ground; 50,000 men with thousands of vehicles, a monster, and yet it is interested only in its neighbours on the right and on the left. What happens an army or two further on is hardly noticed by the Corps. But the Air Force officer sees much, much more and thinks further. What is the large fighting front of a Corps even to a little Leutnant flying long-range reconnaissance? The width of a thumb, no more. That is the way it is on the battlefield, and how it must be in the High Command.'

Gen Karl Koller

There was precious little good news for German airmen after the failure of 'Citadel'. The Hamburg firestorm ignited by RAF Bomber Command at the end of July 1943 signalled a miserable life ahead for many families whose sons were serving in Russia. US bombing of the great Messerschmitt factory at Wiener-Neustadt on 13 August resulted in a four-hour row between Hitler and Hans Jeschonnek, and the V-weapons experimental site at Peenemünde was being bombed as the Germans fell back from Kharkov. At the end of his tether, Jeschonnek committed suicide, lowering morale still further in high places.

Jeschonnek had been the great advocate of concentrating offensive air power in support of ground forces and during 1943, at least 80% of Luftwaffe combat flying was devoted to 'tactical co-operation with the Army.'[248] This left too little effort for air defence of the Reich and it was increasingly seen as a waste of the Luftwaffe. German aircraft losses in Russia, which grew from 487 in June 1943 to 911 in July and 785 in August, came far more from attrition and Soviet ground fire during close-support operations than from VVS air attacks or AAA fire.[249]

Rather than play second fiddle to overstretched ground forces, many German air commanders saw the 'proper' use of air power exemplified by the American Operation 'Frantic'. 'Frantic I' was mounted on 1 August 1943 when 177 USAAF B-24 Liberators were launched from North Africa bound for the Ploeşti oil fields in Romania, then estimated to be supplying 60% of Germany's crude oil requirements. Over Bulgaria, clouds broke up the defensive cohesion of the B-24 formations, which were being tracked by German radar. Denied the element of surprise, 54 Liberators were shot down by German and Romanian air defenders, but the loss of 532 American aircrew was accepted because the refinery was never again to operate at full capacity. Ploeşti was to be targeted a dozen more times before the war's end, and this ability to sever the strategic sinews of an opponent's war machine was seen as the mark of a truly independent air force.

Many felt that von Richthofen should have become the new Chief of Air Staff, but he would have been too forceful to play second fiddle to the increasingly ineffectual Göring. After much discussion, the post was given to Gen Günther Korten, a 45-year-old former World War 1 gunner who had trained at Lipetz in 1928. Korten had moved from Fliegerkorps I to take over command of Luftflotte 1 only on 12 June, but he represented a new start in that he disagreed with the Jeschonnek line of giving air priority to the battlefronts and maintaining the offensive at all costs. In favouring strategic bombing and fighter defence, the avuncular Korten wanted to emulate the UK-based RAF and create separate functional home defence, army support and strategic bombing forces. He started by transferring the Bf110/Me410-equipped ZG26 and ZG72, and Bf109Gs of JG3 and JG11 back from the East to defend the Reich. Next he established a Ground Attack Command. Up to now, 'tactical support forces' had covered a multitude of types ranging from the latest Fw190s and Me410s to Hs123 museum pieces. Dive-bombers had come under the aegis of the *General der Kampfflieger*, and the operating authority for ground-attack units had been the *General der Jagdflieger*, which was counterproductive because bomber and fighter barons lacked interest in what might be termed their stepchildren. The new *General der Nahkampfflieger*, Oberst Ernst Kupfer and then Gen Hubertus Hitschhold, set about updating the anti-tank units and replacing now obsolescent Ju87s with Fw190s. That this transition did not progress speedily was not so much because Stuka specialists like Hans-Ulrich Rudel were adept at destroying tanks (Rudel was eventually to destroy 519 tanks), but rather because increasing bomber attacks on the Reich forced the retention of versatile Fw190s for homeland air defence.

Korten's ultimate objective — to reduce Luftwaffe army support operations to a minimum in order to undertake meaningful strategic bombing operations — appealed to Hitler, who wanted the mass bombing of London to take revenge for German suffering. However, Korten had set his heart on strategic bomber raids against crucial industrial nodes such as Soviet power stations and aero-engine factories. Hitler was eventually persuaded to back *Aktion Russland* by Armaments Minister Albert Speer, who understood Korten's logic. Notwithstanding the hammering that panzers had inflicted on Soviet armoured forces at Kursk, German intelligence estimated front-line Soviet tank numbers as 9,500 on 1 November 1943, rising to 11,000 by the following April.[250] Similarly, although the Germans claimed to have destroyed 3,110 VVS aircraft during July, Luftwaffe intelligence reported 23,000 Soviet front-line aircraft in November 1943, increasing to 29,000 within five months. With Luftwaffe combat power in the East standing at 2,762 aircraft in

January 1944, it was obvious that victory against such numerical superiority could not be achieved simply by combat at the front.

Despite opposition from the OKW, which still thought in terms of maximum air cover and support for the armies in the field, bomber units were withdrawn for retraining once bad weather restricted air activity. On 26 November 1943, Göring authorised the concentration under Fliegerkorps IV of 'the bulk of the heavy bomber units operating in the East, reinforced by special target marking formations.' Fliegerkorps IV was then under the command of Jeschonnek's former chief of operations staff, Gen Rudolf Meister. Meister had been an air observer in World War 1 who had trained in the USSR from 1928-30, and seven heavy bomber Gruppen were initially allocated to what became known as 'korps Meister'. I.,II./KG3, II.,III./KG4, I.,III./KG55 and III./KG100 were expected, after refit and training, to operate forward out of Bobruysk, Orsha and Baranovichi in Combat Zone Centre to give the OKL a strike force of over 300 aircraft. II./KG4 with its He111Hs was to become a special pathfinder Gruppe, though the intention was to dedicate another *Kampfgruppe* to this task because some raids would need 50 pathfinders.

Fliegerkorps IV ceased to operate as a close-support force in early December, and was ordered to be ready for strategic bomber operations by February 1944. Some units got up to speed quite quickly. I./KG55, which left the mid-Crimea and its support role for Seventeenth Army in mid-December, took only 23 operational He111Hs to its new base at Ilez near the Polish-Soviet border. By mid-January, the Gruppe had recovered almost to its established strength of 37 aircraft and its crews were ready for a strategic

night bomber conversion training programme involving massed take-offs and formation navigation and bombing.

Albert Speer's Ministry and German intelligence put together a comprehensive schedule for attacking Soviet production and war reserves. It was estimated that, with careful selection of key targets, Meister's bombers would eliminate 50-80% of Soviet productive capacity, which was put at 3,500 tanks and 3,000 combat aircraft per month. But this dream faded in the harsh glare of political and operational reality. Although 60% of the Luftwaffe's operational bombers were serving in the East, *Aktion Russland* was far beyond Luftwaffe capabilities. Luftwaffe intelligence had to admit that destruction of the massive aero-engine factories at Kuibyschev, Kasan and Ufa would require 'stronger forces' than were in the offing, and that was before Hitler demanded that a fleet of over 400 bombers attack London in January 1944.

Then there was the lack of proper target intelligence on Soviet industrial capabilities. Back in 1941, Rowehl's high-level reconnaissance missions had penetrated only up to 300km and, as late as May 1944, Speer was pressing Korten to ensure 'that air reconnaissance of the Ural district be speedily undertaken'. Aircrew needed this too. Gorky had virtually no flak protection when the Luftwaffe attacked in June 1943, but by early 1944 the

Below:
Ju87Ds of I./StG5 en route to bomb a target near Leningrad early in 1943. Each Stuka is carrying a 250kg bomb under the fuselage, and two underwing AB250 small bomb containers, each holding 108 SD-2 anti-personnel bombs or 17 SD-10 anti-armour bomblets. *Price*

industrial city been ringed by 14 heavy and nine light AAA batteries, 50 searchlights, two air defence radars, a well-organised air raid alert and warning system and day and night fighters.

Making every bomb count was vital, given that the Luftwaffe in the East was as extended in December 1943 as it had been in August. In 1943, German industry produced 24,807 aircraft, which enabled the Luftwaffe to field 2,340 in the East at the beginning of 1944. On the other hand, Soviet industry rolled out 34,900 aircraft, of which 8,500 were available to the VVS.[251] In January 1944 the VVS had a two and half times as many aircraft as its opponents.

Soviet strategy for 1944 was first to destroy Axis flanking forces around Leningrad and in the southern USSR, and then turn to White Russia. Leningrad was an important industrial and armaments centre as well as a focal point of the Bolshevik revolution, and back in July 1941 Halder noted in his diary that 'it is the Führer's firm decision to level Leningrad . . . The city will be razed by the Luftwaffe.'[252] A siege force of six or seven infantry divisions trapped three million Leningrad citizens behind an electric wire fence, but on 6 September Hitler ordered Fliegerkorps VIII to vacate its bases in Estonia and fly south, leaving Luftflotte 1 with only 100 fighters and 150 bombers to pit

against 185 Soviet fighters, 600 AAA guns and around 300 barrage balloons. From September to the end of 1941, some 1,500 tons of HE bombs were dropped on the city, which only approximated to the average weight deposited on a German city *every night* during the last year of the war.

By the end of 1941, the Luftwaffe had shot its bolt in that it had expended 71% of all HE bombs and 96% of all incendiary bombs dropped on Leningrad during the entire war. Thereafter, Luftflotte 1 was alternately employed helping to throw back Red Army attempts to relieve the city during 1942 and 1943, and in trying to enforce the blockade. Many Soviet diaries reveal how terrible the incessant German bombing and artillery shelling could be, and the inhabitants' main lifeline was a truck route from the Moscow railway line, and thence over Lake Ladoga by ferry or its famous ice road in winter. Luftflotte 1 lacked the aircraft to bomb this route with sufficient intensity to close it down, and six parallel tracks cleared across the ice reduced vulnerability to air attacks, as did the fact that bomb holes refroze quickly.

The German air effort in the north became ever more desultory as air assets were committed increasingly in support of more important air battles in Combat Zone South. After KG53 was transferred in November 1942, the Luftflotte 1 command post at Roupti near Luga was frequently reduced to sending a single German aircraft to attack industrial targets in Leningrad. Upwards of a million Leningraders perished during the siege, but as the

Below:
AAA battery fire lights up the night skies of Leningrad. *SCRSS*

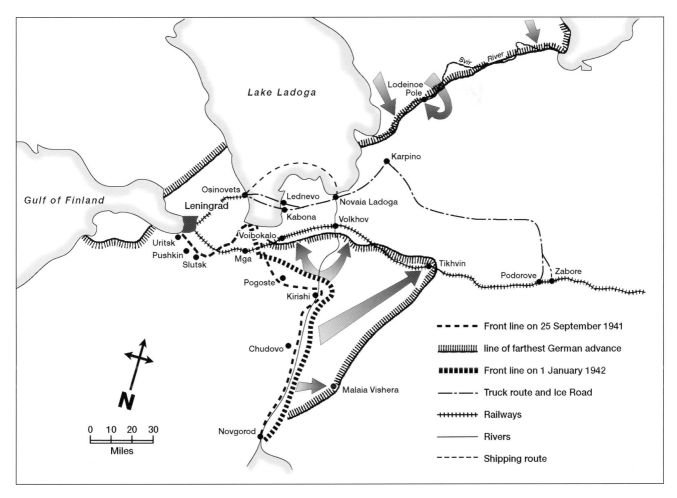

Front line on 25 September 1941

line of farthest German advance

Front line on 1 January 1942

Truck route and Ice Road

Railways

Rivers

Shipping route

Above:
The Leningrad front line on 25 September, 1941.

months passed and suffering intensified, terror of bombing and shelling lost its force and both Party elite (who could often wangle airlift flights out) and the masses were driven together in a common resolve to survive. 'One day in December in 20 degrees of frost,' recalled a Leningrad factory director in 1941, 'we had our windows blown out by a bomb, and I thought to myself: "No, we can't really go on, almost without food!" And yet, somehow we did.' Erich von Manstein was not surprised. 'As for Hitler's belief that the city could be compelled to surrender by terror raids by Fliegerkorps VIII, we had no more faith in this than von Richthofen.'[253]

German Army Group North, which had constructed a strong, multi-layered defensive line 250km deep, was hit by troops of the Leningrad and Volkhov Fronts on 14 January 1944. In support were the 13th and 14th Air Armies, ADD bomber units, 2nd Guards Fighter Corps and aircraft from the Baltic Fleet, making over 1,200 Soviet aircraft in total. The Luftwaffe still had plenty of fight and was occasionally capable of launching 1,000 sorties a day on the Eastern Front. However, over Combat Zone North Col A. A. Matveyev's 275th Fighter Air Div was not overly troubled as it flew top cover for Soviet ground troops. During the first day the VVS flew 284 sorties, putting 47 German AAA and field artillery batteries out of commission and destroying many mortars and ground troops. From his mobile command post located within the

220th Tank Brigade's area, Col F. S. Khatminsky was in constant radio contact with his forward officers in tanks, who directed ground-attack aircraft onto targets as the situation demanded. Il-2s operated over the battlefield for up to 35 minutes at a time, making up to six passes against their targets. The fact that *Shturmovik* commanders such as Lt G. M. Parshin could get away with this showed the extent to which the Soviets controlled the skies.

When Fliegerkorps I moved south to the Ukraine, it was replaced by Fliegerführer 1 at Pleskau in August 1942, which in turn gave way to 3.Flieger-Div in December 1943. By February 1944, 3.Flieger-Div controlled I./SG1 at Wesenberg, I.,II./SG3 at Pleskau, I./SG5 at Dno, NSGr.1 at Idriza, NSGr.3 at Pleskau, NSGr.11 at Jöhwi, II./JG5 at Dorpat and I., IV./JG54 at Wesenberg. The NSGr (*Nachtschlachtgruppen*) operated the German equivalents of the Soviet U-2 biplanes, with Ar66 and Go145 primary trainers misused as light night bombers. Sixteen Staffeln were to operate Ar66 biplanes in the nocturnal attack role, including three by Estonians, two by Latvians and a unit manned by pro-German Russian volunteers. Several hundred Go145s divided between 13 Staffeln were also modified for this pretty brave if thankless role, and it was symptomatic of the decline of the Luftwaffe that by October, 3.Flieger-Div was reduced to trying to stem the Red Army with just II.,III./SG3, III./SG4, NSGr.3 and NSGr.5.

In the drive to free Leningrad, ADD bombers dropped 876 tons in two nights on longer-range targets and on 19 January, a direct hit from a Baltic Fleet Aviation 500kg (1,102.5lb) bomb demolished 3.Flieger-Div's command centre at Pleskau, disrupting communications and killing 30. While giving direct support to advancing troops, the VVS also bombed German reserves moving up to the front. Fired up after years of being under the cosh, the VVS played up its new-found air superiority for all it was worth:

'On 16 January 1944, M. F. Sharonov led his squadron on a ground attack against retreating enemy columns along the highway between Pavlovsk and Stekolny station. The fascists sent a shower of anti-aircraft fire against our first fighters. The squadron commander made eight runs against the enemy column and his fliers followed bravely after him, destroying both men and equipment with machine gun fire. The commander's aircraft was hit and tongues of flame appeared in the cockpit. The daring lover of the Motherland was true to his oath. He guided his burning aircraft onto a concentration of enemy troops and at the price of his life, destroyed a large number of German soldiers and officers. By order of the Presidium of the Supreme Soviet, M. F. Sharonov was posthumously awarded the title Hero of the Soviet Union for his feats in the struggle with the fascist German invaders.'

During the first stage of the offensive up to 30 January, Gen S. D. Rybalchenko's 13th and Gen I. P. Zhuravlev's 14th Air Armies flew more than 4,500 sorties, often down at 100m in bad weather. More than 70% of these missions were in direct support of ground troops, who ended the siege of Leningrad after 880 days, the longest ever endured by a modern city.

On 31 January there were about 240 Luftwaffe aircraft on the Leningrad front. This was double the figure at the beginning of the operation, and there would be 400 in the area by the end of February, but it was too little, too late. With the help of the transport air regiments of the Civil Air Fleet and 13th Air Army, the long-range ADD delivered 278 tons of equipment and 383 individuals to partisan groups who, among other contributions, derailed 133 German trains bringing men and supplies. As the weather improved, so did the VVS sortie rate. Over 1,100 sorties were flown in the final days of February to repel German attacks and protect the 2nd Strike Army. Throughout, aerial reconnaissance was vital in maintaining the momentum of the offensive in bad weather over a marshy and wooded area. The discovery of German troop concentrations and defence lines was left to fighters during the day and the evergreen little U-2 biplane crews at night. By flying about 30,000 sorties and dropping 4,500 tons of bombs, Soviet airmen and women helped their ground colleagues destroy the Sixteenth and Eighteenth German Armies and liberate the Leningrad region by 1 March. But by hanging on to key positions, the Wehrmacht staved off early Soviet attempts to drive into Latvia and Estonia.

Concurrently, the Stavka was running a powerful offensive in the Ukraine. After the fall of Kiev, the Germans were in the process of concentrating men and aircraft in the south to recapture Soviet bridgeheads on the right bank of the Dnieper and to re-establish communications with forces cut off in the Crimea. Much to German surprise, the Soviets launched a pre-emptive attack on Christmas Eve 1943 to liberate the whole right bank of the Dnieper. Three German Army Groups and Luftflotte 4, with 1,460 aircraft or 54% of those on the Eastern Front, found themselves up against the 1st, 2nd, 3rd and 4th Ukrainian Fronts, supported by the 2nd, 5th, 17th and 8th Air Armies respectively, with 2,360 aircraft. Air Marshal Novikov co-ordinated air operations, and the stage was set for some stubborn battles involving more than four million men, 4,400 tanks and over 3,800 aircraft.

By 30 December, the combined effect of Soviet artillery, armour, infantry and air power had pierced the front by an area 300km wide and up to 100km deep. Simultaneously, the VVS hit railway targets and Axis airfields. 2nd Air Army alone flew some 4,200 sorties, including 2,500 against German tanks. As ever, the Germans placed their firefighting hopes in the Luftwaffe, but the Soviet Fighter Air Corps successfully fought them off.

By 28 January 1944, troops of the 1st and 2nd Ukrainian Fronts had encircled seven German divisions at Korsun-Shevchenkovsky. It was time for a 'touch of the Stalingrad whip' as 2nd Ukrainian Front commander Gen Ivan Konev put it, but the Germans responded by sending the 3rd, 11th and 4th Panzer Divs to relieve the situation, followed two days later by 13th Panzer Div with 16th and 17th Panzer Divs assembling around Rizino. Soviet armour found it difficult to finish off the German tanks, and Stalin summoned Novikov to Stavka. 'Tell me, Comrade Novikov, can aircraft stop tanks?' 'It's possible,' Novikov replied, recalling the hollow-charge shells fired by Il-2s to knock out German tanks in the Kursk salient. 'Then tomorrow fly down to Vatutin (commander 1st Ukrainian Front) and take the necessary steps to stop the tanks.'

Fliegerkorps VIII delivered around 250 tons of food and supplies daily to sustain the 50,000 men in the pocket. Knowing that the Germans were mobilising to relieve the encircled force, Novikov organised four 'destruction zones' covered by fighters while his aircraft interdicted the German reinforcement and supply chain and bombers struck airfields beyond the outer encirclement ring. Yet the panzers sent to relieve the encircled force at Korsun-Shevchenkovsky succeeded against an inexperienced tank army in breaking into the outer ring. Emergency help was need from the VVS, with Gen I. I. Vorobyev of the 53rd Army sending the following radio message: 'Smash the tanks and armoured vehicles around Sobolevka and Tolmach — they are the enemy's. Don't touch the artillery — it is ours.' The mass of Soviet artillery and air power co-ordinated by radio and orchestrated by Novikov under precise navigational control came up trumps, with the Il-2 *Shturmoviki* of 2nd Air Army being particularly successful against the tanks.

With relief efforts thwarted, German troops formed into columns to fight their way out to the southwest. They were hammered in the mud of the early spring thaw, with only 32,000 troops reaching the safety of their own lines. On 21 February, three days after the Korsun 'pocket' ceased to exist, Novikov was at the 1st Ukrainian Front command post where Marshal Zhukov had arrived to co-ordinate forthcoming operations. The phone rang and Zhukov took the call from Moscow. 'Alexander Alexandrovich,' he said to Novikov, 'you have just become the first ever Air Chief Marshal.'[254]

Concurrently, the 3rd and 4th Ukrainian Fronts reached Krivoi Rog and the Ingulets River. By the end of February, the Soviets had thrown Axis forces back along much of the length of the Dnieper, and in two months the 2nd, 5th, 17th and 8th Air Armies had flown 31,836 sorties, of which 13,176 were against troops. Meanwhile, the fighter units withdrawn to defend the Reich were never replaced and Fliegerkorps IV was out of the battle gearing up for strategic operations. Against Soviet advances, the remaining Luftwaffe units were unable to mount more than 300-350 sorties per day, in part because of bad weather but also because of the poor state of airfields, low serviceability and

Below:
An He177 strategic bomber, carrying its four engines coupled in pairs, belonging to KG1 which operated over Russia in the summer of 1944. *Price*

dislocation caused by frequent unit moves. The retreat of aircraft parks and supply depots to central Poland, exacerbated by congested communications, degraded maintenance and serviceability still further.

By mid-March the Soviets were seriously threatening the Romanian oil fields. Political unrest in Hungary led the Germans to position bombers at Vierine and single-engined fighters at Belgrade and Nish as a 'demonstration of intent' against Budapest, and to support airborne landings in Hungary and Bulgaria if the need arose. Soviet pressure along the whole front forced the Luftwaffe into smaller combat groups to provide everyone with a modicum of air cover, leaving more gaps for the Soviets to exploit. By this stage the main Luftwaffe forces in southern Russia were concentrated east of the Lower Bug in the Ukraine, in expectation of further Soviet advances from Krivoi Rog towards the Dnieper Estuary combined with an effort to clear the Crimea. The concentration of Fliegerkorps I and VIII in the Yampol area from 17 March left just a depleted Romanian Air Corps to defend the Lower Bug. It was no contest, and the Red Army with VVS support advanced rapidly to capture Nikolayev on 28 March and Odessa on 10 April.

Further north, between the Carpathians and Pripet Marshes, five Soviet armoured corps followed by massed infantry under Marshal Zhukov (Vatutin having been fatally wounded) crossed the Dniester River due south of Tarnopol on 24 March to link up with Marshal Ivan Konev's forces, which had earlier crossed the river several kilometres to the east. The German strongpoint at Tarnopol straddled the Red Army's supply route, causing Zhukov some concern. On hearing of this 'thorn in the flesh', Novikov sent two divisions of U-2 biplanes to drop light bombs in daylight, while fighter cover held off whatever Bf109s were still left until Tarnopol surrendered.

As the Red Army advanced towards Lvov, the initial Luftwaffe reaction was weak given that its bomber force, the only element capable of being brought to bear without change of airfield, had fallen to 165 combat-ready aircraft in the whole of Russia, all of which had to be made available in the Ukraine. Zhukov and Konev's forces encircled the German First Panzer Army in a large arc north of the Dniester near Kamenets-Podolski. Once again Hitler ordered a static defence, but First Panzer commander Gen Hans Hube decided to withdraw the entire pocket west. Although the nearest Luftwaffe airfield was 200km away, the Germans maintained a daily airlift of food and supplies to Hube's men, changing airfields inside the pocket as the fluid ground situation demanded and finally air-dropping supplies when there was no alternative means of delivery. By 5 April, First Panzer Army had moved far enough west to join up with the German front.

All this tolled the death-knell for Korten's strategic bombing dreams. Soviet advances from late December 1943 hindered the withdrawal of bomber units, and because the Luftwaffe striking force was less than half of what it had been in 1941, combat air commanders supported their army colleagues in resisting the removal of any remaining credible aircraft. Large numbers of He111s were also diverted for weeks at a time to help Ju52s supply encircled army troops. Consequently, completion of Fliegerkorps IV's training scheme was delayed until March/April 1944, by which time Soviet advances had pushed important targets such as Gorky outside bomber range.

The last substantial German manned bomber offensive, codenamed Operation 'Wren', began on the night of 27 March 1944. Fifty of Meister's bombers attacked the railway junction at Sarny, one of the crucial railway bottlenecks supplying advancing Soviet forces. The fact that Fliegerkorps IV now embarked on a four-month interdiction programme against railways rather than major industrial centres showed the extent to which German planners confused themselves when it came to differentiating between true strategic operations and battlefield interdiction. Korps Meister could operate almost at will because the Soviets never felt the need to develop a sophisticated night defence system, but the Germans could never offset the fact that they lacked a proper strategic bomber. At a time when RAF Bomber Command had a daily average of 1,000 bombers to send over Germany, the only comparable aircraft in the Luftwaffe's inventory — the He177 — did not appear on the Russian front in a workable form until early June 1944. Under the command of Obstlt Horst von Riesen, the He177s of KG1 began operating out of East Prussia with Luftflotte 6, just as Luftflotte 6 aviation fuel stocks were barely enough for just three sorties per aircraft.[255] As

each He177 took six tons of fuel per mission, the chances of any sustained German large-scale bomber operations were dead and buried by the end of July.

Having cleared the Black Sea coast to the mouth of the Dniester, the Stavka was now well placed to retake the Crimea. Hitler, seeing control of the Crimea as vital to protect Romanian oil and to dissuade Turkey from joining the Allies, ordered his Seventeenth Army (six German and six Romanian divisions) to hold its position, supported by Luftflotte 4. The Soviet plan against them called for simultaneous strikes by the 4th Ukrainian Front, from the northern part of the Crimea, and the Independent Coastal Army from the eastern end of the Kerch peninsula. They were supported by Gen K. A. Vershinin's 4th Air Army and Gen T. T. Khryukin's 8th Air Army, and co-ordination of their operations with ADD, PVO and Black Sea Fleet units was undertaken by Stavka representative, Gen F. Ya. Falaleyev. The Soviets threw 2,255 aircraft into the Crimean operation.

The northern force went in on 8 April, followed by the eastern three days later. Although Luftflotte 4 mounted 530 sorties between 12 and 18 April in the 4th Ukrainian Front area, including 150 on 14 April, for the rest of the week it flew only 40-60 sorties a day and then offered no serious resistance to advancing Soviet troops or aircraft.

The Crimean capital Simferopol fell on 13 April. Axis aircraft were then squeezed into the few remaining airstrips in Sevastopol, which soon felt the combined efforts of Soviet bombing and strafing, supported by artillery when Soviet batteries came within range after 17 April. In the six days before the assault on the Sevastopol Fortified Region, ADD and 8th Air Army aircraft dropped over 2,000 tons of bombs and 24,000 anti-tank munitions. By 20 April, the main Sevastopol airfield was no longer usable, and some 200 aircraft, mainly single-engined fighters, had to be written off once the last airstrip was lost on 8 May. The VVS flew over 13,000 sorties in eight days, of which 2,000 were against Axis air and sea evacuation efforts. The Luftwaffe could mount only 700 sorties in the same period. The Red Army captured Sevastopol in 35 days, and a monument was later erected commemorating the manner in which 8th Air Army 'supported the troops on the ground and for their fearlessness, courage and heroism in battle'.

The German Seventeenth Army and its allies avoided another Stalingrad in so far as they left only 60,000 men behind. But evacuation of the Crimea imposed a heavy burden on Luftwaffe units based in Romania. Torpedo-bombers from the western Mediterranean, twin-engined fighters defending Austria, and a few Fw190s from the Balkans — all of 70-80 aircraft — were moved in haste to protect the evacuation from Soviet naval and air attack. Following Soviet night bombing of Constanta — the only remaining large reception port for Crimean traffic — a Staffel of night fighters had to be brought up.

In 599 air contests during the battle for the Crimea, the Luftwaffe lost 297 aircraft and around another 200 were destroyed on the ground. This was a futile drain on Luftwaffe resources because, once again, Hitler insisted on isolated troops defending a precarious position. With too few German fighter and attack aircraft, in concert with Romanian units, defending the indefensible, the result was further high wastage for no meaningful purpose.

With the Crimea reoccupied, the steam went out of the Soviet spring offensive and the Germans held on to Lvov. But there were no natural defences to protect eastern Poland, and Romania's natural barrier, the Dniester, was outflanked from the north. Throughout May, the Germans tried to counter preparations for a new offensive by interdicting the Soviet rail network, including Velikiye Luki in the north and Kiev in the south. Air operations were also undertaken to impose maximum delay on the transfer of Soviet troops back to the mainland from the Crimea.

In mid-May 1944, Novikov received orders to prepare air operations to drive Finland, already suing for peace, out of the war. He flew to Leningrad on 6 June in a two-seat version of the Yak-7 fighter — only a foolish Air Chief Marshal would think he could cope with the latest fighter *and* direct a major war. Novikov took the opportunity to check for himself the quality of his pilots' headsets, which had been giving grief through poor workmanship. He found his set did work badly and, on landing, he ordered Gen N. P. Seleznev, head of VVS procurement, to get a grip of the errant factories.

Not that the Air Chief Marshal's orders were always carried out thoroughly. 'Frantic I' long-range bombing missions flown by the US 15th Air Force out of Italy were so successful that Stalin and Roosevelt agreed to an extension into 'Frantic II', involving UK-based B-17Gs flying 'shuttle missions' deep into Germany, refuelling and rearming in the Ukraine, and then flying another

Below:
Yak-9s lined up at an airfield designated for US 'Frantic' bombing operations in the USSR. Alexander Yakovlev designed the Yak-9 for mass production and durability, relying on the minimum of scarce strategic materials. Yak-9s were designed to outnumber the enemy, not for technical superiority. They were durable fighter/ground-attack aircraft, able to absorb much battle damage and still make it home. In all, 16,769 were built. *IWM*

raid on the way home. The US 8th Air Force sent two bomber wings and a fighter wing to Russia for the first time on 21 June 1944. Led by Col Archie J. Olds Jr, CO of the 45th Combat Wing, the bombers dropped 500lb (227kg) General Purpose bombs on a major synthetic oil refinery and storage facility at Ruhland, just south of Berlin. The 163 B-17s and 70 P-51 Mustangs continued east across Poland before some of the B-17s landed at Poltava, an airfield recently taken back from the Luftwaffe that lay along the main rail line between Kharkov and Kiev. The 390th Bomb Group landed at Mirgorod, 100km west of Poltava, while the escort fighters landed at Pyaritan another 80km to the west. Maj Marshall B. Shore, lead navigator for the force, got out of his shiny B-17 at Mirgorod and noticed three US-built P-39 fighters, donated under Lend-Lease, some 300m away being serviced by young women wearing overalls.

'While standing around in front of our aircraft awaiting transportation to the debriefing, we suddenly saw a German reconnaissance plane. It was an He177 being used for reconnaissance and it approached from the east, flying at about 12,000ft (4,000m) and at maximum combat speed straight for the field. The photographic pass continued to the west in the direction of the German front lines.

'The only means of warning against air attacks was a single line telephone from Poltava. Seeing the He177 fly overhead the Russian women, who we thought were mechanics, jumped into the cockpits of their P-39s. They quickly started engines and raced for take-off without warming up or checking the mag (magneto) drop of their engines like our pilots always did. They climbed on course heading west into the early evening sunset. They did not catch up with the He177 that had been sent out to spy on our shuttle mission bases and just after sunset, but still daylight, the three pursuit interceptors returned, landed on the

grass and taxied back to their parking area. By this time the German reconnaissance crew was reporting on our arrival — what a juicy set of targets they had found.'

Novikov had ordered extra air defences and increased vigilance while the Americans were in the Ukraine, with responsibility delegated to one of his deputies, Gen A. V. Nikitin. But without night fighters or radar control, there was little chance of intercepting Meister's night bombers. Maj Shore and his colleagues were awakened in the early hours by the sound of heavy Russian anti-aircraft fire. A raging thunderstorm over Mirgorod airfield saved their bacon but the crews at Poltava were not so lucky. Approximately 180 He111s and Ju88s belonging to KG55, KG53 and KG27, with KG4 pathfinding, dropped 110 tons of bombs. The Americans did not help by leaving their aluminium-finished B-17Gs (they should have taken those with drab olive camouflage) neatly lined up wingtip to wingtip in a straight line parallel with the single concrete runway. A direct hit on a high-octane refuelling truck, which exploded and burned fiercely, lit up the entire parking area and served as a beacon for those following on. The Germans bombed and strafed with only token resistance from the light Russian anti-aircraft guns. The Russian fire department could not cope and the raid destroyed 43 of the shiny new B-17Gs sent to impress the Russians, damaged a further 26 and burned 200,000 gallons of aviation fuel. Poltava

airfield was littered with unexploded butterfly anti-personnel and phosphorous incendiary bombs that had to be cleared from the field before it could become operational again.[256]

This is not the place to go into detail on the decisive contribution made by the Anglo-US strategic bombing campaign against Germany. Suffice to say that while Allied troops were bravely kicking open the doors, strategic bombing brought the walls tumbling down on that crucial centre of gravity, the infrastructure of the Reich.

*   *   *   *

Allied forces entered Rome on 4 June and two days later, Gen Eisenhower launched the D-Day invasion of Normandy. At 09.00hrs on 8 June, Gen S. D. Rybalchenko's 13th Air Army and Gen I. M. Samokhin's Baltic Fleet Aviation launched 360 aircraft against the first line of the powerful fortified region built by the Finns to defend the Karelian Isthmus. Further north, Novikov worked with Gen I. M. Sokolov's 7th Air Army to provide local air support and co-ordinate 113th and 334th Bomber Div operations with Red Army activities on the Karelian Front.

Below:
Hptm Diekwisch of I./StG5 completes his 700th mission at Alakurtii, Finland, in June 1944. *Goss/Rauchbach Archive*

Above:
Fw190s of I./SG5, Pori, Finland, in June 1944. *Goss/Rauchbach Archive*

The Finnish Army and German 20th Mountain Army were supported by part of Luftflotte 1 and around 360 aircraft — 223 fighters, 106 bombers and 31 recce aircraft — of the Finnish Air Force. The Soviet 13th Air Army and 2nd Guards Fighter Air Corps alone had 757 aircraft, and together with Red Army and Navy troops they were given the task of breaking through the powerful fortified region. On 9 June, a day before the attack began, 215 bomber and 155 ground-attack aircraft, with fighter escort, made a mass raid on Finnish defence points. The bomber groups flew to their target in column by regiment, and the regiments in column by squadrons, staggered by height. Bombs were dropped on a signal from the lead aircraft, while ground-attackers struck in regimental strength five to 10 minutes later. A density of 80-100 tons of ordnance per sq km of target area fell on the defenders.

From 13 to 17 June, the Front Air Force flew 5,623 sorties against strongpoints, men, equipment and reserves in the second defensive line, while naval airmen flew 21,082 sorties. Forty-three German and Finnish aircraft were lost in these five days alone. Although the Finns fought doggedly, the Soviet 21st Army broke through the third defensive zone on 18 June while troops of the 23rd Army cleared the southern shores of the Suvanto-Jarvi and Vuoksi-Jarvi lakes. Luftflotte 1 transferred over 100 aircraft from JG54, StG1 and other units into the area but they could not stop the liberation of Vyborg. By 11 July the VVS had flown about 19,000 missions in support of ground troops and on 25 August, the Finns asked for peace terms. Moscow stipulated that all German forces had to leave the country by 15 September but the Germans refused, preferring to withdraw slowly towards Norway to hold the valuable nickel mines at Petsamo and protect the port of Kirkenes.

Having addressed the northern and southern flanks, the Stavka now turned to the German Army Group Centre under Field Marshal Busch, which still occupied a giant salient extending eastwards around Minsk along the upper reaches of the Dnieper. Known from its shape as the Byelorussian Balcony, this 1,000km front stretched from the Baltic States to the Ukraine, but its flanks were dangerously exposed because the OKW had stripped Busch of infantry, tanks and artillery in anticipation of a Soviet summer offensive in the south.

From Leningrad, Air Chief Marshal Novikov flew straight to Byelorussia to help plan the destruction of Army Group Centre. He worked with his old comrade in arms, Marshal Zhukov, on the 1st and 2nd Byelorussian Fronts, while Gen F. Ya. Falaleyev was once again the Stavka air representative with Marshal Vasilevsky on the 1st Baltic and 3rd Byelorussian Fronts. Five air armies — the 1st, 3rd, 4th, 16th (and 6th assigned to the second phase of the operation) — were set to deploy 5,683 operational aircraft in the greatest concentration of tactical air power to date in the war. And they were to be supplemented by 1,000 bombers drawn from eight ADD bomber corps.

The first phase of the Byelorussian offensive, named Operation 'Bagration' after a Georgian (like Stalin) hero of the war against Napoleon, called for the four Soviet Fronts to break through the German-held salient at six points. Once German resistance had been crushed, the second phase was expected to carry Soviet forces westward into Poland, the Baltic States and East Prussia. It may have been no coincidence that 'Bagration' was scheduled to start on 22 June, three years to the day since the Germans launched 'Barbarossa'.

The Soviet aircraft industry rolled out 16,000 aircraft in the first six months of 1944, allowing the VVS to fully replenish its air armies after heavy Luftwaffe-inflicted attrition during the previous winter. On 1 June 1944, total Soviet military aircraft strength (including ADD and Naval Aviation) stood at 13,428. For 'Bagration', the VVS was able to assign 2,000 ground-attack aircraft alone to the five participating air armies.

On the other side, the Luftwaffe had a total of 2,085 aircraft spread between four Air Fleets that were still trying to cover a vast Eastern Front of over 2,400km in length. Working from north to south, Luftflotte 5 had 105, Luftflotte 1 had 360, Luftflotte 6 had 775 and Luftflotte 4 had 845.[257] From its HQ at Rzeszów, some 140km west of Lvov, Luftflotte 4 was responsible for the tactical airspace south of Lvov plus air defence of Romania and eastern Hungary. The quick interchange of aerial forces that had been notable during operations in the Ukraine, was now much more difficult between Fliegerkorps VIII north of the Carpathians and Fliegerkorps I defending the Dniester south of Iasi. Mountains and fractured communications also divided the supply and ground organisations of the two Fliegerkorps just when life was really getting difficult.

The main concentration of German bombers was in the Centre — Luftflotte 6 had 370, Luftflotte 4 had 35 and the other two Air Fleets had none. On the other hand, there were relatively strong

Below:
Soviet partisan paratroopers before take-off for a drop behind German lines. *Author's collection*

ground-attack and fighter forces in the south because that was where Hitler felt the main Soviet thrust would fall. One account says that Luftflotte 6 had just 40 combat ready fighters on 22 June.[258] Overall, the Luftwaffe in the East was outnumbered seven to one in total aircraft, around six to one in operational combat aircraft, and by over 10 to one in air defence fighters.[259] It was also getting desperately short of aviation fuel to put in them.

Before 'Bagration', aerial reconnaissance was a VVS priority to give commanders information about the enemy and his dispositions. Alexander Golovanov's bombers hit German targets in the rear for 10 days before the offensive opened, while VVS bombers flew 1,472 missions against Luftflotte 6 airfields around Minsk, Baranovichi and Bobruysk. In among the mass of male aircrew, female pilots now operated from squadrons where all the engineering, armaments and support personnel were women, and their night harassment forays contributed to the 24,000 missions flown by female pilots throughout the war. Concurrently, 374,000 partisans set about destroying supply dumps and generally creating havoc in Byelorussia.[260]

On 17 June, a captured Russian cipher officer revealed that three corps of fighter aircraft, including one from the Crimea, had just arrived in Smolensk. But there was little that the Luftwaffe could do and in three devastating days after 22 June, massive

Above:
The strain shows in the faces of these young He111 crews of 9./KG53 at a briefing at Radom sometime between May and 9 July 1944. R. Bauer via Goss/Rauchbach Archive

Soviet attacks engulfed the German flanks and then the centre, smashing what did not turn and flee. Fast-moving Soviet tank corps, each armed with 168 tanks, anti-tank battalions, Katyusha rockets and AAA artillery, went into battle with the infantry clinging dangerously to rails on the tanks' sides. The Germans were flung back and on 27 June the 4th Air Army commander, Gen Vershinin, sent the following plea to Novikov: 'The air force has been employed in direct support of ground forces. Everything is proceeding normally. But, Comrade Chief Marshal, my heart aches. The Germans are escaping in continuous columns, there are road jams and crowds, and we have nothing to hit them with, as we should. We have not had targets like this since the Crimea. If it is possible, I ask that the neighbouring air armies of Comrades Rudenko and Khryukin send part of their forces to destroy these columns...' In answer to his prayer, about 2,000 missions were flown in six days against retreating Axis troops.

Of 50 single-engined fighters just returned to defend Germany from strategic bomber attack, 40 were immediately brought back. But the main demand was for ground-attack aircraft to try to stop the Russian columns, and 85 Fw190s were moved from the Italian Front which left the German army in that theatre almost completely denuded of strike support. Forty more aircraft were moved from Normandy, where they were having little impact on the build-up of the Allied bridgehead, while a further 70 were moved up from Luftflotte 4.

But these reinforcements were to no avail. With the VVS flying 3,000 missions over five days to seal the escape route to Minsk, Red Army pincers encircled over 100,000 German officers and men on 3 July. Hitler's demands for an airlift went unheeded: the Me323 giant transports were grounded and the entire Luftflotte 6 hamstrung by lack of fuel. The following day, Army Group Centre ceased to exist as a military entity. The secretary of the White Russian Communist Party wrote afterwards that 'this region gives a shattering impression of mass destruction and a demonstration of our Air Fleet's power'. The VVS flew 55,011 sorties between 22 June and 4 July, averaging 4,500 a day. Golovanov's bombers — essentially a force of Il-4s, B-25 Mitchells, A-20 Havocs and Li-2s (Soviet versions of the Douglas DC-3 converted for night bombing) — proved especially effective in attacking breakthrough zones. These aircraft lacked the legs to operate as strategic bombers but as everything from now would be tactical, in December 1944 Golovanov's ADD was redesignated the 18th Air Army and subordinated directly to Novikov.

Pressing on towards Lvov and Stanislav, Zhukov had in his sector alone 80 divisions, 10 armoured corps, four armoured brigades, 13,900 guns and mortars, 2,200 tanks and 3,000 aircraft, making a total troop strength of about 1,200,000. On 28 July this unstoppable force liberated the fortress of Brest-Litovsk, whose defenders had been among the first to face German attack on 22 June 1941. North of the Pripet Marshes, the Red Army pushed the Wehrmacht back across the Berezina River, driving as far as Lithuania and the middle Niemen River by 10 July. Notwithstanding reinforcements, Luftwaffe strength from the Baltic to the Black Sea had reduced to 1,760 by the end of July. The average daily flying effort never exceeded 500-600 sorties, which was far too little to help the hard-pressed ground forces. Sustainability was further undermined when Bialystok, an important focal point of Luftwaffe air activity, fell in early August.

While liberating White Russia, part of Latvia and Lithuania and eastern Poland, the VVS flew 153,000 sorties in the largest air operation of the entire war. Forty-two percent of these sorties were expended against the Luftwaffe, with 2,000 German aircraft claimed in the air or on the ground. 'Bagration' showed how much the Soviets had learned and the extent to which they had adapted in three years. They now amassed tactical air power on an unprecedented scale to achieve absolute air supremacy, before working hand-in-glove with the army to hand out the sort of defeats inflicted on them in 'Barbarossa'. As the VVS war machine swept forward, its impact on what remained of the Luftwaffe showed how the mighty had fallen. JG51, along with JG52 and JG54, had spent the bulk of its existence in the East. The JG51 staff report for 25 June 1944 made grim reading. 'The airfield at Orsha was subjected to a heavy raid. In spite of the fact that the enemy was expected, not one aircraft could take off. The command post burned down after a direct bomb hit and control over the units was lost for some time.'

Hptm Helmut Lipfert of JG52, with 143 kills at the time, recorded a more personal dilemma: 'From Kharkov we went to Radom, from there to Mzurawo and back to Kharkov again. On 21 August we took-off for the long trip across Hungary to Romania . . . but again we couldn't stay long in our former combat zone because Russian tanks were approaching our airfield. Since all contact with corps (Fliegerkorps I) had been lost, I had to take matters into my own hands. Under no circumstances did I want to be accused of cowardice, but abandoning a position without permission was a risky affair. I sent a Bf109 back to corps but the first T-34s had already rolled past the airfield before it returned. It was a damned ticklish situation. If I stayed at the base with my half Gruppe, we would certainly be overrun by the Russians and the machines and pilots would be lost. There were 18 or 19 machines on the airfield but I had only 12 pilots! If I began evacuating the field and the Russians were halted again, then my court martial was almost certain.'[261]

On 20 July 1944, Gen Korten was just briefing on an air reconnaissance report at the Wolf's Redoubt when two pounds of explosive detonated. Hitler survived but Korten was impaled by a jagged table fragment and died two days later. Werner Kreipe, a Hanoverian who was one of the youngest Luftwaffe generals, took his place. Kreipe would have made an excellent Chief of Air Staff but he was too young to have allies in the ruling clique at the Führer's HQ and after a heated argument with Hitler on

19 September, Kreipe was told that he no longer enjoyed the Supreme Commander's confidence. The head of the Luftwaffe Operations Staff, the able Bavarian Karl Koller, moved into the post. In the absence of Göring, who had taken to his bed, Koller had borne the brunt of Hitler's increasingly uncompromising attacks. 'He strongly reproaches the Luftwaffe,' wrote a despondent Koller in his diary on 8 August. 'The reasons are our lack of aircraft, technological shortcomings, and non-completion of replacement Staffeln etc . . . How am I to know what claims the Reichsmarschall and Gen Korten made, or undo the wrongs committed from 1939-42 through the total absence of any planning? It's a hard lot to have to answer for these errors.'[262]

Although the Luftwaffe was still able to achieve short-term tactical successes against advanced or vulnerable Soviet spearheads, from now on there were never enough latest-generation German modern aircraft materially to affect Soviet operations, timings or outcomes. Between 20 and 29 August, Army Group South collapsed completely with over 400,000 prisoners captured. The pro-German Romanian Government fell on 23 August when King Michael tried to save his throne by going over to the Allies, which angered Hitler so much that he ordered the aerial bombardment of Bucharest. By 2 September the Ploeşti oil fields, Germany's last major source of crude oil, were in Soviet hands. The crushing of Army Group Centre liberated the last vestiges of German-occupied Russia, and from now on nothing stood between the Red Army and the conquest of Berlin.

Oppsite top:
'It's not going well, guys . . .' In the KG53 briefing room at Radom in 1944. Front row, left–right: Obstlt Fritz O. Pockrandt, Geschwaderkommodore KG53; Maj Ludwig Grözinger, Kdr IV./KG53 April 1943-August 1944, died 15 February 1945; Maj Richard Fabian (ex-Kdr III./KG53 from February 1941 to April 1942). *Bauer via Goss/Rauchbach Archive*

Opposite bottom:
A Yak-9 of the French 'Normandie-Niemen' fighter group. On 28 November 1944, the French unit received the Niemen suffix on Stalin's orders to mark its involvement in the crossing of this river by Soviet armies. The aircraft is piloted by Lt Marcel Albert, holder of the Gold Star of a Hero of the Soviet Union. Top-scoring unit ace with 22 confirmed and one probable, Albert survived the war as both a 'Hero of the Soviet Union' and Commander of the Legion of Honour. *IWM*

CONCLUSION

'Quantity has a quality all its own.'
Vladimir Ilyich Lenin

As the Red Army struck along the main axis from Warsaw towards Berlin, the VVS deployed 10 air armies and mustered 15,815 aircraft, not counting substantial reserves. Soviet air superiority pilots flew the latest Yak-9 and La-7 fighters while their ground-attack colleagues were now operating Il-10 *Shturmoviki*. Operational training standards were of a high order and even with the Luftwaffe on the ropes, the Soviets were professional enough to build 55 dummy airfields with 818 mock aircraft deployed on them. VVS air armies flew 92,000 missions during the taking of Berlin, over half of them at night and in bad weather.

German industry produced 8,295 aircraft in 1939 and notwithstanding all the bombs dropped on it thereafter, Albert Speer managed to increase output to 39,807 in 1944.[263] The Russian front lost its absolute priority for the Germans after September 1943, with the most modern German aircraft being concentrated against the RAF and USAAF. By the beginning of 1944, front-line German strength in the East had dropped to some 1,800 aircraft, set against 2,600 in the West. As the Allies converged on Berlin, the Luftwaffe fused its commands and set up an air defence system that simultaneously looked both ways. The ability to switch German fighters rapidly from west to east forced Soviet air defenders to fight 1,317 air engagements in the battle for Berlin, during which they lost 527 aircraft to German fighters and AAA guns. The highest scoring Soviet ace, Ivan Kozhedub, closed his score on 62 when he forced down two Fw190s over Berlin on 17 April 1945.

At the very end, the Luftwaffe had 1,798,500 personnel under arms, and Gen Stumpff, who was responsible among other things for operations against the Russians, still had some 2,000 aircraft. But his units were broken, scattered and disorganised. When the Red Army invaded East Prussia, the VVS could mount as many as 10,000 sorties a day using the most modern combat aircraft, while the Luftwaffe was incapable of any meaningful air operations. The Air Ministry had left Berlin for the so-called 'Redoubt' in the Bavarian and Austrian Alps, and some saw it as symbolic that the OKL's alternative HQ ended up in a lunatic asylum near Munich.

*   *   *   *

The Soviet Union's poor performance in 1941 is often put down to it being 'backward'. That is unfair. The USSR was not backward technologically, and the excellent aircraft that soon rolled out of factories east of the Urals proved the point. Where the Soviets were backward was in the way they used military

technology in June 1941, and the Stavka knew this. As the Soviet-German non-aggression pact was being signed in August 1939, Marshal Voroshilov announced in the Supreme Soviet that 'today's army . . . is densely packed with multifarious complex mechanisms and weaponry'. To transform this expanding force into a modern fighting machine capable of getting the best out of emerging doctrine and sophisticated communications, Voroshilov announced that he was going to extend the training period for junior commanders to three years.[264] It was no coincidence that the new breed of professional Soviet military officers, trained in the science of modern all-arms warfare and able to undertake the sort of pitched battles of manoeuvre and firepower in which the Germans had hitherto excelled, arrived in the field around the time of Stalingrad and Kursk.

Throughout the air war over Russia, VVS Front and ADD aircraft flew 3,124,000 sorties fighting air battles, supporting ground troops, bombing the enemy's rear, reconnoitring, supporting partisans and other assignments. About 30,450,000 bombs were dropped on the enemy, totalling over 666,000 tons. In comparison, RAF Bomber Command dropped a cumulative bomb load of 675,674 tons on Germany up to May 1945. Between 1941-5, air-to-air combat accounted for 77% of all German aircraft destroyed during the war. The VVS increasingly attacked German airfields prior to and during major ground operations, and when resultant successes and AAA claims are factored in, total German aircraft losses in the East amounted to 77,000, which was 250% greater than the losses on all other theatres. While German air power was finally silenced for lack of aviation fuel, the Luftwaffe was brought to its knees on the Russian Front.

Many unsung heroes were as responsible for this as dashing aircrew. During 1943-4, Soviet industry turned out four times as many aircraft as before 1941. In 1943, the VVS repair service could work on around 540 aircraft per day, but by 1945 that had increased to more than 4,000. The average number of sorties flown by the VVS in 1943 was 150% more than in June 1941, and by 1945 it was three times greater. In 1941, the VVS lost one aircraft every 32 sorties; in 1945 it was one every 165. On the German side, for one Luftwaffe aircraft lost every 25.5 sorties in 1942, it was down to one in 11 by 1945. On top of that, the German flying rate dropped by 40% between 1942 and 1945.

The official Soviet air history gave the main reasons for their victory as 'the constant improvement in air personnel training and the invaluable experience gained in battle. The air force command, the commanding officers and the staffs at all levels came to understand the nature of their operations and could apply their knowledge in the concrete conditions on the battlefield. During operations, the air force improved its organisational structure, its control and co-ordination with the ground forces. Later on new equipment, improved morale and battle training at all levels had a beneficial influence on the operational skills of the air force . . . Control of the air was one of the most important air force assignments. Experience showed that control of the air was one of the most important conditions for successful ground offensive operations.'

While Hitler was more than happy to fly around his domain, Stalin flew only once — to Tehran to meet Roosevelt and Churchill in November 1943. Thereafter, he refused to take to the air again, preferring to travel by train in an armoured carriage with an armed guard. But suspicion of flying did not impair Stalin's judgement when it came to military air matters. He was willing to hear the truth, no matter how unpalatable, if sensibly expressed with conviction. Marshal Zhukov was emphatic on this point. 'After Stalin's death, the idea is current that he never heeded anybody's advice and decided questions of military policy all by himself. I can't agree with that. When he realised that the person reporting knew what he was talking about he would listen and I know of cases where he reconsidered his own opinions and decisions.'[265]

The official history made it clear that 'the Supreme Command gave great importance to air power and concentrated its largest forces in the major offensive zones'. Stavka reserve units, consisting of 18 air corps at the end of 1943 and 30 by 1945 'were employed with great mobility and made it possible to have great superiority over the enemy . . . The Stavka provided flexibility for creating the most favourable situation in the air, which made the air force more effective in destroying the enemy's major troop concentrations.'[266]

An interesting aspect from a Western perspective was that the VVS was never allowed independent status, nor was it ever used

Below:
The bitter end. Under watchful Soviet eyes, Generaloberst Hans-Jürgen Stumpff, who commanded Luftflotte 5 in Norway and Finland until November 1943 and then was commander of Luftflotte Reich, responsible for homeland air defence, signs surrender terms on behalf of the Luftwaffe in the German Academy of Military Engineering in Berlin at 15 minutes after midnight on the morning of 9 May 1945. Marshal Zhukov, who was in charge of proceedings, wrote that Stumpff was 'a short man whose eyes were full of impotent fury'.
Author's collection

extensively as a strategic bombing force. During the entire war in the East, Soviet long-range bombers flew only 215,000 sorties, or about 4% of all VVS combat flights, against targets in their opponent's rear. To defeat the Germans, the Soviets did not clutch at panacea targets such as oil refineries or aircraft factories or undermining German civilian morale. Instead, the Soviets went for massing enormous firepower at selected points to break and encircle enemy defence lines or troop concentrations. In other words, the VVS served along with tanks, artillery and rockets as one component of a military machine designed to 'enable' Soviet troops to crush their opponents.

The lack of a strategic force to bomb Berlin did not worry the Stavka because they knew that Hitler would be beaten only when Soviet boots marched down the Unter den Linden. Where the VVS developed to a unique extent was in co-ordinating several front air armies, long-range aviation and naval aviation to inflict swift and decisive defeat on an enemy. Air Chief Marshal Novikov, working with his subordinate commanders, demonstrated this most emphatically during the final Berlin offensive of 1945. No previous offensive had employed the 7,500 combat aircraft assembled for this last air battle. Some 6,700 were with the 4th, 16th and 2nd Air Armies, together with at least 800 of Golovanov's 18th Army bombers. Sergei Rudenko's 16th Air Army was by far the largest, with its two bomber corps and four bomber divisions, two Shturmovik corps and two Shturmovik divisions, and four fighter corps and five fighter divisions deployed across 165 airfields. The task of forging these air armies, unit by unit, into a co-ordinated, effective air battle plan across three fronts required considerable expertise and attention to detail. The VVS may have been the Red Army's aerial shield and artillery, linked organically with ground forces rather than in spirit with the bomber barons in the West, but that is what defeated Germany in the shortest possible time.

During the night of 23 February 1946, Air Chief Marshal Novikov, twice hero of the Soviet Union and one of the greatest air commanders of World War 2, was arrested as part of Stalin's purge of the victors. Stripped of rank and decorations, he was interrogated for days and nights by the KGB before being condemned to almost six years in strict isolation in prison. Released after Stalin's death to rejoin the Soviet Air Force and command Long-Range Aviation, Alexander Novikov died in 1976. However, the combined-arms offensive stamp he helped to imprint on Soviet force structure and doctrine remained to the end of the Cold War.

*   *   *   *

Harking back to the official Soviet reasons for their air power victory, the Germans could claim nothing like that. The Luftwaffe was initially employed along classic air power lines with destruction of Soviet air forces, followed by direct support for armour and infantry, sustaining rapid advances along the whole front. This worked like a dream until the Germans reached the Dnieper river line in autumn 1941. Hitler's 'Barbarossa' Directive spoke of a 'short campaign', but once the Soviet Union did not surrender and its political and military elite traded space for time, the Germans had no Plan B to fall back on.

At the end of 1941, when the Soviets began their counter-offensive and the USAAF joined a far-from-defeated RAF, the Luftwaffe should have revamped its whole strategy. Victories in Russia had only extended the Luftwaffe's vast area of operations, yet no effort was made to bring the German aircraft industry up to a sustainable war footing, or to introduce new and improved aircraft to match those about to roll off the line in Manchester, Michigan and Magnitogorsk. On the contrary, new production of bombers, fighters, dive-bombers and close reconnaissance aircraft — the types primarily needed in Russia — was *less* than losses from June to December 1941.

The disconnection between future German aircraft requirements and actual attrition was made worse by the increasing use of the Luftwaffe to co-operate with, and then directly support, the army in the East. As von Richthofen's Fliegerkorps VIII was the Luftwaffe's only true air support corps, there was no alternative other than to misemploy twin-engined bombers. These were the Luftwaffe's backbone, designed to carry out operational and strategic air warfare, but when forced to operate at low-level in close support of the army, these large and ponderous beasts sustained heavy losses and frequent damage from Soviet ground forces that could not believe their luck.

Of the 56 close-reconnaissance Staffeln in place at the start of 'Barbarossa', only 19 were still operational by the end of 1941. Moreover, Luftwaffe- and Koluft-controlled units did their own things, leading to duplication or gaps in coverage. Long-range cover was also degraded as reconnaissance aircraft were used as battlefield bombers. By the end of March 1942, all close-range and long-range reconnaissance, AAA and air-signals units assigned to the army were progressively returned to Luftwaffe command.

As infantry and armour ran up against more dogged Soviet resistance, German troops could only make headway when supported by the Luftwaffe. To make matters worse, the German army got used to generous air support even against Soviet forces that were too small to justify air attack or which could have been just as easily destroyed by artillery. In many ways this stemmed from the narrow-mindedness of the High Command, largely comprised of army officers noted for their loyalty rather than understanding the big picture. As the war in the East dragged on, increasingly dissipated and inappropriate close-air support co-operation became the Luftwaffe's Verdun.[267]

The blame for this state of affairs started right at the top. Hitler could be an inspirational leader in adversity and his grasp of technical detail was formidable: his oft-quoted insistence on using the Me262 as a bomber, based on his strong doubts about whether the jet would be of any real use against more agile Allied fighters, was not without foundation. But Hitler remained indifferent to the importance of air superiority until Germany came under the hammer, by which time the air war in Russia was as good as lost.

After assuming command of the army in December 1941, Hitler came to see tactical air power as a means of overcoming any land crisis. Time and again the Supreme Commander ordered his men to hold on to fortified points as islands of resistance in the midst of enemy held territory, which meant sacrificing aircraft and crews to protect or air supply units enveloped while fulfilling the remit 'to retreat not a step'. Eventually the Luftwaffe in the East became completely subordinate to the army, with control of flying concentrated at the tactical Fliegerkorps level or in the hands of *ad hoc* close-support leaders created to support army units.

After 1945, many senior Luftwaffe officers tried to blame their convincing defeat on the fact that strategic air warfare played no part in Germany's campaign against the Soviet Union. If only the 28 twin-engined bomber Gruppen had been pulled out of the front line and placed under a unified bomber command, they argued, a meaningful strategic air offensive could have been undertaken against Soviet railway lines and factories which would have seriously degraded Soviet war fighting potential.[268] But this was a smokescreen. Germany lacked the manpower and resources to take on the USSR, the USA and the UK simultaneously, and it could never have sustained a strategic bomber force to hit the UK and USSR while providing sufficient tactical air power to take and hold ground in western Europe, North Africa, the Balkans and the USSR from the North Cape to the Caucasus. Strategic bombing in concert with troops going forward was the winning combination in World War 2. But if you could only afford one, the Soviets were right to concentrate on troops going forward. The Germans were capable of neither by the middle of 1943.

It was bad enough that German aircraft losses during the first six months in the East exceeded production by about 20%, but even replacement aircraft were soon not up to attacking the right tactical targets. In general terms, a bomb powerful enough to destroy a 28-ton T-34 tank usually could not be delivered with sufficient accuracy to score a direct hit. Conversely, any weapon accurate enough to hit a vehicle — for example, a 20mm cannon — was not powerful enough to pierce armour. There were interdiction targets aplenty that the Luftwaffe could have gone for, such as supply dumps, railway marshalling yards or troop concentrations in the rear areas, but they were largely left untouched because the Luftwaffe was ordered to 'firefight' on the battle area to placate army officers who, in the main, were incapable of looking beyond their guns. And in neglecting the development of air-delivered weapons to stop the heavily armoured tanks that the Soviets soon rolled out in droves, the Luftwaffe ended up incapable of either bombing the factories or killing off their output. The Germans learned the hard way that if aircraft are sent against targets that are unlikely to be destroyed by the weapons carried, that attack will generally be unsuccessful, *no matter how desirable the destruction of those targets might be.*

In their Yak and LaGG fighters, and Il-2s, Pe-2s and Tu-2s, the Soviets came up with winners that only got better with time. On the other hand, the Luftwaffe increasingly had to make do with elderly designs or quick fixes. It was Göring who ordered in February 1940 that only those aircraft developments 'that can be completed in 1940 or will produce results at the latest in 1941' should be continued. The Wehrmacht High Command repeated this edict in October 1941, which meant that while the VVS knew that things could only get better, no promising developments were in train to improve the lot of the Luftwaffe in the East at the beginning of 1942.

Unlike the Il-2 which could soak up punishment, hand out a formidable punch and was capable of development, the German equivalent — the tank-busting Hs129 — was an innovation going nowhere. Its twin engines were so unprotected that 75% of losses

came from hits there from infantry weapons. Moreover, the tiny Hs129 airframe would not readily accept either more powerful engines or heavier weapons. The failure to get the awesome Rheinmetall 50mm cannon into service on the Me410, despite Hitler's enthusiastic endorsement, was another example of the disjointed and amateurish nature of Luftwaffe procurement.

In contrast to Novikov's team, the Luftwaffe High Command administered, it did not lead. Blinded by the brilliant early results achieved in the skies and in the field, Göring and the OKL failed to plan an air armament programme to sustain a long war, or to provide a credibly powerful air defence system behind which it could flourish. By late 1942, many German aircraft listed as combat types over Russia were 1930s-vintage biplanes and other obsolescent models. The once-proud Luftwaffe was reduced to footling measures such as shifting Ju88 night fighters out to try and counter Soviet U-2 biplane night intruders.

Notwithstanding able air commanders such as Milch, von Richthofen, Kesselring, Korten and Koller, some senior German air appointments were downright bad. Jeschonnek was too immature and shortsighted for the responsibilities placed upon him as Chief of Air Staff, and Ernst Udet's appointment as chief of technical development initiated a chain of ruinous procurement decisions from which the Luftwaffe never recovered. The choice of Josef Schmid as the mouthpiece of Luftwaffe Intelligence during the vital years of 1938-42 resulted in seriously flawed assessments which effectively undermined German air strategy in both 'Barbarossa' and the Battle of Britain. These appointments were made by Göring, who preferred to surround himself by unthreatening favourites rather than run the risk of being upstaged by a united, professional air staff. The blind faith and optimism of those at Hitler's HQ, and the unshakeable belief that victory in Russia was just around the corner, created an atmosphere in which any attempt to paint a true air picture was branded as defeatism. Time and again, plans and programmes drawn up by the more responsible members of the OKL were rejected, and decisions were taken over their heads that bore no relation sound air policy or doctrine.

At the next level down, while the VVS was revamped to concentrate air power where it was most needed, the Luftwaffe stuck with the system whereby Luftflotten acted autonomously to control their own strategic, tactical and air defence forces, and associated logistic support organisations. Each Luftflotte supported an Army Group within its own geographic region, which worked well while Germany fought on one front and ruled the skies. But over Russia, Army Groups tended to commit their Luftflotte on a whim. There was no equivalent of the Stavka air representative empowered to bang heads and co-ordinate air assets from various Air Fleets to deliver maximum mass and value to a crucial operation. Regional fragmentation prevented the Luftwaffe from combining to solve USSR-wide problems, for which the Soviets must have been very grateful.

At the sharp end, Luftwaffe personnel fought well and were formidable opponents. The Luftwaffe's ground organisation, supply chain and signals structure were highly effective and well co-ordinated. A group of generally outstanding operational air commanders, backed by flexible staffs who could think on their feet, exploited the inherent flexibility of air power to move 'their' units between different fronts rapidly and expeditiously. This administrative and logistic flair went a long way towards enabling German air power, numerically inadequate to meet its full commitments, to cope for far longer than Hitler had a right to expect.

Kursk, the Luftwaffe's last organised defence, was also the first co-ordinated air offensive by the VVS. Soviet air armies with large strategic reserves now enjoyed strategic mobility to achieve air superiority quickly and concentrate air power when and where it mattered. Kursk was where the VVS, going up, met the Luftwaffe on its way down. Never again did Fliegerkorps VIII, still the only true German close air support force, appear in battle en masse. From now on, the Luftwaffe was fully preoccupied with buttressing increasingly leaky German defence efforts. Once Luftwaffe units could no longer go ahead of advancing ground forces and were shifted from side to side wherever a crisis developed, German airmen lost the ability to accomplish any meaningful missions along the extended Russian front or to give any attention to troop concentrations in the enemy's rear.[269]

As growing Allied air pressure in the West and Mediterranean coincided with Soviet advances after 'Citadel', the Luftwaffe was forced to rely more than ever on last-minute transfers and quick fixes. And as an over-extended and over-taxed Luftwaffe fell ever more behind, the VVS progressed to paralysing German airfields and ground support organisations, to severing their logistic chain and, above all, improving the support provided to its own ground forces. Being also very good at camouflage, deception and improvisation, the Soviets prevented the Luftwaffe from ever cutting the steady flow of manpower, arms and equipment to Red Army units at the front. Nor could the Luftwaffe stop the infiltration of Russian troops into Axis-occupied areas, or stem the menace of partisan activity.

After 1943, Hitler became ever more detached from reality. The Luftwaffe, harassed on three fronts and over the Reich, and increasingly short of petroleum and modern aircraft, was compelled to commit its remaining resources in hundreds of futile air battles against an enemy enjoying overwhelming qualitative and quantitative superiority. The final blow was the haemorrhaging of experienced aircrew, many of whom had kept the Luftwaffe going since 1939. JG54 lost 112 fighter pilots killed or captured over Russia in 1943 alone, and things got worse as the Luftwaffe was forced to provide fighter cover for all bombing, dive-bombing, destroyer and air transport missions. It even had to bring forward its instructor pilots to plug the increasingly large gaps in aircrew expertise.

Ironically, the VVS learned the importance of winning and maintaining air superiority from the Luftwaffe. The Soviets lost nearly 28% of the 74,300 fighters put into VVS service between 1941-5. The history of the VVS after 1943 is a clear tribute to the tactical and organisation skill with which the Soviets exploited their air superiority, harrying the rapidly fading Luftwaffe hither and yon by constant and ever-shifting pressure along the front. The Stavka kept air superiority against Axis operations as a top priority, unlike some very senior German army officers who failed to realise that once they relinquished control of the air, the fate of the Wehrmacht and thereby Germany was irrevocably sealed.

For all that the Soviet response to the German Blitzkrieg experience was often primitive and makeshift to Western eyes, the VVS stayed the course and proved to be highly efficient, effective and ultimately victorious in a war not of its making. It did not matter that individual Soviet aircrew were often not as good as their German counterparts. For example, every day in April 1944 a VVS reconnaissance Pe-2 appeared over Daugavpils, Latvia, scouting German airfields and installations. It appeared regularly between 07.00 and 08.00hrs such that the Germans dubbed it 'the reconnaissance duty officer'. Soviet liaison pilots also tended to navigate by following railway tracks, and as this became known throughout the Luftwaffe, hundreds of Russian liaison aircraft were shot down, especially by Fw190s. But if Soviet aircrew could still be individually ponderous in 1944, they were collectively very effective. The fact that Hptm Erich Hartmann of JG52 became the highest scoring ace ever with 352 kills, all in the East, could not disguise the fact that the Luftwaffe was a busted flush. Unlike the Soviets, the Germans were not prepared for the long haul. Soviet victory came as a result of transformation in the way the Red Army and VVS went to war; German defeat came about because it became embroiled on too many fronts and lacked the inclination to transform itself until it was too late. Increasingly denied the fuel to train and fight, and lacking the reserves to rest its people properly, the Luftwaffe sunk under the strain of trying to meet a growing number of tasks that it could not fulfil. The writing was on the wall when Hans Jeschonnek remarked at the beginning of 1942 that first Russia would have to be defeated, and then it would be possible to concentrate on training.[270]

The last Luftwaffe Chief of Air Staff, Gen Karl Koller, wrote the epitaph for all German airmen in the East. 'We remained voices crying in the wilderness. Priorities were made to build up the largest air force possible after the close of the Russian war. Millions of soldiers were to be released from the Army and were to be sent to the German aircraft industry and to the German Air Force. In the meantime, however, air armament was put way down on the list; first were submarines, then came tanks, then assault guns, then howitzers or Lord knows what, and then came the Air Force. Meanwhile, the Russian war was eating away men, material, armament and aircraft and the only thing that remained for the Air Force was a promise that was never kept. Its task was to make sacrifices.'[271]

SELECT BIBLIOGRAPHY

Official Histories

British Air Ministry, *The Rise and Fall of the German Air Force (1933-1945)*, 1948

Glantz, D. M., *Kharkov 1942*, Soviet General Staff Study, Ian Allan Publishing, 1998

Glantz, D. M., & Orenstein H. S., *The Battle for Kursk 1943*, Soviet General Staff Study, Frank Cass, 1999

Lederrey, E., *Germany's Defeat in the East*, London: The War Office, 1955

Plocher H., *The German Air Force Versus Russia, 1941*, Arno Press, 1968

Plocher H., *The German Air Force Versus Russia, 1942*, Arno Press, 1968

Plocher H., *The German Air Force Versus Russia, 1943*, Arno Press, 1968

Wagner, R., (ed) *The Soviet Air Force in World War II*, David and Charles, 1974

Books and Magazines

Aders, G., *History of the German Night Fighter Force 1917-1945*, Jane's, 1979

Andersson, L., *Soviet Aircraft and Aviation 1917-1941*, Putnam, 1994

Baumbach, W., *Broken Swastika*, Robert Hale, 1960

Bekker, C., *The Luftwaffe War Diaries*, Macdonald, 1964

Bergstrom, C. & Mikhailov, A., *Black Cross, Red Star*, Pacifica Military History, 2000

Boog H., et al, *Germany and the Second World War, Vol IV The Attack on the Soviet Union*, Clarendon Press, 1998

Boyd, A., *The Soviet Air Force Since 1918*, Macdonald & Jane's, 1977

Brookes, A. J., *Photo-reconnaissance*, Ian Allan, 1975

Bullock, A., *Hitler and Stalin, Parallel Lives*, Fontana, 1998

Churchill, W. S., *The Second World War*, Cassell, 1951

Claasen, A. R. A., *Hitler's Northern War: The Luftwaffe's Ill-Fated Campaign, 1940-1945*. University Press of Kansas, 2001

Copp, D. S., *Forged In Fire*, Doubleday, 1982

Corum, J. S., *The Luftwaffe: Creating the Operational Air War, 1918–1940*. University Press of Kansas, 1997

Danchev, A. & Todman, D., (eds), *War Diaries, 1939-1945, FM Lord Alanbrooke*, Weidenfeld & Nicolson, 2001

Detwiler, D. S., (ed), *World War II German Military Studies*, Garland Publishing Inc, 1979

Dierich, W., *Kampfgeschwader 'Edelweiss'*, Purnell, 1975

Douhet, G., *The Command of the Air*, Faber and Faber, 1943

Erickson, J., *The Soviet High Command*, Macmillan, 1962

Erickson, J., *The Road to Stalingrad*, Phoenix, 1998

Faber, H., (ed) *Luftwaffe*, Sidgwick and Jackson, 1979

Glantz D. M. & House J., *When Titans Clashed*, University Press of Kansas, 1995

Green, W., *Warplanes of the Third Reich*, Macdonald, 1970

Hallion, R. P., *Strike from the Sky: The History of Battlefield Air Attack 1911-1945*, Shrewsbury Airlife Publications, 1989

Hamilton, N., *Monty, Master of the Battlefield*, Hamish Hamilton, 1983

Hardesty, V., *Red Phoenix*, Arms and Armour Press, 1982

Hayward, J. S. A., *Stopped at Stalingrad*, University Press of Kansas, 1998

Higham, R., Greenwood J. T., & Hardesty V., *Russian Aviation and Air Power in the Twentieth Century*, Frank Cass, 1998

Howard, M., *The Concept of Air Power, Air Power History, Winter 1995*, Vol 42 No 4

Irving, D., *The Rise and Fall of the Luftwaffe*, Little, Brown & Co, 1973

Irving, D., *Hitler's War*, Hodder and Stoughton, 1977

Kesselring, A., *The Memoirs*, William Kimber, 1953

Knoke, H., *I Flew for the Führer*, Corgi, 1957

Lee, A., *The Soviet Air Force*, Duckworth, 1950

Lee, A., (ed) *The Soviet Air and Rocket Forces*, Weidenfeld and Nicolson, 1959

Lee, A., *The German Air Force*, Harper & Bros, 1946

Lewin, R., *Ultra Goes to War*, Hutchinson, 1978

Manstein, E., *Lost Victories*, Arms and Armour Press, 1982

Mark, E., *Aerial Interdiction in Three Wars*, Centre for Air Force History, 1994

Meilinger, P. S., *Ten Propositions Regarding Air Power*, US Air Force History and Museums Program 1995

Mikoyan S. A., *Memoirs of Military Test-flying and Life with the Kremlin's Elite*, Airlife, 1999

Muller, R., *The German Air Force in Russia*, Nautical and Aviation Publishing Company of America, 1992

Murphy, P. J., *The Soviet Air Forces*, McFarland & Co, 1984

Murray, W., *Strategy for Defeat, The Luftwaffe 1933-1945*, Air University Press, 1983

Neulen, H. W., *In the Skies of Europe*, Crowood Press, 2000

Nowarra, H., *Heinkel He 111*, Jane's, 1980

Overy, R. J., *The Air War 1939-1945*, Europa, 1980

Overy, R. J., *Air Power, Armies, and the War in the West, 1940*, USAFA Harmon Memorial Lecture, 1989

Pennington, R., *Stalin's Falcons: the 586th Fighter Aviation Regiment*, Minerva, Vol XVIII, Fall/Winter 2000

Price, A., *Luftwaffe Handbook*, Ian Allan, 1977

Prien, J., *Jagdgeschwader 53*, Schiffer, 1998

Raeder, E., *Struggle for the Sea*, William Kimber, 1959

Rudel, H. U., *Stuka Pilot*, Corgi, 1957

Shukman, H., (ed) *Stalin's Generals*, Grove Press, 1993

Smith, P. C., *Junkers Ju87 Stuka*, Crowood Press, 1998

Tedder, Lord, *Air Power in War*, Hodder and Stoughton, 1948

Tippelskirch, *Geschichte des Zweiten Weltkriegs*, Atheneum, 1951

Van Dyke, C., *The Soviet Invasion of Finland 1939-40*, Frank Cass, 1997

Warlimont, W., *Inside Hitler's Headquarters 1939-45*, Weidenfeld and Nicolson, 1964

Wells, H. G., *The War in the Air*, 1908

Werth, A., *The Year of Stalingrad*, Hamish Hamilton, 1946

Werth, A., *Russia at War, 1941-1945*, Barrie & Rockliff, 1964

Whelan, J. R., *Hunters in the Sky*, Regnery Gateway, 1991

Wood D. with Dempster D., *The Narrow Margin*, Arrow Books, 1969

Zhukov, G., *The Memoirs of Marshal Zhukov*, Jonathan Cape, 1971

NOTES TO CHAPTERS

Notes to the Introduction

1. *The Oxford Companion to the Second World War*, p1151; Glantz, D. M., & House, J. M., *When Titans Clashed*, p.284
2. Russian Federation Military News Bulletin, *Victory Day: Importance, Results, Lessons*, April 2002
3. Wood, D., with Dempster, D., *The Narrow Margin*, p.269

Notes to Chapter 1

4. Boyd, A., *The Soviet Air Force Since 1918*, p.24; Higham, R., Greenwood J. T., & Hardesty, V., *Russian Aviation and Air Power in the Twentieth Century*, p.40
5. British Air Ministry, *Rise and Fall of the German Air Force*, p.8
6. ibid, p.35
7. Bullock, A., *Hitler and Stalin: 'Parallel Lives'*, p.481
8. Boyd, *op.cit.*, p.35
9. Bullock, *op.cit.*, p.636
10. *Mein Kampf*, p.533
11. British Air Ministry, *op.cit*, p.21
12. Overy, R., *The Air War 1939-1945*, p.22
13. *ibid*, p.28
14. Below, *At Hitler's Side*, pp.69, 74
15. Boog, H., et al, *Germany and the Second World War, Vol IV*, p.335
16. *Industrie-Vorplanung bis 1.4.1945*, Reichsluftfahrtministerium GL.1 No. 710/40, 15 Oct 1940
17. Personal diary, 3 July 1941; Halder Diaries, 30 March 1941
18. Glantz & House, *op.cit.*, pp.40-41
19. Quoted in Langer, W. L., & Gleason, S. E., *The Undeclared War*, p.538
20. Danchev, A., & Todman, D., *War Diaries*, p.166

Notes to Chapter 2

21. Glantz & House, *op.cit.*, p.31
22. Unlike the UK and US where paratroops came under the army, German paratroops were commanded by the Luftwaffe
23. A vast, low-lying waterlogged region in southern Byelorussia and northern Ukraine covering approximately 270,000 square km
24. Training and replacement flight
25. Bergstrom, C. & Mikhailov, A., *Black Cross, Red Star*, p.30
26. Boog, *op.cit.*, p.764
27. *The German Air Force Versus Russia, 1941*, p.85
28. Erickson, J., *The Road to Stalingrad*, p.111
29. Copyright Hans-Ekkehard Bob
30. Whelan, J. R., *Hunters in the Sky*, p.44
31. Knoke, H., *I Flew for the Führer*, pp.45 49
32. Wagner, R., *The Soviet Air Force in World War II*, p.35
33. Murray, W., *Strategy for Defeat, The Luftwaffe 1933-1945*, p.81
34. By comparison, on the first day of the 1967 Six-Day War, the Israeli Air Force neutralised numerically superior Egyptian, Jordanian and Syrian air forces by destroying some 450 aircraft parked on 25 Arab airfields plus 58 in the air
35. Wagner, *op.cit.*, p.35
36. Kesselring, A., *The Memoirs*, p.90

Notes to Chapter 3

37. Van Dyke, C., *The Soviet Invasion of Finland 1939-1940*, pp.105, 194
38. *Protivo-vozdushnaya oborona* or Counter-Air Defence
39. Bergstrom & Mikhailov, *op.cit.*, pp.267-270
40. Whelan, J., *Hunters in the Sky*, p.42
41. Smith, P. C., *Junkers Ju87 Stuka*, p.114
42. Nearly every two-engined Russian bomber was called a Martin bomber because of the passing similarity between the Tupolev SB-2 and the American Martin Maryland: they were both powered by Wright Cyclones
43. Rudel, H., *Stuka Pilot*, pp.28-29
44. OKL Situation Report No 652 of 22 June 1941
45. Kaberov, *A Swastika in the Gunsight*, p.8
46. Shukman, H., (ed), *Stalin's Generals*, Grove Press, 1993
47. Hardisty, V., *Red Phoenix*, p.12
48. Kesselring, *op.cit.*, p.90
49. Bergstrom & Mikhailov, *op.cit.*, p.47
50. Plocher, H., *The German Air Force Versus Russia, 1941*, pp.34-35
51. British Air Ministry, *op.cit.*, p.165
52. Wagner, *op.cit.*, p.26
53. Boog, *op.cit.*, p.364
54. Plocher, *op.cit.*, p.35
55. OKW Directive, 18 December 1940

Notes to Chapter 4

56. Kesselring, *op.cit.*, p.90
57. GFM von Richthofen, *War Diary*, unpublished
58. Halder, *War Diary*, p.466
59. Guderian, *Recollections*, p.152
60. Situation Report No 789 of 29 July 1941, p.25
61. Kesselring, *Short Report of FM Kesselring Concerning the Employment of the Luftwaffe in the East*, 22 February 1955, Karlsruhe Document Collection
62. Kesselring, *The Memoirs*, p.123
63. Report on combat readiness of flying units as of 12 July 1941, GenQu,6.Abt.,15 July 1941
64. Clark, A., *Barbarossa*, p.90
65. Erfurth, W., *Der finnische Krieg 1941-1944*, Munich 1978, p.88
66. Staffel-Chronik der III. Jagdgeschwader 54, 7. Staffel, p.29
67. Warlimont memorandum, quoted in Clark, p.106
68. Situation Report No 666 of 6 July 1941, p.28
69. Situation Report No 662 of 2 July 1941
70. Neulen, *In the Skies of Europe*, p.123
71. Erickson, J., *op.cit.*, p.204
72. Plocher, *op.cit.*, p.68
73. OKL Situation Report No 731, 9 September 1941, p.34

Notes to Chapter 5

74. Plocher, *op.cit.*, p.127

75. Situation Report No 754 of 2 October 1941, pp.33-34

76. Halder, *Diary*, VII, 18 August and 18 September 1941

77. Guderian, *Recollections*, p.185

78. Kesselring, *op.cit.*, p.95

79. Situation Report No 757 of 4 October 1941, p.18

80. Situation Report No 773 of 22 October 1941, p.12; files of Gen Otto Dessloch

81. Kesselring, *op.cit.*, p.95

82. Plocher, *op.cit.*, p.35

83. Wagner, *op.cit.*, p.400

84. Kesselring, *op.cit.*, p.117

85. Glantz & House, *op.cit.*, p.58

86. Situation Report No 660

87. von Waldau, *Diary*, p.50

88. *ibid*, 6 July 1941, pp.56-57

89. Clark, *op.cit.*, p.90

90. Diary, 11 July

91. Milch documents, 53, p.742

92. Speech by FM Milch to the Industrial Council, 18 September 1941

93. *Hilfsfreiwilliger* were volunteer auxiliaries employed for driving, construction and similar tasks

94. Plocher, *op.cit.*, p.60

95. Berkstrom & Mikhailov, *op.cit.*, p.197

96. Gen Bruno Lörzer, Order of the Day, 13 November 1941

97. Kesselring, *op.cit.*, p.97

98. Peter C. Smith, *Junkers Ju87 Stuka*, p.120

99. Irving, D., *The Rise & Fall of the Luftwaffe*, p.144

100. ibid, p.116

101. Hardisty, *op.cit.*, p.71

102. Diary, 23 July 1941

103. Kesselring, *op.cit.*, p.97

104. Forerunners to the Luftwaffen-Felddivisionen established in autumn 1942

105. Asher, Lee, *The Soviet Air Force*, p.55

106. Erickson, J. *op.cit.*, p.235

107. Werth, *Russia At War*, p.220

108. Wagner, *op.cit.*, p.400; Bekker, C., *The Luftwaffe War Diaries*, p.377

109. Overy, R., *The Air War 1939-45*, p.49

Notes to Chapter 6

110. In gratitude for Condor Legion assistance during the Spanish Civil War, Gen Franco sent 17 of his best fighter pilots to help the Luftwaffe over Russia in early October. 15.(Span)/JG27 shot down 10 VVS aircraft for the loss of six before the pilots returned to Spain in January 1942

111. Manned by Croats. After the German attack on the USSR, Croat leader Paveliç offered volunteers to fight on the Eastern Front. In the beginning, the 10th and 11th Fighter Sqns and 12th and 13th Bomber Sqns formed the Croat Luftwaffen-Legion. As all Croat airmen had formerly flown with the Royal Yugoslav Air Force, they were able to deploy to the Eastern Front in October 1941. Fighter pilots went to JG52 and bomber crews operated Do17Zs with KG3 from Vitebsk, Vyazma and Rzhev

112. Because the Soviets' divisions were smaller, their Armies were seldom more than equivalent to a Wehrmacht Corps

113. Douhet, G., *The Command of the Air*, Faber and Faber, 1943

114. Simpkin, R. E., *Deep Battle: The Brainchild of Marshal Tukhachevsky*, Brassey's, 1987, p.43

115. *ibid*, p.139

116. *Tyazhelyy bombardirovshchik* — Heavy bomber

117. *Tyazhelaya bombardirovochnaya aviatsiya*

118. *Dalniy bombardirovshchik*

119. Irving, D., *op.cit.*, p.54

120. Werth, A., *Russia at War 1941-1945*, p.182

121. Boog, *op.cit.*, p.813

122. Murray, W., *Strategy for Defeat*, p.98

123. Wagner, *op.cit.*, p.79

124. Boog, *op.cit.*, p.372

125. Steiner, B. H., *Bernard Brodie and the Foundations of American Nuclear Strategy*, University Press of Kansas, 1991, p.94

Notes to Chapter 7

126. Below, *op.cit.*, p.117

127. *Generalluftzeugmeister* conference, 23 June 1942

128. Glantz & House, *op.cit.*, pp.91-93

129. Hardisty, V., *op.cit.*, p.65

130. Irving, *op.cit.*, p.117

131. Erickson, *op.cit.*, p.208

132. Gen F. Morzik, *Airlift Operation Demyansk Report*, 8 January-19 May 1942

133. I Flakkorps reports to OKW dated 20 and 29 May 1942

134. Glantz, *Kharkov 1942*, p.245

135. Plocher, vol 2, p.181

136. Dierich, W., *Kampfgeschwader Edelweiss*, p.70

137. ibid, p.237

138. Erickson, *op.cit.*, p.350

139. VIII Fliegerkorps Ops Report No 7519, dated 2 June 1942

140. Plocher, 1942, p.193

141. Baumbach, W., *Broken Swastika*, p.123

142. Manstein, *Lost Victories*, p.58

143. Baumbach, *op.cit.*, p.124

144. Pabst, H., *War Diaries, Reports from Russia, 1942*

145. Fliegerkorps VIII report to C-in-C Luftwaffe, 12 July 1942

146. Baumbach, *op.cit.*, p.124

147. *raion aviatsionnogo bazirovaniya*

148. Murphy, *The Soviet Air Forces*, p.42

149. *batalon aerodromnogo obsluzhivaniay*

150. Murray, *op.cit.*, p.119

151. Plocher, vol 1, pp.23-24

152. Becher, p.290

153. Overy, *op.cit.*, p.52

154. *Vozdushnaya armiya.*

155. Kozhevnikov, pp.83-86

156. Murphy, Ed., *op.cit.*, pp.45-6

Notes to Chapter 8

157. Danchev & Todman, *op.cit.*, p.300

158. Erickson, *op.cit.*, p.355

159. Prien, J., *Jagdgeschwader 53*, vol 2, p.412

160. Tieke, W., *Der Kaukasus und das Öl*: p.30. *Fliegerverbindungsoffiziere* were assigned down to Panzer div level

161. Tippelskirch, *History of the Second World War*, p.285

162. Hayward, *Stopped at Stalingrad*, p.150

163. ibid, p.184

164. Hardesty, p.101

165. ibid, p.101

166. Richthofen Diary, 21 August 1942

167. Pabst, *op.cit.*, 23 August 1942

168. Richthofen Diary, 23 August 1942

169. Wagner, *op.cit.*, p.97

170. Neulen, *op.cit.*, p.100

171. Plocher, vol 2, p.233

172. Zhukov, G., *The Memoirs of Marshal Zhukov*, p.138

173. Hayward, J. S. A., *op.cit.*, p.195

174. Hardesty, *op.cit.*, p.104

175. Wagner, *op.cit.*, p.103

176. Chuikov, p.113

177. Plocher, vol 2, p.241

178. Kozhevnikov, p.96

179. Bullock, A., *Hitler and Stalin, Parallel Lives*, pp.394, 804, 851

180. Erickson, *op.cit.*, p.253

181. Halder, *Diary*, 24 September 1942

182. Wagner, *op.cit.*, p.135

183. Hardesty, *op.cit.*, p.106

184. *ibid*, p.106
185. Fiebig, *Diary*, 21 November 1942
186. Below, *op.cit.*, p.159
187. Plocher, *op.cit.*, p.275
188. Letter dated 11 March 1955, quoted in Plocher, vol 2, p.275
189. Morzik, *Die deutschen Transportflieger*, pp.155-156
190. Muller, *op.cit.*, p.94
191. Wagner, *op.cit.*, p.146
192. Hardesty, *op.cit.*, p.119
193. Faber, *Luftwaffe*, p.239
194. Muller, *op.cit.*, p.95
195. Manstein, *op.cit.*, p.347
196. ibid, p.395

Notes to Chapter 9
197. Danchev & Todman, *op.cit.*, p.243
198. *ibid*, p.242
199. OKL Ops Staff Establishment Order, 7 April 1941, plus recollections by Oberst Wild
200. *Seenotbereichskommando IX*
201. Fliegerführer Ostsee, Situation Report No 21, dated 2 September 1941
202. *Admiral Schwarzes Meer* Situation Report, 16-31 March 1942
203. Known in the USAAC as the P-40.
205. Arkhangelsk is blocked to almost all sea traffic for around 190 days a year
206. Werth, A., *The Year of Stalingrad*, p.64
207. 600,000 tons went via the Persian Gulf and 500,000 tons through Pacific ports
208. Claasen, A. R. A., *Hitler's Northern War*, p.201
209. Werth, *op.cit.*, pp.34, 37, 41-2
210. Luftflotte 5 War Diary, 10 July 1942

Notes to Chapter 10
211. Dessloch was rebuilding I Flakkorps in the region after the withdrawal of his Luftwaffe Group Caucasus
212. Richthofen Diary

213. Murray, *op.cit.*, p.156
214. The US delivered 2,343 combat aircraft to the Soviets in 1942, plus an additional 1,383 in the first five months of 1943. *USAAF Statistical Digest*, Dec 1945, pp.129-130
215. Wagner, *op.cit.*, pp.148-150
216. Luftflotte 4 Operations Book and StG2 War Dairy, 20-24 April 1943
217. Wagner, *op.cit.*, pp.153-4
218. Pennington, R., *Stalin's Falcons*, p.84
219. Rudel, *op.cit.*, pp.107-8
220. Interview by Jon Guttman, *Aviation History Magazine*, September 2000
221. Vershinin, *The 4th Air Army in Combat for the Motherland*, 1965, p.9
222. Muller, *op.cit.*, p.106
223. British Air Ministry, *op.cit.*, p.224

Notes to Chapter 11
224. Irving, *op.cit.*, pp.201-2
225. Manstein, *op.cit.*, p.496
226. Murray, *op.cit.*, p.254
227. Muller, *op.cit.*, pp.117-118
228. *The Power Fuel Situation in Germany 1939-1944*
229. Zhukov, G., *op.cit.*, p.431
230. Glantz & House, *op.cit.*, p.64
231. Glantz & Orenstein, *The Battle for Kursk*, p.240
232. *ibid*, pp.252, 260
233. Zhukov, *op.cit.*, p.456
234. Rudenko, S., *The Gaining of Air Supremacy and Air Operations in the Battle of Kursk*, p.191
235. Glantz & Orenstein, *op.cit.*, p.254
236. ibid, p.271
237. ibid, p.192
238. Hallion, *Strike from the Sky*, p.258
239. War Diary, 5 August 1943
240. Hallion, *op.cit.*, p.241
241. Wagner, *op.cit.*, p.172
242. Glantz & Orenstein, *op.cit.*, p.254

243. Irving, *Hitler's War*, p.538
244. Glantz & Orenstein, *op.cit.*, pp.252, 260
245. Wagner, *op.cit.*, pp.180-1
246. Zhukov, *op.cit.*, p.477
247. Hardesty, *op.cit.*, p.165

Notes to Chapter 12
248. 8th Military Science Branch, OKL, *Overview Concerning the German Conduct of Aerial Warfare*
249. British Air Ministry, *op.cit.*, p.236
250. Muller, *op.cit.*, p.157
251. Overy, *op.cit.*, p.150; Wagner, *op.cit.*, p.215
252. Halder, entry for 8 July 1941
253. Manstein, *op.cit.*, p.264
254. Shukman, *Stalin's Generals*, p.169
255. Muller, *op.cit.*, p.215
256. Shore, Marshall B., *'Our Russian Adventure'*, The 390th Memorial Museum Foundation
257. British Air Ministry, *op.cit.*, p.357
258. Irving, *Hitler's War*, p.647
259. Hardesty, *op.cit.*, pp.190-191
260. Zhukov, *op.cit.*, p.521
261. Lipfert, H., *War Diary*, p.127
262. Irving, *op.cit.*, p.685

Notes to Chapter 13
263. Overy, *op.cit.*, p.150
264. Van Dyke, *op.cit.*, p.43
265. Zhukov, *op.cit.*, p.464
266. Wagner, *op.cit.*, pp.362-3
267. Boog, *op.cit.*, p.820
268. For example, see Faber, *Luftwaffe*, pp.223-6
269. 8th Military Science Branch, OKL, *Survey of German Air Operations*, 1944, p.8
270. Boog, *op.cit.*, p.832
271. British Air Ministry, *op.cit.*, pp.407-8

INDEX